RACE, ETHNICITY, AND ENTREPRENEURSHIP IN URBAN AMERICA

SOCIOLOGY AND ECONOMICS
Controversy and Integration

An Aldine de Gruyter Series of Texts and Monographs

SERIES EDITORS

Paula S. England, *University of Arizona, Tucson*
George Farkas, *University of Texas, Dallas*
Kevin Lang, *Boston University*

Values in the Marketplace
James Burk

Equal Employment Opportunity:
Labor Market Discrimination and Public Policy
Paul Burstein (ed.)

Industries, Firms, and Jobs
Sociological and Economic Approaches
[Expanded Edition]
George Farkas and Paula England (eds.)

Towards a Structure of Indifference
The Social Origins of Maternal Custody
Debra Friedman

Beyond the Marketplace:
Rethinking Economy and Society
Roger Friedland and A. F. Robertson (eds.)

Social Institutions:
Their Emergence, Maintenance and Effects
Michael Hechter, Karl-Dieter Opp and Reinhard Wippler (eds.)

The Origin of Values
Michael Hechter, Lynn Nadel and Richard E. Michod (eds.)

Race, Ethnicity and Entrepreneurship in Urban America
Ivan Light and Carolyn Rosenstein

Parents' Jobs and Children's Lives
Toby L. Parcel and Elizabeth G. Menaghan

Power, Norms, and Inflation: A Skeptical Treatment
Michael R. Smith

RACE, ETHNICITY, AND ENTREPRENEURSHIP IN URBAN AMERICA

Ivan Light and Carolyn Rosenstein

ALDINE DE GRUYTER

New York

About the Authors

Ivan Light is Professor of Sociology at the University of California, Los Angeles. His research on urban and immigrant enterprise has been widely published in major journals and in edited volumes. Dr. Light is the author of *Ethnic Enterprise in America* and *Cities in World Perspective*, and coauthor of *Immigrant Entrepreneurs: Koreans in Los Angeles, 1965–1982*.

Carolyn Rosenstein is Research Associate in the Department of Sociology, at the University of California, Los Angeles, where she has held previous positions with the Center for Pacific Rim Studies and the Institute for Social Science Research. Dr. Rosenstein's analyses of immigration data have been published in major journals.

ALDINE DE GRUYTER
A division of Walter de Gruyter, Inc.
200 Saw Mill River Road
Hawthorne, New York 10532

This publication is printed on acid free paper ∞

Library of Congress Cataloging-in-Publication Data
Light, Ivan Hubert.
    Race, ethnicity, and entrepreneurship in urban America / Ivan
Light and Carolyn Rosenstein.
        p.   cm. — (Sociology and economics)
    Includes bibliographical references and index.
    ISBN 0-202-30505-8 (acid-free paper). — ISBN 0-202-30506-6 (pbk.
: acid-free paper)
    1. Minority business enterprises—United States.
2. Entrepreneurship—United States.   3. Community development,
Urban—United States.   4. Businessmen—United States.
5. Immigrants—United States—Economic conditions.   I. Rosenstein,
Carolyn Nancy.   II. Title   III. Series.
HD2346.U5L545   1995
338.6′422′0973—dc20   95-3418
                                                                                      CIP

Manufactured in the United States of America

10 9 8 7 6 5 4 3 2 1

Ivan Light fondly dedicates this book to Allison Grant and Muriel Hale Grant, who helped out when help was needed.

Carolyn Rosenstein dedicates this book to Richard, Wendy, and Rachel, for their love and support; to Ivan Light for his faith and patience with the many interruptions to our work due to my many life cycle crises; and to Harold Segal, Michael Schlink, Sonja Chandler, Armando Giuliano, and William Power, for helping me survive those crises.

Contents

Preface

Our book approaches entrepreneurs as if they were herd animals. Although this approach conflicts with the popular notion that entrepreneurs are supremely individualistic, it is unavoidable when one adopts a statistical approach. Such an approach examines the capacity of groups to produce entrepreneurial responses to opportunity conditions. Our objective in this endeavor is to build theory rather than to explain the world as it was in 1980. That new theory would feed into practical agendas of how to increase the wealth of ethnic and immigrant minorities and to rebuild American cities, serious matters. But, even more importantly, it would also influence the underlying image of how economies operate, thus affecting social policy throughout the world. That scientific issue is semiindependent of the actual economic conditions that existed in 1980. Those conditions are of scant concern in this book, which succeeds to the extent that, based on the experience of 272 American cities in 1980, it creates theoretical ideas that clarify the present and future while suggesting agendas for social action.

The book utilizes a gigantic data set that summarizes the behavior of one hundred million Americans. Building that data set was expensive. The Sociology Division of the National Science Foundation put up the money. Without that money, that work and this book would not have been completed. The National Science Foundation is the only organization that supports pure research in sociology. The authors thank the National Science Foundation for its support. However, the authors bear exclusive responsibility for errors of fact, interpretation, or method.

We worked on this book for several years, imposing a burden on our spouses, children, and grandchildren, all of whom saw less of us than they otherwise would have during that period. Moreover, when they did see us, they had to listen to more talk about entrepreneurship than they wanted to hear. We thank all these people for their emotional and practical support in this prolonged period.

1

Why Entrepreneurs Still Matter

Entrepreneurs are innovators. Starting a new firm is one entrepreneurial innovation; expanding a firm is another; and changing the manner of doing business is a third (Wilken, 1979:62–63). Entrepreneurs differ in the number, frequency, and importance of their innovations. Some make many, frequent, important innovations; others make few, infrequent, trivial ones. Additionally, innovations may be pioneering or imitative. Original innovations begin a sequence of related innovations. Derivative innovations follow from an original innovation but modify the original. Thus, Henry Ford's (1922:8) automobile assembly line was an original technological innovation. Ford's high wage policy was a derivative factor innovation necessitated by the prior technological innovation.

The scorn directed at entrepreneurial imitation is unjustified. First, as Drucker (1985:220) observes, some imitators surpass the originators in their understanding of a novelty's implications. Moreover, even slavish imitators are also innovators to the extent that their imitations even minutely depart from prevailing business practice. As long as a practice is not already taught in business schools, its adoption is somewhat innovative. In this sense, Japanese imitations of Western products were innovative, even if derivative. As Lockwood (1954:581) long ago observed, Japanese borrowing involved "purpose, criticism, and a creative synthesis." Westerners' scorn of Japanese imitation represented an ethnocentric exaggeration of what Westerners did well (original innovation) and deprecation of what the Japanese did well (imitative innovation). From the market's point of view, however, both originality and imitation earn the reward of entrepreneurship.

The most significant entrepreneurs make frequent, original, and important innovations. These are the elite entrepreneurs. People like Henry Ford or Thomas Edison merit this designation. At the opposite extreme, one identifies a huge nonelite whose innovations are derivative, infrequent, and inconsequential but who are, nonetheless, innovators in at least some minimal sense. Almost all entrepreneurs belong to the undistinguished multitude. Indeed, undistinguished entrepreneurs are a surprisingly numerous part of the total work force. In 1989 approximately one-quarter of the American labor force either was currently self-employed or had been self-employed in the past (Steinmetz and Wright, 1989:974). Many employees were former entrepreneurs who had failed in business. Another 57% of working class respondents and two-thirds of male employees also reported that they would like to be self-employed some day.[1] These are would-be entrepreneurs. Summing the would-be entrepreneurs, the failed entrepreneurs, and the current entrepreneurs, we have an actual majority of the American labor force.

Carland, Hoy, Boulton, and Carland (1984; also Kallen and Kelner, 1983:13) seek to restrict the appellation "entrepreneur" to the innovative elite. Wilken (1979:60) and Kilby (1971:27–29) also distinguish entrepreneurs from the self-employed on the grounds that only entrepreneurs innovate. Faithful to Schumpeter, this flimsy distinction collapses when challenged. Thus, Drucker (1985:21) proclaims that "not every new small business is entrepreneurial or represents entrepreneurship," specifically noting that "another Mexican restaurant" in the suburbs just "gambles on the increasing popularity of eating out." In contrast, according to Drucker (1985:27–28) a real entrepreneur "always searches for change; responds to it, and exploits it as an opportunity." The obvious objection is that the increased popularity of eating out is a bona fide change that justifies an entrepreneurial response. Therefore, a restaurant owner qualifies as an entrepreneur.

Existing entrepreneurship theory is elitist. The elite theory of entrepreneurship has yielded a prolonged and fruitless search for confirmatory evidence in personality psychology. If entrepreneurs were special, so the theory goes, personality tests should distinguish them from the merely self-employed (Wilken, 1979:16). But, despite 30 years of searching, evidence of personality differences between entrepreneurs and the self-employed persistently fails to materialize. Reviewing the long search, Brockhaus (1982:50) declares that "all recognized research to date does not allow a causal connection to be specified between these [psychological] tests and entrepreneurial success." McLure (1990:159, 160) finds that neither "risk-taking" nor "need for autonomy" distinguishes successful entrepreneurs from the less successful. Indeed, McLure (1990:161) concludes that successful entrepreneurs have "approximately the same psychological profile as the unsuccessful entrepreneurs." Chell, Haworth, and Brearley (1991:37) acknowledge that 30 years of "research findings on entrepreneurial traits have yielded equivocal results."

Additionally, innovation is harder to measure than is realized. In an illustrative effort to measure it, Marsh and Mannari (1986) studied 50 manufacturing plants in southwest Japan. They measured entrepreneurship by the owner's plans for expansion and patent applications, finding that some firms were nonentrepreneurial as thus defined. However, Marsh and Mannari's measure of entrepreneurship tapped only quantitative and technological innovation, the latter but one aspect of product innovation. Marsh and Mannari ignored qualitative innovation, factor innovation, and market innovation, which Wilken (1979:62) regards as equally important forms of entrepreneurship. They made no effort to measure these forms of entrepreneurial innovation. Possibly some of the "nonentrepreneurial" firms were innovating in the ignored dimensions. That result could happen if an owner had no plans for expansion, but proposed introducing new technologies, tapping new markets, or introducing new accounting methods. Therefore, when Marsh and Mannari (1986) declared some firms "noninnovating," they did so without having examined all possible dimensions of innovation.

This example illustrates the hazard of attempting to distinguish entrepreneurs from the self-employed by measuring innovation. Although the class of business owner/operators admittedly contains wide variation in the extent of innovation, with only a minority delivering frequent, important, and original innovations, one can rarely exclude any owner/operator from the class of entrepreneurs on the grounds that he or she achieved *no* innovation in *any* sphere of business operation. After all, even a new pizza topping is an innovation (Abrams, 1978). Given the difficulty of measuring innovation, and the numerous dimensions of the concept, we deem it useless to distinguish entrepreneurs from the self-employed on the ground that only entrepreneurs innovate. One might, with equal justice, declare that no one who does not sing as well as Maria Callas sings.

Among the entrepreneurs, one appropriately distinguishes gradations of importance. Archer (1991:797) distinguished three. At the top she identified an "industrial/merchant elite" who represented 21% of all self-employed. Below them, she identified a solid stratum of "general merchants and proprietors" who were 51% of all self-employed. "Petty merchants and proprietors" represented the lowest level. They were 28% of all self-employed. Following Schumpeter, who thought that only "one man or a few men" had the vision to become entrepreneurs (Schumpeter, 1991:413), the most extreme discrimination simply distinguishes elite entrepreneurs of world-historical importance from all others. Hughes (1965:3) declares that these great entrepreneurs are "the handful, the vital few" who "change the allocation of resources over time." Cornelius Vanderbilt, Michael Milken, and Donald Trump presumably belong to that vital few; owner/operators of pizza restaurants do not. However, owners of pizza parlors also change the allocation of resources, increasing demand for mozzarella cheese and pepperoni sausage. Therefore, resource allocation does not distinguish them from the vital few.

Traditional entrepreneurship's elitism yields a great man theory of economic history as bankrupt as the great man theory of political history. We agree that the important differences between rich and poor entrepreneurs and between big innovators and small innovators merit attention (Aldrich and Weiss, 1981). But we deny that these are differences of kind rather than of degree. The important differences between rich and poor entrepreneurs usually reflect the level at which each entered the business system rather than each one's innovation or business acumen. After all, even at his most successful, Donald Trump was not more successful than many owner/operators of pizza restaurants whose origins were as humble as Trump's were patrician; Trump was only bigger in the scale of his operations, not more successful. An entrepreneur who turns $100 into $10,000 has multiplied capital as effectively as did one, like Trump, who turned $5,000,000 of inherited wealth into $500,000,000.[2]

Finally, it is simply untrue that every major business innovation bears the stamp of some elite entrepreneur. In many cases, major innovations have been the product of an entrepreneurial movement whose members were individually unknown. For example, of the major business changes that have influenced the United States in this century, one of the most prominent has been the growth of fast food restaurants, frozen foods, and take-out foods (Morgan and Goungetas, 1986:92). All these retail industries have responded to the need of American households to reduce the time spent in meal preparation, but other entrepreneurial solutions to this problem (boarding houses, apartment hotels) were business failures (Cowan, 1983: Ch. 5). Naturally, some famous entrepreneurs stand out. Founder of Kentucky Fried Chicken, Inc., Harlan Sanders is an identifiable participant in the movement, as is Ray Kroc of McDonald's. But neither Sanders nor Kroc started fast food.[3] Viewed in terms of the historical development, both Kroc and Sanders were only late-coming leaders of a much larger and innovating social movement that gradually transformed the eating habits of a nation.[4] Their celebrity entrepreneurship joined a process that a multitude of unsung entrepreneurs had initiated before them and continued after them.

In the pizza industry, one also finds that celebrity entrepreneurs were only late arriving leaders in a movement much larger and older than themselves. The Italian pizza has become a staple of the American diet. No one knows who invented pizza, popularized it, and brought it into the mainstream (Minervini, 1973:19–20). Admittedly, Tom Monahan of Domino's Pizza deserves recognition as a celebrity entrepreneur in pizzas. In 1990 Domino's operated a national system of 5,473 restaurants, and delivered pizza to homes everywhere (Buckley, 1991:44). Nonetheless, although Monahan did a lot for pizza, he cannot be assigned exclusive credit for the industry's success without stripping credit from those numerous but unnamed restaurateurs who coparticipated in pizza's development before, during, and after Monahan's rise to entrepreneurial celebrity. Whoever invented and popularized pizza surely earned a space in Schumpeter's hall of elite entrepreneurs, if such a hall existed. In point of fact, numberless obscure restaurateurs deserve that recognition. Taken together, they share the elitist distinction. Celebrity entrepreneurs like Monahan could not have succeeded without those nameless predecessors.[5]

The invention and popularization of Chinese food offer a comparable story. Nineteenth-century Americans did not eat Chinese food. Rather, they loathed it because of its disgusting ingredients and the unsanitary conditions under which they imagined it was prepared (Light, 1974a; Tannahill, 1973:265).[6] The invention of "chow mein" in the 1890s began the popularization of Chinese food in America. The inventor's name is unknown, but, a century later, the dish he popularized has eventuated in a Chinese food industry to which virtually every urban North American is exposed (Zelinsky, 1985:62–63; Tuchman and Levine, 1993). If some innovating entrepreneur had introduced Chinese food into the American diet, producing the huge change by himself, that person would deserve Schumpeter's recognition for heroic entrepreneurship. In reality, successive generations of Chinese restauranteurs relentlessly accomplished that objective. Taken together they deserve Schumpeter's recognition. How can those individual Chinese restaurateurs be declared noninnovative in view of the massive innovative effect of their collective enterprise?

CAUSALLY SIGNIFICANT ENTREPRENEURSHIP

Although entrepreneurs have political and cultural significance, and these are important aspects of the role, we address the economic significance of entrepreneurs. The economic significance of entrepreneurs resides in their independent contribution to the economic development and growth of their region and of their own ethnoracial group (Knight, 1921:283). The entrepreneurship of Chinese restaurateurs accomplished both goals. On the one hand, Chinese restaurants changed a nation's diet while increasing its GNP.[7] On the other, Chinese restaurants also improved the economic well-being of Chinese Americans, the product's main producers.

We claim that entrepreneurs *independently* affect the rate, form, and location of economic development. That is, the quality and abundance of the entrepreneurs available are important causes of economic growth and development. As Granovetter (1990:105) has stressed, one must reject the assumption that "entrepreneurial activity is somehow automatically called forth by economic circumstances." Instead, the *sociology* of entrepreneurship posits markets that depend for entrepreneurs upon exogenous and noneconomic societal conditions. This dependence defines what Wilken (1979:4–6) has called the "causal significance" of entrepreneurship. Entrepreneurship is *causally significant* when problematic and noneconomic. It is problematic when its availability enhances or its unavailability inhibits economic growth and development. It is noneconomic when its availability wholly or partially depends upon political, institutional, and cultural circumstances that markets cannot govern. Therefore, the sociology of entrepreneurship concerns the extent to which and the conditions under which entrepreneurship is causally significant.

The null hypothesis proclaims that entrepreneurship is predictable and economic in origin. If markets always create the entrepreneurs they need, then the sociology of entrepreneurship has no purchase.[8] In point of fact, many important writers do credit markets with this capacity. For example, Piore and Sabel (1984:68–69) claim that Westinghouse would have produced the electric light industry had Edison not done so first.[9] If Westinghouse were ready, and behind Westinghouse still others, and all entirely mercenary in their motives, then Edison's entrepreneurship was not causally significant in the creation of the electric light industry. That is, extrapolating Piore and Sabel's view, market demand for artificial lighting generated a multitude of technoentrepreneurs, each of whom sought to pioneer the product, and one of whom was bound to succeed. In that sense, the market created its own electricity entrepreneurs so the critical agents were neither problematic nor exogenous to the economic process.

The issue turns on whether entrepreneurs can be taken for granted. Obviously, entrepreneurs produce business innovation as surgeons produce surgery, druggists pills, and welders rivets. We assume that surgeons, druggists, and welders will be there when markets for their services exist, so why not entrepreneurs? Entrepreneurship is not causally significant when markets reliably create the quality and number of entrepreneurs they require. Causal significance arises only when noneconomic factors independently affect the *supply of entrepreneurs* (Alexander, 1967). The supply of entrepreneurs is their number and their quality within a serious span of time.[10] Conversely, causal significance is absent when and to the extent that entrepreneurship itself is a fungible, fully elastic factor of production that markets reliably create to serve them (Kilby, 1971:2–6). In that limiting case, the market provides itself with needed entrepreneurs by the usual price signals. When their money returns rise, entrepreneurs enter the market; when their returns decline, they exit the market. In effect, market demand then creates all the entrepreneurs needed to fulfill it. To fulfill a market demand means to fulfill all the potentialities immanent within it. Under this circumstance, entrepreneurs represent an essential element in the innovation process but one that, like oxygen, is reliably present while operating on the surface of the earth.

We dispute that argument, claiming instead that entrepreneurs are causally significant in Wilken's sense. Three examples illustrate causally significant entrepreneurship's impact upon economic development, now and in the past. In traditional China, Confucianists disesteemed money handling, long hours of labor, and competition, all elements of the entrepreneur's role. As a result, traditional China could not overthrow the anticompetitive guild system as the Occident finally succeeded in doing (Light, 1983: Ch. 3). In China's case, public disesteem of the entrepreneurial role reduced the supply of entrepreneurs to such an extent that virtually none came forward to challenge the guilds.[11] Therefore, markets could not create the entrepreneurship needed to serve them. Because entrepreneurial innovation was negligible, China did not break out of economic traditionalism until integrated into the capitalist world economy centuries later. To the extent that lack of entrepreneurs in traditional China inhibited the kingdom's economic development, entrepreneurship was causally significant. To the extent that public disesteem of the entrepreneur's role stifled entrepreneurial supply, China's late development was a product of public attitudes toward entrepreneurs, a noneconomic condition. In this case, entrepreneurship was causally significant because the shortage of its supply stifled economic development.

Advanced market societies award entrepreneurs public approval and esteem. As the popularity of Ross Perot demonstrated again, no nation exceeds the United States in public esteem for entrepreneurs. Yet, even in the United States, the public still despises some entrepreneurs. Toxic waste dumpers, child pornographers, and cocaine vendors are despised entrepreneurs who encounter police sanctions and public hostility (Smith, 1978, 1980). Ironically, except for the sanctions of disesteem and incarceration, pornographers and cocaine vendors would earn no more than owner/operators of dry cleaning establishments or pizza parlors and, like them, would operate retail establishments in shopping malls (Witkin, 1991). Additionally, except for the sanctions, their products would be so cheap that children could buy all they want. Naturally, to expand childrens' consumption of cocaine and obscene films undermines the public interest; therefore, this suppression of entrepreneurship is justified (Burr, 1986). But the wisdom or unwisdom of suppressive policy is not our point. Rather, these illegal markets illustrate a condition of chronic if partial market failure caused by public disesteem and imprisonment—independent, noneconomic determinants of entrepreneur supply.

Entrepreneurship also reaches causal significance when, as a result of favorable attitudes toward the entrepreneur's role, societies produce more entrepreneurs than the market needs rather than less. For many decades American sociologists puzzled over the atavistic persistence of entrepreneurial values and aspirations in the labor force, despite the declining money returns of the entrepreneur role and its dwindling numbers.[12] Given the nation's laissez-faire traditions, it was easy to understand entrepreneurial ambition as a cultural residual of an economically by-gone era. Thus, Riesman (1950) juxtaposed the "inner-directed" old-fashioned individualism of yesterday's entrepreneurs with the extroversion of corporate executives, finding in this contrast a shift in modal personality from the former to the latter. Similarly, Miller and Swanson (1958:123) found that achievement imagery in the American middle class had shifted away from self-employment toward bureaucratic careers in corporate hierarchies. Bell (1976:84) identified the Puritan tradition as a self-destructive rationality whose adolescent heirs had discarded planning and work in favor of "voluptuary hedonism."

Entrepreneurship's protracted decline neatly illustrated cultural lag, the belated adjustment of superstructure to changes in productive relations.[13] A small business economy had needed entrepreneurial motivations in the labor force. When the economic basis of small business deteriorated, socialization lagged behind, continuing to produce entrepreneurial aspirations among life-long wage workers. The temporary result was a glut of disappointed aspirants for small business, a situation of market failure. Ultimately, the surplus of aspiring entrepreneurs reached back to the socialization system, and parents ceased to encourage their children to prefer self-employment. As salaried workers corrected their aspirations, so went the argument, the social origins of American business owners declined. But, until equilibrium was restored, a period of several generations, the United States produced more entrepreneurs than the market could absorb. Since the cause was noneconomic, a lag of socialization values, entrepreneurship was causally significant by its proliferation rather than by its absence.

WEBER, SCHUMPETER, AND MARX

The founder of entrepreneurship research, Max Weber (1958, 1978) claimed that Puritan theology had once encouraged believers to adopt the entrepreneur's role and to redefine the role's content. As a result,

Weber claimed, European capitalism received a stimulus that enabled it to break away from guild traditionalism, a restraint that frustrated capitalism elsewhere in the world. In Wilken's terms, Weber identified a causally significant entrepreneurship because he linked theology, a noneconomic determinant, to the supply of entrepreneurs. Since capitalism required entrepreneurs to complete its triumph, Puritan religious beliefs played an independent role in the triumph of capitalism. If Weber is right, then Protestant sects expedited the transition from feudalism to capitalism in Europe, vastly enhancing economic growth and development in the process. Even if capitalism would ultimately have triumphed in Europe without the assistance of Protestantism, the triumph might have required generations more to accomplish. One could measure the importance of Puritan entrepreneurship in the delay of years, generations, or centuries that would otherwise have been required to effect the transition to capitalism, calculating the cumulative reduction in gross world product that each delay occasioned.[14]

Although he introduced the subject of entrepreneurship into sociology, Weber's influence upon subsequent research in entrepreneurship was equivocal. Like others of his generation, Weber also believed that mature market capitalism outgrew its infantile dependence upon noneconomic sources of entrepreneur supply. First, like Alfred Marshall, his contemporary, Weber believed that large bureaucratic organizations were the model of the future (Aronson, 1991:117; Hage and Powers, 1992: Ch. 2). This view was antientrepreneurial in implication because big organizations need few entrepreneurs. Second, Weber (1958:181–183; 1:368) supposed that "victorious capitalism" of the twentieth century no longer needed the support of "religious asceticism." To the extent that entrepreneurs were still needed, Weber implied that mature capitalism relied upon market signals to produce the needed entrepreneurs from a population securely attached to materialistic ideals. As a result, the market could take over from society the job of supplying its own entrepreneurs.[15] Implicit in Weber's vision is the presumption that mature capitalism had molded a labor force in whom entrepreneurship had been culturally legitimated and enshrined. In the shadow of this cultural change, entrepreneurship became a fungible, elastic, and inexhaustible labor commodity. Therefore, entrepreneurship had lost its historic connection to noneconomic sources of supply and therewith its causal significance.

Whereas Weber had only foreseen a bureaucratized world, shorn of magic and romance, Joseph Schumpeter drew out the destructive implication of such a world for causally significant entrepreneurship (Cauthorn, 1989: Ch. 1; MacDonald, 1971). Schumpeter (1934, 1988) distinguished entrepreneurship from economic innovation, treating entrepreneurship as just one method by which economic innovation could occur. Schumpeter also supposed that large, professionally managed, corporately organized business firms would continue to replace small owner-operated firms as the dominant industrial combination in advanced market societies (Cauthorn, 1989:18–21, 58–59). However, giant corporations' management would assume entrepreneurship's duties. That is, professional managers would take over the entrepreneur's task of planning innovation, evaluating its risks, and executing the plans. Salaried scientists would assume the entrepreneur's technical and research responsibilities. Salaried accountants would assume the entrepreneur's financial functions. Salaried psychologists would assume the entrepreneur's labor management responsibility. Having broken down the entrepreneur's role into sequential steps, the usual process of work simplification, giant corporations would hire managers to perform the ci-devant entrepreneur's various tasks. Committees would take over the task of integration. Committees would perform the entrepreneur's innovative function more efficiently than entrepreneurs, just as proletarians were more efficient than craftsmen. Salaried managers would provide the manager's labor relations, financial, and technical roles more efficiently than entrepreneurs. Therefore, Schumpeter (1988:256, 261, 266; 1943:132; 1991:417–418) anticipated the technological/organizational obsolescence of entrepreneurs in this century.

Uninterested in entrepreneurship, Karl Marx was most interested in the bourgeoisie, and in an unusual demonstration of political convergence, his pessimistic evaluation of its future agreed with the conclusions of the conservative Schumpeter and of Weber, the liberal. Marx (1965: Ch. 32) analyzed the "historical tendency of capitalist accumulation" in terms of progressive reduction of small capital on the one hand, and of proportional and absolute growth of big capital on the other. Marx (1965:763) expected this progressive reduction would be "accomplished by the—immanent laws of capitalistic production itself, by the centralization of capital." That is, overlooking their political influence, Marx supposed that big firms had preponderant economic strength arising from market power, economies of scale, and access to capital such that big firms vanquished and absorbed smaller competitors. When small firms disappeared, entrepreneurs would disappear too because small firms provided the vehicle for entrepreneurs.

Marx's prediction proved remarkably successful. Small business declined, and big business increased as he had anticipated. C.W. Mills (1951:24) long ago showed that there had occurred a steady decline of agricultural and nonagricultural self-employment in the United States between 1870 and 1940.[16] After Mills wrote, the decline of self-employment in the American labor force continued until 1973. In that year, a slim majority of American farmers continued to be self-employed, but less than 7% of nonfarm workers were still self-employed, trends that were also visible in Europe (Ray, 1975; Browning and Singelmann, 1978:482). Given these century-long trends, analysts agreed that the probability of self-employment and the economic rewards of the entrepreneur's role had declined. Bechofer and Elliott (1985:185–186; see also Steinmetz and Wright, 1989:981) declared the property-owning small middle class "an anachronism, a vestige of the simple commodity form of production which attended the transition from feudalism to capitalism." [17] Therefore, like others, they expected entrepreneurship to slide into oblivion (Light, 1984:195). Indeed, as Bell (1973:66) noted, even conservatives accepted the view that in market economies firms grow in average size, economic power converges around the largest firms, and big firms swallow little ones. When these events unfolded, entrepreneurs lost their causal significance for economic development and change.

We can summarize the destructive implications of classical theory in three propositions. First, in the course of modernization, a market economy outgrows its infantile dependence upon noncommoditized, supply-side sources of economic innovation, organizing innovation as a routine function of the enterprise. In this manner, mature capitalism provides itself with needed entrepreneurs, releasing itself from the primitive necessity of depending upon exogenous societal provision by means of religious sects, social movements, or ethnic minorities.

Second, advanced market capitalism produces a homogeneous, culturally modern labor force within which entrepreneurial skills and motivations exist in ample supply to accommodate any need. The flexible supply of entrepreneurs guarantees effective market coordination of the entrepreneur population. When high profits signal the market's need for entrepreneurs, those needed always appear promptly in the quality and number required. The market obtains the entrepreneurs it needs.

Third, because small firms are ineffective in production, they ultimately vanish, thus depriving entrepreneurs of their organizational vehicle. The entrepreneurs vanish as their vehicle, the small firm, totters into oblivion.

RESURGENT ENTREPRENEURSHIP

As all these classical expectations materialized to a significant extent, economists and social scientists lost interest in entrepreneurship research, deeming the subject of interest only to historical sociology or third world and development research (Light, 1979; Corley, 1993:12–14).

"In the early 1970s there were sound grounds for concluding," writes Boissevain (1984; see also Waldinger, 1986:249) "that the decline of the small enterprises was a universal and continuing process." However, in the 1980s, the classical view of entrepreneurship came under broad criticism after long decades of unquestioned acceptance. Disputing the classic prescriptions, these writers claimed that entrepreneurship and small business remained too important to ignore and was likely to remain so for the foreseeable future (Borjas, 1986:486; Waldinger, 1986:249; Weiss, 1988:4). Even some Marxists came around to this view (Steinmetz and Wright, 1989:981–983; Rainnie, 1985).

Grounds for this revisionist claim emerged on the demand side and on the supply side. On the demand side, researchers discovered new evidence of the continued profitability of small and medium business firms. Whatever else they accomplished, these firms provided vehicles for entrepreneurs, thus rebutting the classical expectation that entrepreneurs would lose their function in mature capitalism. The new demand-side evidence falls most easily under four headings: numerical resurgence, aptitude of technology, organizational responsiveness, and political encouragement. Of these, numerical resurgence was the most basic. Marx's prediction to the contrary, the protracted decline of self-employment ended in 1972. Table 1.1 shows that, in the period 1972–1988, the American self-employed increased for the first time in a century, rising from 6.8 to 8.3% of the nonfarm labor force and then stabilized (Aronson, 1991:18; Becker, 1984; Light, 1984; Haber, 1985a:12). The same reversal occurred in Australia at approximately the same time (Castles et al., 1991:21). Boissevain (1984:20; also Mars and Ward, 1984:6) has reported that Common Market countries also registered a net increase in number of entrepreneurs and family workers in 1978, thus reversing their postwar trend of decline. Marceau (1989b:51) reported that in 1974 half of the largest 200 French firms were still family controlled, and that family capitalism had declined much less in France than expected. In Italy, Martinelli and Chiesi (1989:112) stress the high "entrepreneurial vitality" that has added thousands of new firms every year in the last two decades.[18] All this evidence was incompatible with the classical expectation that small and medium firms would disappear because they were unprofitable.

In approximately the same period, the mean size of business firms in the United States began to decline. In manufacturing, the mean number of employees per firm declined from 66 to 52 between 1970 and 1983. Among all industries, mean employees per firm declined from 16 to 14 in the same 13-year period. Admittedly, these reversals of historic trend were slight, but any reversal proves that the protracted decline of entrepreneurship had stalled in the mature capitalist economies. Some Marxists

Table 1.1.   Self-Employed Workers in the United States, 1948–1988 (Number in Thousands)

	1948	1958	1968	1972	1979	1988
Nonagricultural						
Employed	51,975	56,863	72,900	78,929	94,605	103,021
Self-employed	6,109	6,102	5,102	5,332	6,652	8,519
% Self-employed	11.8	10.7	7.0	6.8	7.0	8.3
Agricultural						
Employed	6,309	4,645	3,266	3,005	2,993	3,169
Self-employed	4,664	3,081	1,985	1,789	1,580	1,398
%Self-employed	73.9	66.3	60.8	59.5	52.8	44.1

Source: Fain (1980: 4, 1985: 108); U. S. Bureau of the Census, Statistical Abstract of the United States, 1990 (110th edition). Washington DC: USGPO, 1990, Tables 639 and 640.

reinterpreted Marx to retract and correct the expectation of small business disappearance while maintaining the spirit of Marx's analysis.[19]

Previous estimates of the self-employed population also turned out systematically to have underestimated its size and economic viability (Lindner, 1992:123). The 1980 U.S. Census enumerated 8,641,000 self-employed persons in the United States. Deriving its data from tax returns, the U.S. Internal Revenue Service counted 12,701,597 sole proprietors in 1980. Since some self-employed were partners, the number of self-employed ought to have exceeded the number of sole proprietors. In fact, it was only two-thirds as large. The disparity is known to result from different methods of enumeration, a problem discussed in President Ronald Reagan's (1984) report to Congress. Similarly, the Current Population Survey ignores part-time business owners whose main work is wage or salary employment. Using the Census Bureau's Survey of Program Participation, Haber, Lamas, and Lichtenstein (1987) were able to enumerate the part-time self-employed, thus permitting estimates of those uncounted in the CPS. They reported (1987:18) that self-employment was 60–75% more frequent than had been reported in the CPS. U.S. government publications have acknowledged the undercounts of the self-employed, and pledged to develop a "small business data base," which accurately tabulates them. Because entrepreneurs were undercounted, social scientists thought them less numerous than they actually were.

Studies of the underground economy also damaged the assumption that small business was economically inconsequential in the United States (Portes and Stepick, 1985) as well as in the developing countries (De Soto, 1989).[20] Narrowly defined, the underground economy consists of goods and services that change hands clandestinely. More broadly defined, the underground economy includes illegal activities concealed for obvious reasons, and traditionally uncommodified work such as housework or child care. Utilizing a narrow definition, Guttman (1977:27) estimated that the underground economy concealed 9.4% of GNP from taxation. The Commissioner of the U.S. Internal Revenue Service declared Guttman's estimates compatible with those of the Service, which estimated that $300 billion escaped taxation in 1981. The Internal Revenue Service also estimated that it lost between $60 and $70 billion in taxes on unreported earned income in 1988 (Akst, 1991). Since most of the purchasing units were small business enterprises, the discovery of the underground economy magnifies the importance of the small business sector.[21] The underground economy assumes special importance for the entrepreneurship of disadvantaged groups whose workers lack the resources required to own and operate firms large enough or legal enough to enumerate (Light, 1979; Jones, 1988).

Some evidence suggests that small business in the United States created more jobs than big business in the 1970s and 1980s (Acs and Audretsch, 1990:151). Birch (1981, 1987) compared the number of jobs created in U.S. metropolitan areas by 5.6 million big and small firms in the period 1969–1976. Of all new jobs created, small firms with 20 or fewer employees created 80%. Confirming Birch's results, Teitz, Glasmeiser, and Svensson (1981) studied job creation in California between 1975 and 1979. They found that firms with fewer than 20 employees created 56% of jobs in this period. According to Greene (1982:6), small business created 3 million jobs in the preceding decade whereas the 1,000 largest firms in the U.S. economy "recorded virtually no net gains in employment." In 1990 firms employing fewer than 100 employees accounted for two-thirds of all new employment while firms with 10,000 or more employees created only 3% of new jobs.[22]

The failure rate among small firms is high so that the life expectancy of the jobs they create is low. Big firms create many fewer jobs than small firms, but they retain longer the jobs they do create. Brown, Hamilton, and Medoff (1990:88–90) find that when job losses are subtracted from job gains, small firms did *not* create more than their share of jobs. We disagree. After all, even a failing firm provides months or years of employment before it finally fails. Acknowledging that a large share of small firms is always failing, we conclude that the economy contains a *permanent sector* of failing enterprises on whom the employment chances of many workers always ride. Put differently, if that failing sector abruptly vanished, unemployment rates would increase. In that sense, the employment contribution of small business, including failing ones, is meaningfully and permanently greater than that of big business.

The revised evidence of the small and medium business sector's revival, size, and economic importance promoted revisionist explanations. Some demand-side analysts called attention to the liberating potential of computer technology (Acs and Audretsch, 1990: Ch. 6). A major industrial trend of the 1970s and 1980s was flexible specialization, which referred to small and medium firms that employed the latest computer technology. This technology permitted them to produce a variety of products in small batches, and to switch rapidly among them. Flexible specialization characteristically occurred in industrial districts populated by numerous small and medium firms, each headed by an entrepreneur (Piore and Sabel, 1984:282; Scott, 1988:41–42, Ch. 6). Flexible specialization accounted for some of the most outstanding entrepreneurial revivals of the 1970s and 1980s, especially garment manufacturing. Hage and Powers (1992:7) find that of the 26,000 "high tech" firms in the United States, 92% were small firms.

Another line of research attacked the exaggerated claims that had been made for the efficiency of bureaucracy. Reviewing the evidence, Weiss (1988:24–25) concluded that "the economic case" for economies of scale was "not at all established." Keeble and Wever (1986:28) even detect a general trend toward "more decentralized, small-scale forms of economic organization—in advanced capitalist societies." Zucker's (1983) evidence showed that some of the nineteenth century's vaunted bureaucratization arose from follow-the-leader institutionalization, a process of social conformity, rather than from the strictly productive advantages of great organizational size. Granovetter (1984:323) even discovered that "contrary to the myth of bureaucratization," size of workplace in the American economy hardly increased between 1920 and 1970. Even in manufacturing, the bastion of large firms, Granovetter found no decrease in the proportion of workers in smaller establishments between 1923 and 1966. At no point in the twentieth century did more than one-third of manufacturing workers actually find employment in establishments larger than 1,000 workers. As the productive advantages of bureaucracy were reassessed, and the myth of bureaucratization debunked, sociologists openly questioned the classical idea that big organizations are always more efficient than small ones.

The organizational responsiveness of small and medium firms afforded another revisionist theme. New evidence showed that big firms innovate with difficulty (Stein, 1974:52–58; Hartley and Hutton, 1989) despite the theoretical advantages of bureaucracy. In a careful analysis, Acs and Audretsch (1990:57, 147) found that small firms innovate better than large firms in at least some environments. In several key industries, notably genetic engineering technology and desk-top computers, old-fashioned entrepreneurship has been the driving force of industrial innovation.[23] Without the small, entrepreneur-driven firms, personal computers would not have been developed in the 1970s (Takahashi, 1990). In junk bonds, a sphere of wild financial entrepreneurship during the 1980s, salaried managers became de facto entrepreneurs within the brokerage firms that ostensibly employed them (Bruck, 1988:19, 32, 52). Multinational giants had research and development laboratories staffed with salaried scientists, just as Schumpeter predicted, but biotechnology emerged from the garages of old-fashioned entrepreneurs (Kenney, 1986).

In addition to the technological and organizational arguments, Weiss (1988: Ch 4; see also Aronson, 1991:97) developed a political explanation for the revival of small business. Drawing on the dramatic case of the "Third Italy," the central Italian small business district, Weiss found technological explanations incomplete. To complete the explanation, she stressed (1988:79) the "importance of extra-economic factors," notably the influence of the Italian state in shaping a small business economy by law. Ideologically committed to an artisanal and small business economy, Italy's Christian Democrats introduced laws intended to encourage small firms. Through cheap loans, loan guarantees, low taxes, reduced cost welfare benefits, exemptions from recordkeeping requirements, and bankruptcy provisions, successive Italian governments in the 1950s and 1960s laid down a political basis for the subsequent dramatic resurgence of small firms in the Third Italy.

THE SUPPLY SIDE OF ENTREPRENEURSHIP

On the supply side, evidence proved conclusively that the proclivity for entrepreneurship was not evenly spread over all labor force segments. Women continued to lag men in entrepreneurship, although Loscocco and Robinson (1991:512) reported that during the 1980s "the increase in the number of women owning small businesses was five times greater than that for men." Other research showed the uneven participation of ethnic and immigrant minorities, thus rebutting the classical expectation that mature capitalism would recruit entrepreneurs equally from men and women as well as equally from all ethnoracial and religious groups (Aronson, 1991:8).

Seventy years after Weber's pronouncement, advanced market economies still contain many cultures, some of which are more entrepreneurial than others.[24] Partially for this reason, uneven entrepreneurship has remained a fact of development even in the advanced countries. To the extent that the labor forces of even mature market economies still contain groups that do not share an economic culture, metropolitan labor markets contain uneven entrepreneurial endowments. In that case, market signals can produce suboptimal supplies of entrepreneurs within and among metropolitan areas with some areas more responsive than others. After all, the same market demand generates unequal numbers of entrepreneurs when labor forces consist of groups whose propensity for entrepreneurship is unequal. For example, if high-proclivity groups predominate in Wausau's labor force, then market demand will evoke all the entrepreneurs needed to maximize economic growth in Wausau. However, if low-proclivity groups predominate in Newark, Newark's labor force might not produce enough entrepreneurs to fulfill the immanent economic potential of the city's market demand. In that case, Newark's rate of economic development would be impaired and Wausau's enhanced. Here entrepreneurship is problematic, noneconomic, and causally significant.

In point of fact, metropolitan labor forces in North America consist of groups whose proclivity for entrepreneurship is still unequal. Immigrants in the United States, Canada, and Australia continued to manifest higher rates of self-employment than the native born, a proclivity they have displayed for at least a century (Borjas, 1986:486; Simon, 1989:71–74; Castles, et al., 1991:30). Since immigration has not disappeared in the course of modernization, and shows no sign of disappearing, immigration repetitiously recreates cultural heterogeneity in the labor forces of advanced market societies. The labor market's heterogeneity engenders unequal responsiveness of participant groups to market demand for entrepreneurs in apparent defiance of classical theory.

Although the foreign born generally exceed the entrepreneurship of the native born, several immigrant and ethnic minorities produced rates of entrepreneurship appreciably higher than the foreign born in general. Langlois and Razin (1989:345) found that Canadians of German or Dutch origin were more frequently self-employed than other immigrants. In Los Angeles, Light and Bonacich (1988: Chs. 1, 7, 8) found that 23% of foreign-born Koreans were self-employed in 1980 compared with only 7% of non-Koreans. As another 30% found employment in Korean-owned firms, about 53% of Koreans worked within the Korean economy. Portes, Clark, and Lopez (1981–82:18) found that 20% of Cubans in Miami were self-employed, and another 30% worked in Cuban-owned enterprises. This rate of entrepreneurship was much higher than that prevailing among Mexicans in Miami. Sabagh and Bozorgmehr (1987) reported that 30% of Iranian men in Los Angeles were self-employed in 1980.

Among nonimmigrants, Jews, Chinese, Japanese, Greeks, Italians, and Armenians were reliably higher than average in rate of self-employment. Admittedly, Goldscheider and Kobrin (1980:262–275) found that successive generations of white ethnics in Providence evidenced successively lower rates of self-employment, a result compatible with the concentration theory. Nonetheless, in every generation, Jews led the rank order of ethnic groups in entrepreneurship, suggesting that sociocultural endowment continued to affect each group's production of entrepreneurs.

In Britain, immigrant entrepreneurship also became visible during the 1970s and 1980s. In the depressed centers of larger British cities, Pakistani and East Indian immigrants opened numerous small business enterprises. By the mid-1980s, the rate of self-employment among Britain's Asian minority exceeded that among the native-white population. In addition to equal rights with native-born persons, immigrants in Britain, Canada, and the United States enjoyed complete liberty to initiate firms. But working-age foreigners did not have the same freedom on the European continent where laws commonly forbade foreign workers from becoming self-employed. Possibly because of legal restraints upon foreigners' self-employment, immigrant entrepreneurship developed less on the European continent than in Britain or North America. However, by the early 1980s, Surinamese in Amsterdam, Turks in Berlin, and North Africans in Lyon had become visible in urban business enterprise (Boissevain et al., 1990; Boissevain and Grotenbreg, 1987; Blaschke and Ersoz, 1986a).

CAUSES OF UNEQUAL ENTREPRENEURSHIP

Demand alone is capable of producing intermetropolitan differences in rates of self-employment among ethnoracial or ethnoreligious groups. Conceivably, persisting intergroup differences in entrepreneurship are wholly the product of persisting disparities in the demand environment. In that case one would wrongly infer unequal proclivity for self-employment from unequal self-employment rates. Much literature addresses this issue. Cultural theory fastens upon transplanted cultural endowments of immigrant minorities that explain their entrepreneurship. Derived ultimately from Weber, cultural theory claims that individuals learn their group's values, motivations, and skills in the course of socialization (Woodrum, 1985; Cochran, 1965:93, 100). When a group's values, motivations, and skills encourage business enterprise, cultural minorities produce socialized adults who prosper in business (Min, 1984:344–345). In its most straightforward version, cultural explanation posits international relocation of intact cultural traditions such that entrepreneurial groups in one country remain entrepreneurial in others. Gypsies offer a splendid example. Wherever they debark, Gypsies already know how to tell fortunes, repair pots, and collect salvage (Sway, 1988). Whether in Europe or the Americas, Gypsy practice these trades.

Although a cultural explanation fits classic middleman minorities (Zenner, 1991), whose histories betoken a prolonged tradition of entrepreneurship, cultural explanations are not universally satisfactory. Some entrepreneurial immigrants in the United States (Cubans, Koreans) did not have prior histories of entrepreneurship around the world. Also, where entrepreneurship is legally available on an equal basis to immigrants and nonimmigrants, immigrant self-employment normally exceeds nonimmigrant self-employment. Because the foreign born outperform the native born, we cannot turn to unique cultural traditions for an explanation. More is presumably at work than idiosyncratic cultural traditions. Studying this problem, some sociologists have concluded that disadvantage in the labor market is a frequent cause of some immigrant entrepreneurship independent of cultural tradition (Light, 1979; Min, 1984).[25] Labor market disadvantage encourages compensatory self-employment. For example, Light and Bonacich (1988: Ch. 8) found that Korean wage earners in Los Angeles County received only 76% of the return on their education that non-Koreans received. On the other hand, Korean entrepreneurs received 93% of the return on education that non-Korean entrepreneurs received. Therefore, Koreans had a greater financial incentive to undertake self-employment than did non-Koreans.

REACTIVE ETHNICITY

Young (1971:142) and Hagen (1962) long ago argued that entrepreneurship rises when newly subordinated groups react against real or threatened loss of status. Reactive ethnicity applies this approach to immigrant and ethnic entrepreneurship. Reactive ethnicity is a joint effect of the presenting culture and of the host society's social structure (Auster and Aldrich, 1984). As such, reactive ethnicity is neither an intact cultural transmission nor a labor market disadvantage. It arises in response to alien status in defense of the collective self-esteem of group members.

Reactive ethnicity enhances entrepreneurship by enhancing solidarity. In the first place, ethnicity is itself an ideology of solidarity (Cohen, 1969; Espiritu, 1992). Ethnic entrepreneurs champion disesteemed groups whose conception of their culture's prestige appreciably exceeds that prevailing where they live. For example, reflecting upon his entrepreneurial career in Toronto, an Italian Catholic informant reported that "It was a major factor in my career—attempting to prove that I am worthy of respect and also that Italians are worthy of respect."[26] In addition to the jobs they create for coethnics, often a significant share of total group employment, coethnic entrepreneurs exhibit disesteemed aliens in powerful roles. Although socially disesteemed, alien entrepreneurs are economically powerful, a forceful claim to social recognition in any society. While thus vindicating the alien culture to its own adherents, and providing jobs for its members, alien entrepreneurs also prove a disesteemed group's capacity for leadership as well as its worthiness for citizenship and social acceptance.

Because of these important, group-strengthening services, ethnic solidarity legitimates the coethnic bourgeoisie's right to command coethnic employees. "We must work hard in order to build a solidarity- and wealth-enhancing ethnic economy." Here ethnicity provides immigrant entrepreneurs with what Bendix (1956:13–21) has called an "ideology of management," a valuable business resource. However, industrial paternalism is the price of this economic resource. Ethnic solidarity requires the group's entrepreneurs to adopt a paternalistic attitude toward coethnic workers, offering them training, sponsorship, and patronage they would not accord an outsider. This paternalistic responsibility facilitates subsequent self-employment on the part of sponsored workers (Cobas, Aickin, and Jardine, 1993; Wilson and Portes, 1980:315).

Ethnicity also provides ideological support for mercantile association in restraint of trade. In economic theory, markets destroy cartels by promotion of internal competition. Admittedly, internal competition inhibits cartel formation and survival so the theory is partially correct. However, ethnicity offers a countervailing force that, by uniting the entrepreneurs around an ideology of solidarity, increases the likelihood of cartelization in defiance of market competition (Werbner, 1987; Yu, 1982:67). Precisely insofar as coethnics share an ethnic identity, they acquire some enhanced capacity to cooperate, thus permitting advantageous business cartels capable of strangling competition. This capacity Portes and Sensenbrenner (1993:1324) call "bounded solidarity." Additionally, because coethnics cluster in a handful of trades or professions, an arrangement Hechter (1976:215) has labeled the "cultural division of labor," their share of the entrepreneurs in an ethnic industry is likely to exceed their share of entrepreneurs in the economy. Thus, Light and Bonacich (1988: Chs. 7, 8) found that Koreans in Los Angeles were 1% of the population, 5% of the entrepreneur population, but 35% of beer, wine, and liquor dealers. As a result, the Korean liquor merchants association exerted more market power in the liquor industry than would have been possible had Koreans represented only 5% of the merchant population in every industry.

By enhancing the scope and integration of social networks, ethnic solidarity confers important business resources (Gold, 1992:167–198;

Waldinger, Ward, and Aldrich, 1985:591–592; Hisrich and Brush, 1986:4; Portes, 1987:346; Portes and Sensenbrenner, 1993:1329). First, ethnic networks carry business-related information (Wells, 1991). Because of these networks, coethnic entrepreneurs promptly acquire news of business value such as the relative profitability of different industries or the success of industrial innovations (Portes, 1987:368). Channelling information causes "entrepreneurial chains" from which, according to Werbner (1984:186), a community-wide "culture of ethnicity" subsequently develops. Second, social networks also encourage mutual aid among business owners. Mutual aid ranges from advice to preferential purchasing. Research shows that informal and mutual aid is common among immigrant entrepreneurs (Waldinger, 1986: Ch. 6; Kim and Hurh, 1985:93). By contributing to the viability of individual firms, mutual aid increases the ability of immigrant populations to support numerous business firms.

All business requires trust (Macaulay, 1963; O'Neill, Bhambri, Faulkner, and Cannon, 1987; Zucker, 1986). Multiplex social networks permit ethnics to trust one another in business (Cohen, 1969, 1971). Enhanced trust makes possible many advantageous business arrangements. By expediting the purchase and sale of business firms, social networks help to build economic specialization in the self-employment sector. The specialization, in turn, supports market power. Again, rotating credit associations are an informal financial system that Asian immigrants in the United States have utilized successfully for purposes of encouraging thrift as well as for the assembly of business capital (Light, Im, and Deng, 1990). Although rotating credit systems originate in countries of origin, and thus represent an intact cultural heritage, the continued viability of the traditional credit system requires reconstruction and maintenance of social trust. By buttressing social networks, reactive ethnicity contributes to the viability of rotating credit associations in a developed economic environment.

Social trust also contributes to the proliferation of entrepreneurs among immigrant and ethnic populations by reducing external transaction costs (Landa, 1991; Redding, 1991). External transaction costs generally promote bureaucratization as entrepreneurs evade the external cost by internalizing transactions. This strategy embeds business trust in an imperatively coordinated, centrally managed bureaucracy. Transactional economists suppose that inefficient markets compel firms to choose bureaucracy over market coordination (Acheson, 1986:49). However, the social relations among economic actors are also influential. Ethnic and immigrant entrepreneurs often maintain a transactional environment that minimizes transaction costs within the ethnic economy. Relying upon informal social trust, anchored ultimately in social networks, communities of immigrant and ethnic entrepreneurs transact business cheaply in inefficient markets. In the community of ethnic entrepreneurs, external transaction costs are lower than those prevailing in the general economy. Because of extensive social trust within the ethnic economy, immigrants' firms compete successfully in the general economy.

THE RESOURCES THEORY OF ENTREPRENEURSHIP

Whatever their differences, cultural explanations, disadvantage explanations, and reactive ethnicity explanations all revolve around and attest to the unequal propensity of groups to embrace entrepreneurship. In an attempt at synthesis, the *resources theory of entrepreneurship* reduces earlier approaches to ethnic and class resources of entrepreneurship (Young, 1971:142; Light, 1984; Light and Karageorgis, 1994; Model, 1985:79; Boissevain et al., 1990). Whatever demographic, sociocultural, or socioeconomic features of a group encourage its entrepreneurship represent an entrepreneurial resource. These resources operate singly or jointly (Light, 1984). That is, any group's resource banks may contain only class resources, only ethnic resources, or both. When joint production obtains, both class and ethnic resources contribute to entrepreneurship, but the influences need not be equal and usually are not. When influences are joint but unequal in magnitude, we distinguish class-preponderant or ethnic-preponderant causes.

Ethnic resources are sociocultural and demographic features of the whole group that coethnic entrepreneurs actively utilize in business or from which their business passively benefits (Light, 1984; Chan and Cheung, 1985; Kim and Hurh, 1985; Light and Bonacich, 1988: Ch. 7).[27] Ethnic resources characterize a group, not isolated members. Therefore, if A enjoys a resource, but his coethnics do not, A's resource is not ethnic. Typical ethnic resources include entrepreneurial heritages, entrepreneurial values and attitudes, low transaction costs, rotating credit associations, relative satisfaction arising from nonacculturation to prevailing labor standards, social capital, reactive solidarities, multiplex social networks, and a generous pool of underemployed and disadvantaged coethnic workers (Young, 1971:142; Werbner, 1984:167; Foner, 1985:717). If one observes, for example, that Chinese work long hours, save more of their income than outsiders, express satisfaction with low wages, help one another to acquire business skills and information, follow one another into the same trades, combine easily to restrain trade, utilize rotating credit associations, or deploy multiplex social networks to economic advantage, one is calling attention to the manner in which ethnic resources promote Chinese entrepreneurship (Basu, 1991; Wong,

1987; Bailey, 1987: Ch. 3; Harrell, 1985; Stites, 1985).[28] As the constituent resources are collective, ethnic entrepreneurship acquires a collective rather than individualist character (Cummings, 1980; Fratoe, 1986).

In contrast, *class or bourgeois resources* are the normal cultural and material endowment of bourgeoisies.[29] As such, class resources lack distinctive ethnic character. Any bourgeoisie enjoys them. On the material side, class resources include private property in the means of production and distribution, human capital, and money to invest (Bates, 1985a). But the bourgeoisie also has a vocational culture.[30] In the standard Marxist lexicon, the bourgeoisie is the class that owns the means of production and distribution, a formulation that overlooks their human and social capital. Our formulation corrects this oversight. The standard Marxist definition also overlooks the bourgeoisie's vocational culture. The vocational culture of the bourgeoisie includes occupationally relevant and supportive values, attitudes, knowledge, and skills transmitted in the course of socialization. Bourgeois culture means cultural traits (values, skills, attitudes, knowledge) characteristic of bourgeoisies around the world, and which, furthermore, distinguish a bourgeois from nonbourgeois coethnics while linking him or her to noncoethnic bourgeois.[31] An established bourgeoisie equips its youth with appropriate class resources, both material and cultural, and, having them, the youth are well equipped to prosper in and to reproduce a market economy (Marceau, 1989a). Therefore, if one observes that ethnic or immigrant entrepreneurs had entrepreneurial parents, previous business experience in their homeland, large sums of money available for investment when they arrived, materialistic attitudes and values, and graduate degrees in business administration, these resources define a class explanation of their entrepreneurship. Ethnic resources play no role in such a class-only explanation.[32]

A bourgeoisie usually enjoys both cultural and material class resources, but occasional separations occur, especially among refugees. When these separations occur, an ethnic bourgeoisie has only material or only cultural class resources at its disposition. For example, Portes and Bach (1985) reported that the earliest pre-Mariel Cuban refugees in Miami were of bourgeois origin. Their parents had been wealthy entrepreneurs and business managers in Cuba. However, the Cuban bourgeois refugees arrived penniless in Miami with only their class culture, social capital, and human capital intact. The socialist government of Cuba would not permit them to take their money out of Cuba. Nonetheless, the impoverished Cuban bourgeoisie in Miami promptly reconstituted itself as a property-owning class within a decade.[33] In so doing, the Cuban bourgeoisie made heavy use of the cheap labor of post-Mariel coethnics (Portes, 1987). They also developed an ideology of ethnic solidarity that explained and justified their paternalistic, nonunion policies. The abundant coethnic workers and paternalistic ideology were ethnic not class resources. These ethnic resources supported the Cuban bourgeoisie's class cultural resources, chiefly their business know-how. The Cuban ethnic economy in Miami was, therefore, a joint product of ethnic as well as of class cultural resources. Class resources alone did not create it.

The distinction between class and ethnic resources is essential in order to avoid what Turner and Bonacich (1980:145, 180) have called "unnecessary and wasteful polemics." Ethnic and immigrant entrepreneurship *always* draws on both class and ethnic resources, although the balance can vary with now one, now the other predominant (Light, 1984:202). As a result, an ethnic bourgeoisie is not just a bourgeoisie, nor is an ethnic entrepreneur just an entrepreneur. In Marxist theory, bourgeoisies only have class resources; they do not have ethnic resources. In reality, bourgeoisies enjoy both ethnic and class resources. Since these endowments are not universal, the bourgeoisies of the world differ importantly one from the other.

The availability of ethnic resources changes the entrepreneurship of a bourgeoisie. First, ethnic solidarity provides a legitimating ideology for ethnic entrepreneurs (Wong, 1987:128): "We Shanghainese must help one another in business." Second, ethnic entrepreneurs convert social characteristics of their group into economic resources, thus creating employment and income independent of class resources. This social alchemy converts characteristics of no economic value into economic value. In effect, ethnic entrepreneurs convert ethnic difference and social marginality into an economic resource.[34] Finally, ethnic entrepreneurship improves the economic status and hastens the economic mobility of the entire ethnic population, even the employees (Light et al., 1994). The entrepreneurs have high earnings, but employees benefit because their employment chances are expanded beyond the secondary labor market, the normal boundary of their employability (Nee and Sanders, 1985:87–88). Hess (1990:11) even reports that Korean garment manufacturers treated Korean employees better than Mexican employees.[35]

SUMMARY AND CONCLUSION

The classical literature of entrepreneurship predicted its obsolescence. For this reason, researchers ignored the subject for decades. However, the renaissance of entrepreneurship in the last two decades requires reattention to the subject. This revisionist effort has created a growing but poorly integrated theoretical literature that rejects the classical synthesis but falls short of adequacy on its own. One reason is inattention to the articulation of demand and supply issues. On the demand side, researchers debunked classical theory's unrelentingly negative prognosis for the economic viability of small and medium business. However, they accepted classical theory's expectation that entrepreneurship would lose its causal significance in consequence of cultural homogenization. Classical theorists expected entrepreneurship to shed its dependence on ethnic minorities, and demand-side revisionists have accepted this part of classical theory. Demand-side theorists implicitly and sometimes explicitly stripped entrepreneurship of its causal significance.

Arguably correct, this demand-side view conflicts with extensive evidence of the persistently unequal proclivity of groups for entrepreneurship. To explain this inequality, sociologists have turned to class and ethnic resources. Resources theory posits a pluralistic society within which ethnoracial groups have uneven class and ethnic resources at their disposal. Now the most widely accepted explanation of intergroup disparities in entrepreneurship, resource theory's distinction between class and ethnic resources is pivotal (Myers, 1983:14; Light, 1984; Min and Jaret, 1985:432; Kim and Hurh, 1985; Fratoe, 1986:7, 13; Wong, 1987:122-128; Waldinger, 1988; Yoon, 1991; Cobas and DeOllos, 1989; Boissevain et al., 1990).[36] Class resources are the usual endowment of a bourgeoisie, e.g., money to invest, human capital, and ownership of productive means. Existing theory adequately recognizes these material resources. But class resources also include cultural endowments unique to the bourgeoisie, especially vocationally relevant knowledge, attitudes, skills, beliefs, and values. In contrast, ethnic resources are features of the whole group, including all the social strata therein, that entrepreneurs passively or actively utilize in their business. Ethnic resources include ethnic ideologies, industrial paternalism, solidarity, social networks, ethnic institutions, and social capital.

Although contrasting, demand-side and supply-side factors need not exclude one another in that both operate in the same economic environment, reinforcing or contradicting one another. To claim that entrepreneurship remains causally significant in American society, as we do, does not require us to deny the technological, political, or organizational explanations for entrepreneurship's resurgence. We claim only that demand for entrepreneurs still encounters a labor force whose entrepreneurial resources vary from group to group. As a result, the same demand generates more entrepreneurship in some groups and localities than in others. In essence, we dispute the notion that demand for entrepreneurs is now invariably a sufficient explanation for the level of entrepreneurship observed. We dispute this notion on the ground most unfavorable to our claim, an advanced market economy.

On the other hand, even if demand-side and supply-side causes coproduce entrepreneurship, existing literature offers no guidance to how much weight one ought to assign to each. Possibly, cultural homogenization has proceeded to such an extent that resources and disadvantage matter little in the generation of entrepreneurs even if they cannot entirely be discounted. In that case, markets would routinely generate enough entrepreneurs to serve them, but one would find infrequent occasions in which markets still depended upon exogenous, causally significant entrepreneurship for this achievement. The classical theory would be almost correct on this point, and the resources theory a quibble.

But it is also possible that exogenous sources continue to provide some or most of the entrepreneurs needed, in which case economic outcomes still depend heavily upon ethnic diversity. Moreover, to the extent that some ethnoracial groups do not generate enough entrepreneurs, they could suffer the consequence of aborted economic development and stymied economic mobility. In fact, this alternative is the one we endorse. We maintain that entrepreneurship is still so significant that entrepreneurial resources still affect the aggregate economic development of society as well as the economic chances of individual groups within it.

NOTES

1.   This American level is high. Only "one-fourth of the Hungarian population" expresses an aspiration for self-employment. See Lengyel (1989:80).

2.   In addition to valuable experience and contacts in the construction industry, Donald Trump's father handed young Donald several million dollars at the age of 23 (Trump, 1987: Ch. 1). Obviously, young Donald made his inheritance grow. Trump became richer and more visible than Antonio Lopez, owner/operator of El Grito taco stand in Torrance, California. But to label Trump more successful than Lopez, whose father was an itinerate *campesino*, is to confuse scale with success. Conceivably, Lopez was more successful than Trump if by success we mean the ability to multiply in one's lifetime the financial endowment one received from one's parents.

3.   "Ray Kroc did not invent fast food. He did not invent the self-service restaurant. And his first McDonald's restaurant was not the first McDonald's" (Love, 1986:10).

4.   "Businessmen do not think of themselves as leaders in social movements, but they are" (Ford, 1929:101).

5. "Pepsi Co., Pizza Hut Reach an Accord on Proposed Merger." *Wall Street Journal* (June 17, 1977:24). On the history of the pizza industry (see: Lovell-Troy, 1990, Ch. 2).

6. Indeed, Americans' repulsion toward some Chinese ingredients still occasionally surfaces in popular media. A restaurant in Canton now serves rat 30 different ways. See James McGregor, "Waiter There's a Rat in My Soup," *Wall Street Journal* (May 31, 1991:A1). On other repulsive foods still consumed in China see also *Newsweek* (July 29, 1991:35).

7. Fifty-two percent of Americans claim that Chinese restaurant food is "more healthful" than their usual diet. Since the American diet is unhealthful, this belief could be true even though Hurley and Schmidt (1993) found that the average Chinese restaurant meal contains more than one day's recommended intake of sodium, 70% of a day's fat, and 80% of a day's cholesterol.

8. Constraint on supply does not disappear when a population is ethnically homogeneous or all of its ethnoracial-religious groups have identical entrepreneurship proclivities. For example, declaring that the "quantity of entrepreneurship is not fixed," Taub and Taub (1989:175) find that India's castes all responded to entrepreneurship's financial incentives to the limit of their financial resources. Even if this claim were true, and caste did not influence the rate or quality of entrepreneur formation, India's entrepreneur supply would still be limited by the resources available—and so constrained.

9. Usselman (1992) finds, however, that Westinghouse and Edison were *not* interchangeable. Edison was more theoretical than Westinghouse. If so, the historical fungibility of Westinghouse and Edison is really in doubt, a possibility that strengthens our argument.

10. Even if Westinghouse and Edison had failed, someone else would have invented the electric light by 1994. But had humanity been compelled to wait even a year for the invention, the wait would have been *nontrivial*.

11. Gershenkron (1953–54:9) remarks similarly upon the inhibiting effect in Russia "of the lingering preindustrial value systems, of aversion to entrepreneurs, and to new forms of economic activity in general." He concludes that "an adverse social attitude towards entrepreneurs may thus indeed delay the beginning of rapid industrialization."

12. This argument is developed in greater detail in Light (1984:195–197).

13. These points are amplified in Light (1984).

14. That is, if the absence of Protestantism would have delayed capitalism by one century, then our current standard of living would be that of a century earlier without Protestantism. We would now have electric lights, but no telephones, washing machines, or automobiles. Measured in terms of GNP foregone, the money cost of that century's delay would be astronomical.

15. That is, when their market price rose, entrepreneurs entered the market in appropriate numbers; when their price fell entrepreneurs left the market; and equilibrium was achieved by the usual balance of supply and demand. Markets never suffered a chronic shortage of entrepreneurs. As a result, market demand attained its immanent growth potential with the population of entrepreneurs a function of demand, not supply (Kilby, 1971:2).

16. Light (1974b) discusses Mills in greater detail.

17.   Deeming self-employment atavistic, Marxists also disapproved of it morally and politically. As Gorz (1982:55) explained, a working person's dream of professional autonomy represented an obstacle to working class consciousness that "proletarian militants" long resisted and condemned for this reason. See also Clegg, Boreham, and Dow (1986:82).

18.   For a review of books dealing with the Third Italy, see Orru (1991).

19.   "In other words, small firms should not be viewed as anachronistic survivors of a bygone age, destined for destruction. They have a role to play in the advanced, though crisis-ridden economies of the late twentieth century" (Rainnie, 1985:3). On the other hand, Clegg, Boreham, and Dow (1986: Ch. 4) hang onto the orthodox Marxist view of a petit bourgeoisie in decline.

20.   Studies of third world economies had long ago reached the same conclusion. See: Light (1983: Ch. 14) and De Soto (1989).

21.   For a dissenting view, see Harding and Jenkins (1989). However, their dissent is motivated as much by policy-driven fear that public officials will misuse research on this subject as much as by scientific skepticism.

22.   *U.S. News and World Report* (June 3, 1991:52).

23.   Calvo and Wellisz (1980) make a plausible theoretical case for the advantages of youth and small size in technological innovation.

24.   For documentation, see: Fratoe and Meeks, 1985.

25.   We explore disadvantage in Chapter 6.

26.   Ironically, if Torontonians had exhibited a higher opinion of Italians, Italians would have manifested less reactive entrepreneurship. The quotation is from Kallen and Kelner (1983:74).

27.   Kim, Hurh, and Fernandez (1989:91) properly observe that to explain intergroup differences in self-employment in terms of resources, one must specify the resources alleged to cause high self-employment. Yoon (1991) operationalized ethnic resources as follows: an entrepreneur received loans from family and/or friends, participated in a rotating credit association, was in partnership with a coethnic, participated in a business network of family and kin, has coethnic suppliers, and worked long hours of unpaid labor. Yoon defined class resources with the following variables: an entrepreneur used personal savings to finance his or her own business, brought money with her or him from homeland, and obtained bank or government loans for his or her business.

28.   On China, see Harrell (1985) and Stites (1985:227–246).The same claim is made for many groups. (See also Hess, 1990: Ch. 6:11; Cobas and De Ollos, 1989:409; Young and Sontz, 1988; Portes, 1987; Foner, 1985:717.)

29.   Pierre Bourdieu collapses gender, ethnicity, and generation into class, a strategy that conceals the distinction between class and ethnic resources. See Brubaker (1985:762).

30.   Pierre Bourdieu has analyzed the high culture of the bourgeoisie, but neglected its vocational culture as though bourgeoisies only attended art openings and poetry readings. For a comprehensive review of Bourdieu's voluminous work, see Brubaker (1985).

31.   Yoon (1991) disputes the distinction between class culture and ethnic culture, arguing that class culture often coincides "with the cultural values and attitudes of an ethnic group." He gives the example of Korean Americans, all of

whom value education, hard work, and thrift, thus rendering these allegedly class values into cultural values.

32. For an economist's critique of resources theory, see Bates (1994a).

33. Their achievement was analogous to that of the postwar Hungarian bourgeoisie that, stripped of its wealth by the communist government, emerged a generation later with independent property, strictly on the basis of their class culture (Szelenyi, 1988).

34. For a related argument, see Coleman (1988).

35. "Interviews suggest that Korean homeworkers are less subject to unreasonably low wages and payment difficulties encountered by Hispanics. The Koreans interviewed report that they have never heard of a case of a Korean homeworker who was not paid by a Korean contractor. They say that if a Korean contractor ever failed to pay a Korean homeworker, the news would spread quickly to the other Korean homeworkers, and the contractor would have great difficulty securing workers in the future" (Hess, 1990:11).

36. In a related effort, O'Brian and Fugita (1984:522) distinguish ethnic interests from class interests in their analysis of Japanese American farmers in California.

2

Urban Entrepreneurs in America

Although building upon two decade's research, resources theory's basis in evidence still suffers methodological and measurement limitations. Existing theory depends almost exclusively on case studies and selective comparisons (Paulin, Coffey, and Spaulding, 1982:359). Case studies are intensive examinations of one group's entrepreneurship in a single locality. Selective comparisons juxtapose one or more categories or groups in one or more localities (Kim, Hurh, and Fernandez, 1989; Gold, 1988a; Boissevain et al., 1990). Neither case studies nor selective comparisons provide overviews, and, at a certain phase of a subject's development, overviews become essential.[1] Case studies fill gaps in knowledge or resolve theoretical problems. But, to locate the gaps requires a broad view, and, even when pieced together, selective comparisons and individual case studies cannot always convey the whole picture any more than an album of photographs can replicate the Grand Canyon. Lacking overviews, researchers selected cases for study on grounds of convenience, the absence of previous research, and even topicality.

As case study research accumulated, theory developed a backlog of unsolved questions. These questions were those that case studies and selective comparisons could raise, but could not resolve.[2] Unresolved questions concerned the wholes of which the cases were parts. For example, Lieberson (1980:297) proposed that big groups had lower self-employment rates than small groups, but he lacked the evidence to test this idea. By definition, case studies and selective comparisons could not treat whole populations, although they could, and often did, emerge with a sense of the whole's importance. As population questions piled up, they became an intellectual backlog awaiting liquidation.

Existing quantitative research has exposed these problems without resolving them. One reason is the relative recency of quantitative approaches in this subject area. Given the evidence vacuum, just producing information was an achievement. Therefore, some useful quantitative research is purely descriptive (Wicker and King, 1989; Haber, Lamas, and Lichtenstein, 1987; Haber, 1985; Becker, 1984). Other research analyzes the entrepreneurship experience of one or possibly two immigrant or ethnoracial categories without disaggregating localities (Furino and Bates, 1983; Ong, 1981). Still other research provides quantitative treatments of ethnic and immigrant self-employment at the national level without disaggregating locality influences (Fratoe and Meeks, 1985; Portes and Rumbaut, 1990).

Recently, geographers and sociologists have underscored the importance of disaggregating localities as well as comparing groups. Taking a social problems approach to 55 metropolitan areas, Robert Boyd (1990) compared Asians and African Americans in 55 metropolitan areas using the public-use sample of the 1970 and 1980 censuses. Boyd found that African-American self-employment lagged in metropolitan areas in which African-American employment in public service increased most during the decade of the 1970s. Boyd's (1991) paper examined African-American/Asian self-employment earnings in the same 55 metropolitan areas. He found that Asians had more human capital than African Americans, and that they earned more in self-employment than African Americans. However, he found no differences in self-employment earnings between Asians and African Americans net of human capital, concluding that group differences resulted from disparities in level of resources rather than in rates of return to these resources (1991). Boyd also pioneered the use of statistical interaction terms to examine interdependence between level of resources and returns to resources. Boyd's research uncovered many of the issues with which we are now concerned, but he did not theoretically exploit the interlocality comparisons that his data afforded.

Unsurprisingly, geographers were first to stress interlocal comparisons. European geographers have explained local variation in entrepreneurship ignoring group resources (Keeble and Wever, 1986; Rekers, Dijest, and Van Kempen, 1990). That approach brings out geographic influences while ignoring social influences. However, an Israeli, Eran Razin (1988; see also Langlois and Razin, 1989; Hoffman and Marger, 1991) compared foreign-born self-employment in San Francisco and Los Angeles. He found intermetropolitan differences in entrepreneurship that he attributed to locational influences as well as to ethnic differences. Langlois and Razin (1989) concentrated on social influences upon entrepreneurship in Canadian cities. Comparing immigrant self-employment in several cities of Israel, Canada, and California, Razin (1993) again found distinct group and locality influences, but he reported that "locality and ethnicity interact in their influence on self-employment" in Israel as well as in the United States (1993:119). Razin's (1993) most recent work is more theoretical than other work in this field, because Razin first recognized the importance of simultaneous variation in locality and resources.

MEASUREMENT PROBLEMS

On the measurement side, resources theory accepted flawed statistical evidence from official sources. The most obvious problem was the uncritical utilization of the Current Population Survey's (CPS) definition of the self-employed. The self-employed represent the closest approximation to the entrepreneur population available in American statistics (Light and Bonacich, 1988:158), use of which is unavoidable. The CPS definition fell short of validity, but was uncritically accepted anyway. Social scientists routinely accepted statistics based on the CPS definition (Light, 1979:38–40; Light and Bonacich, 1988:10–12). Admittedly, the CPS definition of self-employment improved upon previous measurements of the entrepreneur population, and it vastly exceeds what is still available in European census publications. However, it did not, as was once believed, solve all the measurement problems.

The CPS defines the self-employed as workers who reported that they worked as sole proprietors or partners of an unincorporated business. The CPS question required respondents to declare what they were mainly or principally doing in a criterion week. Therefore, this CPS definition excludes from the self-employed population at least five classes of workers who belonged in that classification. First, the CPS definition excludes employees of their own corporations, treating these workers instead as wage or salary earners. Typically medical doctors, accountants, and attorneys, these so-called employees are really founders and sole owners of the companies that employ them. In Haber's (1985:2) opinion, such workers must be "considered when focussing on the entrepreneurial class."

Second, the CPS excludes from self-employment those wage and salary workers who reported self-employment as a secondary activity (Becker, 1984:14; Sullivan and McCracken, 1988:170; Portes and Rumbaut, 1990:89). Forced to choose between wage worker or self-employed worker, they usually chose wage worker, thus concealing secondary self-employment. Excluding these wage workers undercounts the true entrepreneur population for several reasons. In many cases, full-time entrepreneurs begin as part-time entrepreneurs (Sullivan and McCracken, 1988:171; Ray, 1975:51; Wilensky, 1963:108, 115). Therefore, when part-time entrepreneurs are excluded, results conceal fledgling entrepreneurs whose firms do not yet support them. In the same sense, some full-time entrepreneurs fall back to part-time when wage employment opportunities improve or when business conditions deteriorate. To exclude such workers from the category of self-employment obscures the worklife changes that move people into and out of full-time entrepreneurship, and also underestimates the true entrepreneur population.

Third, the CPS definition of self-employment excludes housewives. Classifying housewives as "not in the labor force," the CPS assumes that housewives had no commercial roles just because they were not actively seeking jobs. Yet, some housewives operated a business from their home on a part-time basis (Dallalfar, 1989). Alas, the CPS definition of self-employment is incapable of detecting these women entrepreneurs, thus tending to underestimate the number of women entrepreneurs. Indeed, it is an open question to what extent the recent surge in women's entrepreneurship does not represent a surfacing of women-owned businesses that were invisible so long as their owners were full-time housewives rather than employees.

Fourth, the CPS definition excludes the unemployed from entrepreneurship. Yet, with or without self-employment earnings, some unemployed workers operated full-time or part-time business firms. In most cases, unemployed entrepreneurs earned little from their own business, and were, for this reason, seeking wage-earning jobs even while eking out a precarious existence from self-employment (Haber, 1985:12). In a few cases, unemployed workers began marginal firms that later became capable of supporting them. In any case, the CPS survey defined away the unemployed entrepreneurs, thus tending to undercount the true entrepreneur population.

Finally, the CPS survey overlooks those who concealed their self-employment. Concealers included criminals self-employed in gambling, drugs, pornography, prostitution, and the like. Additionally, concealers included business owners whose firms, perfectly legal in themselves, violate laws regulating the manner in which business must be conducted. Such firms include off-the-book operations, firms that violate labor standards, and unlicensed firms in fields where licenses are required.

Although unmeasured, the combined effect of these incomplete statistics must be big. When Haber (1985:5) corrected the CPS definition of self-employment to take account of wage and salary workers who also operated a small business, the measured rate of nonagricultural self-employment increased from 7.8 to 13.5% of the employed in 1983. Wage and salary workers who were also self-employed represented 22.1% of business owners. Yet, the CPS definition of self-employment had wholly excluded these persons from the self-employed population.

Haber's correction for part-time self-employment increased the measured self-employment of the less advantaged relative to the more advantaged groups. For example, the rate of self-employment of full-time women entrepreneurs represented only 47% of the self-employment rate of all entrepreneurs; but when part-time entrepreneurs were included, the women's rate increased to 67% of the self-employment rate of the whole labor force. Similarly, among African Americans, the rate of self-employment of full-time entrepreneurs was only 40% of the self-employment rate of the whole population. However, when part-time self-employment was added, the aggregated African-American rate rose to 43% of the total (Haber, 1985:6). Entrepreneurs with less than 4 years of high school represented 16.6% of the full-time, nonagricultural self-employed but 22.6% of the part-time self-employed (Haber, 1985:17).

These measurement problems affect theory. Because theory builds upon evidence, theory depends upon how the CPS defined entrepreneurs. Insofar as CPS definitions undercounted or even excluded disadvantaged entrepreneurs, CPS statistics underestimated true rates of entrepreneurship, exaggerating intergroup differences in entrepreneurial performance. Thus, in 1994, a visitor to Washington, D.C. found hundreds of African-American entrepreneurs in front of the National Portrait Gallery on a fair day. From blankets spread on the ground and impromptu stands, these entrepreneurs sold new and used clothing, appliances, sports and musical equipment, and sundries, as well as food items. Yet, these entrepreneurs did not fit the CPS definition of self-employment, thus causing the official archive to ignore their existence. If one knew only the official statistics, one would concoct a flawed theory of African-American entrepreneurship.

ASSEMBLING THE DATA

We seek to rectify shortcomings of the existing literature in order to place resources theory upon a firmer evidentiary basis, while expanding its theoretical range. Quantitative approaches are particularly useful provided they address theory, rejecting descriptive empiricism. Additionally, useful research should compare localities as well as groups, thus varying supply and demand influences. Finally, quantitative research should generate analytical tools of general utility. Derived inductively from comparison of existing groups, these conceptual tools should create a theoretical language that will permit more advanced discussion.

We designed our dataset to meet these objectives. First, we examine self-employment in the 272 largest metropolitan areas of the United States, thus providing the first panoramic overview of entrepreneurship in America's big cities. Second, we examine whites, African Americans, Asians, and Hispanics in these 272 metropolitan areas, thus comparing the largest ethnoracial categories, as well as all the localities. Third, we employ novel definitions of self-employment, comparing our definitions to the CPS definition where appropriate. The alternative definitions bring out aspects of self-employment overlooked when only the CPS definition is utilized. Finally, we attend to the backlog of hitherto untestable theoretical ideas that have emerged from the existing literature.

Our unit of analysis is the Standard Metropolitan Statistical Area, the basic Census definition of a big central city and its economically and socially related areas.[3] In 1980, there were 317 metropolitan areas in the United States. However, our dataset includes only the 272 largest metropolitan areas. These 272 biggest metropolitan areas contain a population of at least 100,000 and a civilian labor force of at least 40,000. Forty-five metropolitan areas did not meet this test. As a consequence, our dataset contains no metropolitan areas from North Dakota, Vermont, or Wyoming.

Our dataset represents the universe of all big metropolitan areas, not a sample thereof. N is 272. To obtain this universe, we began with the 1980 U.S. Census Public Use 5% Microdataset (U.S. Bureau of the Census, 1983), creating selected demographic, human capital, and labor force variables by aggregating characteristics for the total selected labor force population and each of 47 ethnoracial categories and groups within each of these 272 metropolitan areas. The Census utilized sampling techniques to obtain individual-level data representing about 3.6 million persons (or 72 million in the 100% weighted sample), in the civilian, nonagricultural labor force, age 16 and older, in the 5% PUM dataset. Our dataset *aggregated* this individual-level data into 272 aggregate-level samples. Bearing in mind Robinson's strictures against ecological correlation, we relate aggregated variables to one another at the group rather than the individual level, a legitimate use of aggregate data (Lieberson, 1985:107). Moreover, as Dogan and Pahre (1990:46) have noted, "the computer revolution" has obviated the original objections to ecological analysis and we have taken full advantage of that revolution.

Because the magnitude of the original individual-level, Public Use Microdata (PUMs) exceeded the capacity of UCLA's IBM 3090 computer, we subdivided the gigantic 47-state data file into subsets of one or more states in order to create our research dataset. For each data subset, we selected one variable from the household record—metropolitan area, and 15 variables from the personal record (Table 2.1).[4] We limited the sample to persons 16 years of age and older, who were not prevented from working, who were employed or unemployed in the civilian labor force, and who worked in a nonprimary industry.[5]

Table 2.1. Original Variables Selected From the 1980 Census
5% Public Use Micro-Dataset

Codebook Name[1]	Description
SMSA	Standard Metropolitan Statistical Areas
SEX	0 = male; 1 = female
AGE	0 to 89 years, 90 = 99 years or more
RACE	Thirteen racial categories
SPANISH	Spanish origin
CITIZEN	U.S. citizenship
IMMIGR	Year of immigration
GRADE	Highest year of school attended
FINGRADE	Finished highest grade
DISABIL2	Work disability status: prevented from working
LABOR	Labor force status
INDUSTRY	Industry codes
CLASS	Class of worker
WEEKSU79	Weeks unemployed in 1979
INCOME1	Wage or salary income in 1979
INCOME2	Nonfarm self-employment income in 1979

[1] See U.S. Bureau of the Census (1983).

Categories and Groups

If one cross-classifies the 13 Census "race" codes with the five "Spanish origin" codes (U.S. Bureau of the Census, 1983:76-77), one generates 65 unique ethnoracial groups, e.g., Puerto Rican whites, Puerto Rican Japanese, Puerto Rican blacks, etc. We assigned these 65 to 12 mutually exclusive ethnoracial groups. The assignment of whites, African Americans, Japanese, Chinese, Filipinos, Koreans, Vietnamese, and Asian Indians was simple.[6] We based these assignments upon respondents' self-identification and self-declared non-Spanish origin. Pacific Islanders comprised two racial groups: Hawaiians and Other Asians not of Spanish origin. Mexicans, Puerto Ricans, Cubans, and Other Spanish, could be of several non-Asian, non-Pacific Islander racial backgrounds, so their primary identity was based upon their specific Spanish origins.

Because of the likelihood of response errors, we deleted "Other Mixed Asians."[7] Of course, among 72 million people, some incongruous ethnic identities were bona fide, but more represented tabulation or recording error. For example, if the census reported that a respondent was of Japanese racial background and of Mexican Spanish origin, we deemed this combination more likely to be tabulation error than a bona fide report. Furthermore, since we could not categorize mixed-background respondents in our ethnoracial scheme, we had to leave them out.

We next aggregated all of the Asian groups (except "Other Mixed Asian") into the category "Asians," and followed the same procedure to create the category "Hispanics." The other two categories are "whites" and "blacks" (African Americans). Category means one of four broad ethnoracial aggregates: whites, blacks, Asians, and Hispanics. Group refers to 11 specific racial-national and/or nativity defined subpopulations. The Asian category contains seven groups and the Hispanic category contains four. Each group and category can be further divided into native and foreign born.[8]

Table 2.2 presents descriptive statistics of the 4 categories, 11 national-origin groups, and 32 nativity classifications in the 272 metropolitan areas. Of the nonagricultural labor force of these 272 metropolitan areas, 84.5% were white, 9.1% African American, 1.2% Asian, and 4.6% Hispanic. Great variation existed in the ethnoracial composition of these metropolitan areas. McAllen, Texas, had the lowest percentage of whites (22.5%), but the highest percentage of Hispanics (76.9%). St. Cloud, Minnesota, had the highest percentage of whites (99.5%), and the lowest percentage of African Americans (0%). The highest percentage of African Americans (37.7%) was in Jackson, Mississippi and the highest percentage of Asians (65.1%) was in Honolulu. Sharon, Pennsylvania had the lowest percentages of both Asians and Hispanics.

Each of the seven Asian groups averaged 0.3% or less of the labor force of the 272 metropolitan areas. However, although the Asians' minimum representation in these metropolitan areas was zero, their maximum representation varied a lot. Five of seven Asian groups reached their maximum share of the labor force in Honolulu. Japanese were 32.7% of the Honolulu labor force, Pacific Islanders were 11.1%, Filipinos were 10.4%, Chinese were 8.0%, and Koreans 2.4%. The maximum percentages for the other two Asian groups were in two different mainland metropolitan areas. Asian Indians comprised 1% of the labor force of Jersey City, their maximum, and Vietnamese comprised 0.7% of the labor force of San Jose.

Mexicans comprised, on average, 3% of the labor force in the 272 metropolitan areas, Other Spanish, 1%, and the other two Hispanic groups, Puerto Ricans and Cubans, each comprised less than 0.5%. These four Hispanic groups were not found at all in the labor force of some metropolitan areas. Whereas the highest percentages of five of the Asian groups occurred in Honolulu, the highest percentages of each of the four Hispanic groups were in four different metropolitan areas. Each Hispanic group had its own ethnic capital. An ethnic capital is the met-

Table 2.2. Nonagricultural Labor Force in 272 Metropolitan Areas by Nativity and Ethnoracial Category (in Percentages)

	Total			Native Born			Foreign Born		
	Mean	Min.	Max.	Mean	Min.	Max.	Mean	Min.	Max.
Total[1]	100.0	[2]	[2]	95.3	58.8	99.8	4.7	0.2	41.2
White	84.5	22.5	99.5	82.1	21.7	98.7	2.5	0.1	17.6
Black	9.1	0.0	37.7	8.9	0.0	37.5	0.2	0.0	4.7
Asian	1.2	0.1	65.1	0.4	0.0	51.7	0.7	0.0	13.5
Japanese	0.3	0.0	32.7	0.2	0.0	30.3	0.1	0.0	2.4
Chinese	0.2	0.0	8.0	0.1	0.0	6.1	0.2	0.0	3.0
Filipino	0.2	0.0	10.4	0.0	0.0	4.1	0.2	0.0	6.3
Korean	0.1	0.0	2.4	0.0	0.0	1.1	0.1	0.0	1.4
Vietnamese	0.1	0.0	0.7	0.0	0.0	0.1	0.1	0.0	0.7
Asian Indian	0.1	0.0	1.0	0.0	0.0	0.1	0.1	0.0	1.0
Pac Islander	0.1	0.0	11.1	0.1	0.0	10.0	0.1	0.0	1.1
Hispanic	4.6	0.1	76.9	3.3	0.1	57.3	1.3	0.0	33.6
Mexican	3.0	0.0	74.1	2.3	0.0	55.4	0.7	0.0	21.4
Puerto Rican	0.4	0.0	7.1	0.4	0.0	6.9	0.0	0.0	0.3
Cuban	0.3	0.0	28.9	0.0	0.0	1.3	0.2	0.0	27.6
Other Spanish	1.0	0.0	17.5	0.6	0.0	17.1	0.4	0.0	7.1

[1] Total population equals 3,601,541 (PUMS 5% dataset).
[2] Not applicable, total population equals 100%.

ropolitan area in which the largest share of a group or category is located. Mexicans were 74.1% of McAllen, Texas, Puerto Ricans were 7.1% of Jersey City, Cubans were 28.9% of Miami, and Other Spanish were 17.5% of Albuquerque.

Native and Foreign Born

Next, examining the native born and foreign born, we find that in all 272 metropolitan areas, 95.3% of the nonagricultural civilian labor force was native-born in 1980. However, this percentage varied greatly among metropolitan areas. Gadsden, Alabama's population was 99.8% native born, the highest percentage native born among the 272 metropolitan areas. Miami's population contained 41.2% foreign born, the highest percentage of foreign born in the 272 metropolitan areas.

Although the mean percentage of the native-born and foreign-born Asian and Hispanic groups was small, the local balance of native and foreign born reflected each group's historical experience. For example, of the 65.1% of the labor force of Honolulu that was Asian in 1980, 51.7% were native-born and 13.5% were foreign-born. This imbalance reflects the earlier settlement of Japanese, Chinese, Filipinos, and Pacific Islanders in Honolulu. However, we found slightly more foreign-born than native-born Koreans in Honolulu, a reflection of the Koreans' more recent migration. Unlike all other Asian groups, the highest percentages of native-born and foreign-born Vietnamese and Asian Indians were not in the same metropolitan area for each group. Native-born Vietnamese comprised 0.1% of the labor force of Olympia, Washington, and their foreign-born counterparts comprised 0.7% of San Jose. Similarly, native-born Asian Indians comprised only 0.1% of Gainesville, Florida, but their foreign-born compatriots comprised 1% of Jersey City.

The maximum percentages of each Hispanic native born and foreign born were not in the same metropolitan area, except for Cubans. Foreign-born Cubans made up 27.6% of Miami's labor force, and native-born Cubans made up 1.3% of Miami's labor force. Native-born Mexicans contributed their maximum percentage of the labor force to McAllen, Texas (55.4%); foreign-born Mexicans contributed their maximum percentage (21.4%) to the labor force of El Paso, Texas. The highest percentage of native-born Puerto Ricans (6.9%) in the labor force was in Jersey City, and the highest percentage (0.3%) for their foreign-born coethnics was in Waterbury, Connecticut. Similarly, native-born Other Spanish comprised 17.1% of the labor force of Albuquerque, and their foreign-born counterparts comprised 7.1% of Jersey City.

Table 2.2 shows that some metropolitan areas recorded no African Americans, no Asians, and no Hispanics in their labor force. This result is no error. Because statistics would be unreliable if a metropolitan area had less than 400 persons in the civilian labor force,[9] we deleted any ethnoracial category or group that did not attain this minimum size in a locality. Many metropolitan areas did not have enough representatives of small groups to constitute effective representation. Effective representation means sufficient numbers for statistical reliability.

What constitutes effective representation is arbitrary in that no scientific standard governs the point. However, from a statistical point of view the issue is clear enough. Utilizing the 5 Percent Public-Use Sample of the 1980 U.S. Census, we expected a sample of 20 when true group size was 400 in the metropolitan area. With 20 persons in our sample, a shift of one person caused a 5% change in any result. For example, if 5 of the 20 were self-employed, the self-employment rate of that group would be 25%, but if 6 of the 20 were self-employed, the group's rate would become 30%. In view of this situation, we decided that a threshold of 20 persons in our sample (400 representatives in the labor force) represented the minimum criterion compatible with meaningful measurement. Therefore, we deleted from category and group analysis any localities in which any category or group did not achieve the threshold size of 20 sampled representatives in the labor force.[10]

The number of metropolitan areas with the threshold minimum of each category or group reflects the migration streams that populated the United States. For this reason, whites, African Americans, and Hispanics were more likely to be native born than foreign born, whereas Asians, current immigrants, were more likely to be foreign born than native born. Total, foreign-born, and native-born whites, total and native-born blacks, and total and native-born Hispanics exceeded the threshold minimum in over 200 metropolitan areas. However, total and foreign-born Asians, foreign-born Hispanics, total and native-born Mexicans, and total and native-born Other Spanish had 400 or more persons in only 131 to 180 metropolitan areas. Foreign-born blacks, native-born Asians, and all of the Asian groups, Puerto Ricans, and Cubans, irrespective of their nativity, clustered in less than 100 metropolitan areas, reflecting the recency and concentration of their migration.

Aggregate Characteristics

Our dataset consists of the mean characteristics of each of the 47 categories and groups for each metropolitan area.[11] We calculated means for the original interval-level variables after deleting cases with missing values.[12] Other original variables we converted from categorical or ordinal to interval-level variables before we calculated means.[13] Most categorical variables we first converted into dummy variables to create additional mean variables[14] after deleting missing cases. One can interpret the means of dichotomous dummy variables as percentages.[15]

We also saved the numbers of respondents with valid responses represented by each mean, each category, and each group in each metropolitan area. The final step was to combine the data subsets into one master dataset. This master dataset contained 2,084 variables[16] for each of 272 metropolitan areas. This cross-section summarized the economic behavior of more than 72 million people.

DEFINING SELF-EMPLOYMENT

The 1980 Census provides two ways to identify the self-employed: those who said that they were self-employed and those who reported that they had earned self-employment income. Self-identification is the narrowest definition of self-employment. Respondents indicated in which of seven classes of workers[17] they best fit. Of these seven, two classes indicate self-employment: self-employed worker—business not incorporated, and employee of own corporation.[18] On the one hand, by including professional workers who work on salary for a corporation they own, this definition corrects a shortcoming of the class of worker definition. Many self-employed professionals utilize this legal form. On the other hand, like the CPS definition, this narrow definition still excludes moonlighting wage and salary workers who were self-employed after hours.

The income self-employment definition measures the number of persons who reported gains or losses from nonfarm self-employment.[19] This income self-employment definition is broader than the CPS definition, because it includes both those who engaged in self-employment exclusively and those who did so in addition to wage and salary employment.[20]

In framing our study population, we tried to define an entrepreneur population that would minimize the known shortcomings of the CPS definition, but several remain. First, in selecting our study population, we included only those in the civilian labor force, thereby excluding housewives and the discouraged unemployed. Both categories include persons who were secondarily self-employed. Also unknown is the extent to which illegal entrepreneurs fail to identify themselves as self-employed and/or to report the amount or source of their income. We cannot measure any of these, so our dataset underestimates true self-employment.

We expected the income definition of the self-employed to yield more self-employed workers than did the class of worker definition. We also expected that the income definition would include all the self-identified self-employed. Results surprised us. First, we found that the number of self-employed was approximately equal, whether one utilized the self-identified, class of worker definition, or the income definition of self-employment. This result replicates for all categories what Sullivan and McCracken (1988:171) found among African Americans. Table 2.3 compares the numbers of persons classified as self-employed by either the income or class of worker definitions. Of the 47 categories and groups,[21] 35 had more persons defined as self-employed in terms of the class of worker definition than were defined as such by the income definition. This result held true for the total, white, and Hispanic civilian labor force categories and/or groups, irrespective of nativity. We found only 12 cases in which the income definition identified more self-employed than did the class of worker definition. Filipinos are the only ethnoracial group in which the income definition of self-employment consistently exceeded the class of worker definition. Where there are discrepancies by nativity, it is native-born blacks and Asians (category and three groups), rather than their foreign-born counterparts, who have more workers defined as self-employed in terms of income rather than class of worker.

Since the income criterion defines almost the same number of self-employed as does the class of worker criterion, we expected that most entrepreneurs would report both self-employment income and self-employment work (*c* in Figure 2.1). Conversely, we expected that few entrepreneurs would have only self-employment income (*a* in Figure 2.1) or only self-employment work (*b* in Figure 2.1). Testing this assumption, we percentaged each of these possible definitions of self-employment on

Table 2.3. Total Number[1] Defined as Self-Employed in Terms of Source of Income[2] or Class of Work[3]

	Total		Native Born		Foreign Born	
	Total No. SE Defined by SE		Total No. SE Defined by SE		Total No. SE Defined by SE	
	Income (1)	Work (2)	Income (3)	Work (4)	Income (5)	Work (6)
Total	240,819	255,731	219,171	230,255	21,644	25,472
White	214,296	228,168	201,345	212,514	12,911	15,605
Black	10,381	10,322	9,832	9,772	523	524
Asian	5,502	5,687	1,694	1,574	3,733	4,040
Japanese	1,329	1,291	998	948	298	316
Chinese	1,631	1,752	404	356	1,183	1,342
Filipino	501	440	71	65	414	360
Korean	790	935	12	15	763	908
Vietnamese	92	100	—[4]	—[4]	89	97
Asian Indian	495	496	7	8	475	471
Pacific Islander	214	193	96	72	105	107
Hispanic	9,438	10,444	5,266	5,462	4,111	4,925
Mexican	4,632	4,847	3,195	3,264	1,404	1,549
Puerto Rican	698	805	661	757	28	39
Cuban	1,314	1,738	64	80	1,228	1,635
Other Spanish	2,640	2,905	1,213	1,232	1,351	1,594

[1] The numbers are derived from the 5% 1980 Census PUMS dataset. (Multiply numbers in the table by 20 to replicate 100% of the 1980 U.S. Census population.)
[2] Respondents reported either gains or losses in self-employment income (see *a* + *c* in Figure 2.1).
[3] Respondents reported self-employment work in a business that was not incorporated or as an employee of their own corporation (see *b* + *c* in Figure 2.1).
[4] Excluding native-born Vietnamese, because no metropolitan areas had a minimum of 400 native-born Vietnamese in the labor force.

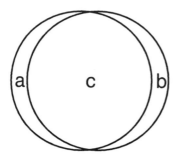 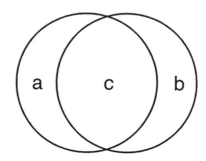

Figure 2.1.   Hypothesis and empirical finding regarding the extent of congruence between those defined as self-employed by income and by class of
worker. Hypothesis (left): Almost all of those who had primary self-
employment work also had self-employment income. Therefore, there were
few who had self-employment income and no self-employment work, and
there were few who had self-employment work and no self-employment
income. Empirical finding (right): For most categories and groups, only
between 50 and 60% had both self-employment work and self-employment
income, 20-30% had self-employment work only, and 20-30% had self-
employment income only. (see Table 2.4).

a, Marginal income-defined self-employed, i.e., all those who had income
gains or losses from self-employment economic activities, but *no* primary
self-employment work. *b*, Marginal work-defined self-employed, i.e., all
those whose primary class of worker status was self-employed, but who
had *no* self-employment income. *c*, Core income-defined *and* work-defined
self-employed, i.e., those whose primary class of worker status was self-
employed *and* who had self-employment income.

the maximum number who could be defined as such, whether because
of self-employment work or self-employment income (*a* + *b* + *c* in Figure
2.1), counting the overlap in definitions only once.

Results again surprised us (Table 2.4). For the total population, only
58% of the self-employed had both self-employment income and self-
employment work (column 3). About 19% of the entrepreneurs reported
only self-employment income (column 1), and 24% had claimed *only* self-
employment work (column 2). These results show how problematic self-
employment is. The *core self-employed* consisted of workers who identified
themselves as self-employed and who also obtained income from self-
employment. Such core entrepreneurs satisfy any definition of self-
employment. However, flanking this core we find two marginal groups
that, when combined, represent 74% of the core self-employed.[22] These
marginal self-employed consisted of those who identified themselves as
self-employed without self-employment income[23] or those who had self-
employment income, but who failed to declare themselves self-employed.

The two styles of marginal self-employment probably reflect different labor market situations. On the one hand, marginals who received self-employment income were probably wage and salary workers who operated part-time businesses after hours. On the other hand, those who defined themselves as self-employed without income might represent unemployed people whose self-employment was an aspiration, not a fact. In some cases, unemployed, nonearning, but aspiring entrepreneurs someday will see their businesses support them. Most never will. Either way, however, at the moment of the Census, the income-only or the work-only self-employed represented aspirants to full membership in the core self-employed population.

The 47 ethnoracial categories and groups differed in the proportion of their entrepreneurs who were marginal or core. The smallest core was the native-born Koreans among whom only 35% of entrepreneurs had both self-employment income and self-employment work. Since native-born Koreans were very few and very young in 1980, the marginality of their entrepreneurial cohort is easy to explain on demographic grounds. Conversely, among foreign-born Puerto Ricans, 67.5% of entrepreneurs were core entrepreneurs, the maximum recorded for any ethnoracial group. Comparing counterpart native-born to foreign-born categories, we found little difference in the size of the entrepreneurial core for all categories and most groups within categories with the following exceptions: large differences in percentage points between the foreign-born and the native-born Koreans, Puerto Ricans, Filipinos, and Pacific Islanders. Of these four groups, with the exception of the Filipinos, the foreign born had higher percentages of core entrepreneurs than their native-born coethnics. Of the other Asian and Hispanic groups, only two had higher percentages of core entrepreneurs among the foreign born than among the native born (i.e., Japanese and Chinese), whereas the other four groups had more core entrepreneurs among the native born than the foreign born (i.e., Asian Indians, Mexicans, Cubans, and Other Spanish).

The foreign born had generally higher percentages of work-only entrepreneurs and lower percentages of income-only entrepreneurs than did the native born. Unemployed and underemployed foreigners were more likely than unemployed natives to operate unremunerated business firms in the hope of ultimate success. Conversely, natives more frequently operated after-hours firms than foreigners, a choice compatible with the nondisadvantaged labor market situation of the natives. Having a job already, natives started a business by working after hours. Lacking a job or, at least, a good job, foreigners more frequently started a business by working at it without pay.

We had expected a large overlap between class of worker and income definitions of self-employment. That is, we assumed that almost

Table 2.4. Marginal[1,2] and Core[3] Self-Employment

	Total			Native Born			Foreign Born		
	Marginal SE		Core SE	Marginal SE		Core SE	Marginal SE		Core SE
	SE Income Only[1] (1)	SE Work Only[2] (2)	Income and Work[3] (3)	SE Income Only[1] (4)	SE Work Only[2] (5)	Income and Work[3] (6)	SE Income Only[1] (7)	SE Work Only[2] (8)	Income and Work[3] (9)
Total	18.9	23.6	57.6	19.3	23.2	57.6	14.9	27.7	57.5
White	18.8	23.7	57.5	19.1	23.4	57.5	13.5	28.5	58.0
Black	21.3	20.9	57.8	21.3	20.8	58.0	21.8	21.9	56.3
Asian	21.3	23.8	54.9	25.2	19.5	55.2	19.6	25.7	54.8
Japanese	21.9	19.6	58.4	23.4	19.3	57.3	17.1	21.8	61.2
Chinese	19.9	25.4	54.7	28.8	19.2	52.0	17.3	27.1	55.6
Filipino	30.8	21.2	48.0	24.4	17.4	58.1	32.1	21.9	46.0
Korean	12.4	26.0	61.7	25.0	40.0	35.0	11.9	26.0	62.1

Vietnamese	25.4	31.3	43.3	—[4]	—[4]	—[4]	24.8	31.0	44.2
Asian Indian	26.4	26.6	47.0	20.0	30.0	50.0	26.5	25.9	47.6
Pacific Islander	26.3	18.3	55.3	35.7	14.3	50.0	20.1	21.6	58.2
Hispanic	16.1	24.2	59.8	18.0	20.9	61.1	13.7	28.0	58.2
Mexican	16.5	20.2	63.4	17.2	18.9	63.9	14.9	22.9	62.3
Puerto Rican	17.5	28.5	54.0	18.1	28.5	53.5	2.5	30.0	67.5
Cuban	11.8	33.3	54.8	11.1	28.9	60.0	11.7	33.7	54.7
Other Spanish	16.9	24.4	58.7	19.7	20.9	59.4	14.3	27.4	58.2

[1] Marginal "SE Income Only" $= a/(a + b + c)$ (see Figure 2.1). The numerator is the number of respondents in metropolitan areas of each respective category or group who could be defined as self-employed in terms of self-employment income (a in Figure 2.1), divided by the denominator. It excludes those who had both self-employment income and work (c in Figure 2.1). The denominator equals the number of maximally self-employed. The maximally self-employed are composed of all, in each respective category or group, who could be defined as self-employed, i.e., those with SE Income Only + SE Work Only + SE Income and SE Work ($a + b + c$ in Figure 2.1). Thus, for each row, columns 1 through 3 = 100%, 4 through 6 = 100%, and 7 through 9 = 100%.

[2] Marginal "SE Work Only" $= b/(a + b + c)$ (see Figure 2.1). The numerator is the number of respondents in metropolitan areas of each respective category or group who could be defined as self-employed in terms of self-employment work (b in Figure 2.1), divided by the denominator. The numerator excludes those who had both self-employment income and work (c in Figure 2.1).

[3] Core "Income and Work" $= c/(a + b + c)$ (see Figure 2.1). These respondents had both self-employment income and work (c in Figure 2.1).

[4] See Table 2.3, note 4.

everyone who would be defined as self-employed by income would also be defined as self-employed by class of work as well. We had not anticipated that only about 60% could be defined as self-employed by *both* of our criteria—income and work, and the other 40% could be defined by only one of the criteria. Unfortunately, since we had anticipated a big overlap when we constructed our research dataset, we could not operationalize variables for each of the alternative definitions of the self-employed for each group and category. Thus, we are unable to compare those who earned self-employment income and declared themselves self-employed, those who had *only* self-employment income, and those who *only* declared themselves self-employed.[24]

Next, we ask whether self-employment rates differ for each category and group, depending on which of three definitions of self-employment are used. These three definitions of self-employment differ from the core and marginal definitions in Table 2.4. Unlike the three definitions in Table 2.4, which are mutually exclusive, the three definitions that we use, beginning in Table 2.5, are overlapping.[25] In Table 2.5, we compare the mean self-employment rates of categories and groups of *all* those who are defined as self-employed by income ($a + c$ in Figure 2.1),[26] by work ($b + c$ in Figure 2.1),[27] and by both income and work ($a + b + c$ in Figure 2.1).[28]

Table 2.5 presents the weighted mean percentages[29] of these three different measures of entrepreneurs for each ethnoracial category and group. These three mean self-employment rates distinguish the income and the work classes of entrepreneur from the maximum percentage of self-employed that would be obtained if *both* criteria are used to define self-employment.

The most persons are defined as self-employed if one uses the "maximum" definition. If one uses either the income or the work definition of self-employment, fewer self-employed emerge. However, because the work and the income self-employed contained mostly the same people, those previously designated "core" entrepreneurs, the two groups usually differed little in self-employment rate. Among all workers in all metropolitan areas, the work-defined self-employed exceeded the income-defined self-employed by about 6%.[30] Among the foreign born, the work group exceeded the income group by 18%, reflecting the foreigners' less comfortable labor market position. In some groups, differences were larger than in categories. For example, among foreign-born Cubans, the work-only group exceeded the income-only group by one-third.[31]

We had expected that the income-defined self-employed would include almost all of the work-defined self-employed, and, thus, would produce higher self-employment rates than the work-defined self-employed. Table 2.3 shows that this expectation was rarely correct. Table 2.5 translates those numbers into self-employment rates, and so the comparisons between the self-employment rates produced by these two alternative definitions are the same as in Table 2.3. For example, for the four categories, we find that the larger numbers of work-defined self-employed produce correspondingly higher self-employment rates for the work definition than the income definition.

Because there are many marginal, income-only and work-only entrepreneurs, in addition to a large core self-employed with self-employment income, a big maximum category emerged in Table 2.4. The maximum category provides the most generous definition of the self-employed population.[32] Table 2.5 also includes the self-employment rates for categories and groups that result from the maximum definition of the self-employed.

Comparing the work-defined self-employed with our maximum estimates, we isolate the part-time self-employed ignored by the work-only definition. These are workers who reported income gains or losses from self-employment in addition to their other sources of income (as represented by just *b* in Figure 2.1). This group is large. Among all workers in all 272 metropolitan areas, the self-employment rate of our maximum definition of the self-employed population exceeds the work definition by 24% (Table 2.5). It exceeds the income definition by 31%.[33]

Previous research has defined the self-employed by self-identification, the CPS definition. Although we have recited numerous shortcomings of this definition, no one knows the detailed characteristics of persons who claimed self-employment, but who did not also report self-employment income or loss. These might be persons who did not report their self-employment income to tax collectors and so declined to report it to the Census, or they might be unemployed or underemployed persons whose claim to self-employment was an aspiration. Comparing the self-employment rates of the income-defined to the maximum-defined for categories and groups also indicates the large percentages who claimed self-employment, but had no evidence of it. Having to choose, we stressed the income-receiving group, ignoring claims to self-employment not validated by self-employment income. Therefore, in most of our analyses, we will define the self-employed as *those who reported income gain or loss from self-employment*. The self-employed include those who are working full-time as self-employed workers in addition to wage earners who supplement their incomes with part-time self-employment.[34] We will refer to these as "income-defined" self-employed, and those whose self-employment identity comes from their class of worker status, we will refer to as "work-defined" self-employment.

Table 2.5. Weighted Mean Self-Employment Rates[1] of Three NonExclusive Self-Employment Types

	Total			Native Born			Foreign Born		
	Total No. SE Income[2] (1)	Total No. SE Work[3] (2)	Total Maximum[4] (3)	Total No. SE Income[2] (4)	Total No. SE Work[3] (5)	Total Maximum[4] (6)	Total No. SE Income[2] (7)	Total No. SE Work[3] (8)	Total Maximum[4] (9)
Total	6.7	7.1	8.8	6.6	7.0	8.6	7.2	8.5	9.9
White	7.5	8.0	9.8	7.4	7.8	9.6	9.9	11.9	13.8
Black	2.5	2.5	3.2	2.5	2.5	3.2	2.9	2.9	3.7
Asian	7.4	7.7	9.7	7.1	6.6	8.8	7.6	8.2	10.2
Japanese	8.4	8.2	10.5	8.4	7.9	10.4	9.0	9.6	11.5
Chinese	9.0	9.7	12.1	8.5	7.5	10.5	9.2	10.4	12.6
Filipino	3.7	3.2	4.7	3.4	3.1	4.1	3.7	3.2	4.8
Korean	13.6	16.2	18.4	4.2	5.3	7.0	14.4	17.1	19.4
Vietnamese	3.1	3.4	4.5	—[5]	—[5]	—[5]	3.1	3.3	4.4

Asian Indian	7.2	7.2	9.8	4.0	4.6	5.7	7.5	7.4	10.1
Pacific Islander	4.1	3.7	5.0	3.6	2.7	4.2	4.6	4.7	5.8
Hispanic	3.9	4.4	5.2	3.7	3.9	4.7	4.2	5.1	5.9
Mexican	3.5	3.7	4.4	3.7	3.8	4.6	3.1	3.4	4.0
Puerto Rican	2.3	2.7	3.3	2.3	2.7	3.2	2.8	3.9	4.0
Cuban	6.8	9.0	10.2	4.5	5.6	6.3	7.0	9.3	10.5
Other Spanish	4.7	5.2	6.3	5.1	5.2	6.5	4.4	5.1	6.0

[1] Self-employment rates are based on the percentage of the civilian labor force of each category or group, in each metropolitan area, that is self-employed. Notes 2–4 describe three alternative definitions of the self-employed to be examined in this table. The weighted, population-level mean self-employment rates are the mean of the total numbers of persons in the civilian labor force in a category or group, in all metropolitan areas, that met the threshold criterion. Weighted means weight metropolitan areas in proportion to their population.

[2] "Total No. SE Income" = $a + c$ (see Figure 2.1). It is the number of each respective category or group who had self-employment income, which includes both those who were and were not self-employed, in terms of the class of worker definition.

[3] "Total No. SE Work" = $b + c$ (see Figure 2.1). It is the number of each respective category or group who were self-identified as self-employed, in terms of the class of worker definition, which includes both those who had and did not have any self-employment income (or losses).

[4] "Total Maximum" = $a + b + c$ (see Figure 2.1). It is the total number of each respective category or group who were self-employed, that is, the sum of the core and two marginal self-employed.

[5] See Table 2.3, note 4.

SELF-EMPLOYMENT INCOME

Next, we examine mean self-employment income of the income-defined and work-defined self-employed. The measure of income-defined self-employment is the mean income gains or losses derived from self-employment of those who reported income or loss. The class of worker income measure is the income gains or losses only for those who also reported that they were primarily self-employed workers. The income-defined self-employed were more likely to have reported income losses from self-employment than were the work-defined. As a consequence, in all cases, the work-defined self-employed reported higher mean self-employment income than did the income-defined self-employed. For example, comparing the unweighted means of the total population (Table 2.6), we find that the work-defined self-employed earned an unweighted mean self-employment income of $14,300 (column 9), whereas the income-defined self-employed earned only $11,800 (column 3), just 83% as much. Presumably the lower income-defined gain includes part-time self-employed who may also have earned income from wages and salaries.

Examining the unweighted, income-defined mean self-employment incomes of the four categories (column 3), one finds a descending rank order with Asians at the top ($14,400) followed by whites ($12,100), Hispanics ($11,900), and African Americans ($8,400). Among the groups, Vietnamese had the lowest mean self-employment income ($7,800), and Asian Indians the highest ($21,000). Conceivably, these ranks reflect differences in resource endowments such that those with more resources obtained higher self-employment incomes than those with less. But, if resources caused self-employment incomes, why should the same category or group display different incomes in different metropolitan areas? This objection does not apply fully to native whites, who had the lowest standard deviation of self-employment income among localities. Additionally, in the 272 metropolitan areas, native whites always reported positive incomes from self-employment. However, all the minorities reported negative self-employment incomes in at least some metropolitan areas. Of those who lost any money, foreign-born whites and Asian Indians lost the most. Moreover, the standard deviations of minority incomes were much larger than that for whites, a sign that the minority groups experienced drastic differences in self-employment income among the various metropolitan areas. The class of worker definition shows a less extreme version of this result. However, class of worker yields fewer negative incomes (column 11) than does the income-defined measure (column 5). Asians, some Asian groups, and some Hispanic groups have positive minimum mean self-employment incomes as do whites and native-born whites.

This result clarifies why whites had generally more income-only self-employment than did minorities. First, the income-defined statistics give a more accurate picture of the secondary self-employed than do the class of worker statistics. In our income-defined data, the native whites presumably undertook secondary self-employment from a position of strength in the labor market. Therefore, their self-employment efforts were less risky, and less frequently eventuated in financial losses. Undertaking self-employment from weaker bases in the labor force, or even as a consequence of unemployment, the foreign born, in general, the foreign whites, in particular, and native-born blacks took greater risks and more frequently suffered income losses from self-employment. However, secondary self-employment is presumably not the whole explanation, because the class of worker definition also records such contrasts. Those who met the class of worker definition less frequently conducted their business on a part-time basis. Therefore, we conclude that foreigners and minorities operated firms at greater risk of losing money than did native whites for reasons unrelated to labor market anchorage.

WEIGHTED AND UNWEIGHTED RATES

We now examine rates of self-employment. Table 2.7 presents descriptive statistics of the mean self-employment rates for both the income-defined and the work-defined self-employed of all ethnoracial categories and groups. Although we stress income-defined self-employment, we include statistics for the class of worker definition because this important comparison is available nowhere else.

Table 2.7 presents both the population-level (weighted) means and the metropolitan area-level (unweighted) means, plus the unweighted standard deviations, minima, and ranges. The unweighted, metropolitan area-level means represent the mean of means, that is, they represent the means of the metropolitan areas in which each category or group had 400 or more persons in the labor force, the threshold minimum. Therefore, the unweighted mean assigns each metropolitan area equal weight regardless of population. Thus, although 50% of Cubans resided in Miami, the unweighted Cuban mean self-employment rate awards equal influence to Miami, Peoria, and all other metropolitan areas in which Cubans resided above the threshold level. In contrast, the weighted, population-level mean self-employment rates are the mean of the total numbers of persons in the civilian labor force in all

Table 2.6. Descriptive Statistics of the Two Measures of the Mean Self-Employment Income (MSEI),[1] for Categories and Groups,[2] in 272 Metropolitan Areas, 1980 (Thousands of Dollars)

| | Income-Defined MSEI | | | | | | Work-Defined MSEI | | | | | |
| | No. of SMSAs (1)[3] | Weighted Mean (2) | Unweighted | | | | No. of SMSAs (7)[3] | Weighted Mean (8) | Unweighted | | | |
			Mean (3)	SD (4)	Min (5)[4]	Range (6)			Mean (9)	SD (10)	Min (11)[4]	Range (12)
Total	272	12.7	11.8	1.7	7.0	11.0	272	15.5	14.3	1.9	8.4	13.2
Native born	272	12.7	11.8	1.7	7.1	11.0	272	15.5	13.3	2.0	8.5	13.2
Foreign Born	269	13.3	12.7	7.8	−5.9	80.9	266	15.4	15.0	8.6	−3.8	78.8
White	272	12.9	12.1	1.9	7.0	10.9	272	15.7	14.6	2.1	8.5	13.2
Native born	272	12.9	12.1	1.9	7.1	10.7	272	15.8	14.6	2.1	8.5	13.1
Foreign Born	243	12.9	13.2	6.5	−10.0	50.5	243	15.8	14.4	8.6	−10.0	85.0
Black	233	9.0	8.4	6.8	−1.8	76.8	225	10.9	10.3	7.7	−3.5	78.5
Asian	172	12.5	14.4	11.3	−0.7	75.7	168	15.8	18.4	12.9	0.9	74.1
Japanese	48	12.1	10.8	6.0	−0.4	24.4	44	15.3	14.6	7.1	−0.4	33.4

Chinese	68	11.6	11.4	7.1	-7.5	40.8	66	14.5	14.5	8.8	1.0	49.0
Filipino	44	11.2	12.4	11.0	-2.2	52.0	40	15.5	16.9	11.9	0.7	49.0
Korean	44	13.5	13.1	7.9	-1.0	39.5	43	15.1	15.0	8.5	0.3	38.2
Vietnamese	23	5.6	7.8	6.9	-0.1	26.5	20	8.2	11.0	10.8	-0.5	50.5
Asian Indian	52	16.5	21.0	19.1	-10.0	85.0	46	22.2	30.0	20.6	3.8	71.2
Pacific Islander	30	9.4	12.0	10.3	-1.3	44.6	24	11.9	16.4	12.8	1.0	59.0
Hispanic	210	11.4	11.9	8.4	-1.0	76.0	203	13.1	14.2	11.2	-1.0	76.0
Mexican	140	10.7	11.6	9.4	-2.8	77.8	130	12.3	13.3	10.6	0.8	74.2
Puerto Rican	67	10.3	9.0	7.3	-2.3	35.1	60	11.6	10.7	8.1	-2.3	35.1
Cuban	41	12.9	11.2	6.2	-1.2	31.1	38	14.3	14.4	8.4	-1.2	40.8
Other Spanish	145	11.6	12.2	9.7	-1.6	48.7	136	13.7	15.4	13.1	-3.7	78.7

[1] The income definition is based only upon the mean self-employment income of all the respondents in each respective category or group who reported income from self-employment, whereas the work definition is based only upon the mean self-employment income of respondents who also reported that they were self-employed workers.

[2] Not included in the table are statistics for native-born and foreign-born blacks or the Asian and Hispanic categories and groups

[3] Excludes metropolitan areas in which any category or group did not have at least 400 persons in the civilian labor force.

[4] The unweighted maximum MSEI can be obtained by adding the range to the minimum MSEI for each category and group.

metropolitan areas that met the threshold criterion. Weighted means weight metropolitan areas in proportion to their total population. For example, when calculating Cuban mean self-employment rate, the weighted statistic gives Miami 50% of influence, a share proportional to its share of the total Cuban population of all threshold metropolitan areas.

The weighted mean is the usual statistic in entrepreneurship studies. The weighted mean is appropriate when one's interest is a summary statement. However, our interest is interlocal variation in self-employment rates. After all, our concern is not what percentage of a group was self-employed in the United States, an obsession of journalists and politicians. Rather, we wish to understand how different metropolitan areas affected the entrepreneurship of ethnoracial groups and categories jointly with features of the groups. Weighted means suppress this knowledge.[35]

In actuality, the effects of weighting are slight. Within the total population, the unweighted mean (6.9% in column 3) exceeds the weighted mean income-defined mean self-employment rate (6.7% in column 2) by only 3%. The unweighted mean work-defined self-employment rate (7.2% in column 8) exceeds its weighted mean (7.1% in column 7) by 1%. However, weighting makes a greater difference among the foreign born than among the native born. For example, the unweighted, income-defined, mean self-employment rate of the native born exceeds the weighted, mean self-employment rate of the native born by only 6%, but the unweighted, income-defined mean self-employment rate of the foreign born exceeds the weighted by 15%.

Chinese and Koreans had the highest weighted and unweighted mean self-employment rates, as well as the largest differences between their weighted and unweighted statistics. The weighted, work-defined mean self-employment rate of Koreans is 16.5% (column 7), whereas the unweighted rate is 12.7% (column 8), a difference of 30% between the two measures. This result indicates that the clustering of Koreans in a few high entrepreneurship metropolitan areas, mostly in California, substantially inflated their weighted mean self-employment rate. Among all the groups and categories, the unweighted exceeds the weighted, income-defined, mean self-employment rates in 14 of 20 comparisons and the unweighted exceeds the weighted work-defined rates in 12 of 20 comparisons.

INTERCATEGORY RATES

Now we compare the mean self-employment rates of the five major ethnoracial categories in Table 2.7. Weighted or unweighted, the class of worker rate exceeds the income-defined rate for whites and Asians. But the class of worker rate does not exceed the income-defined rate for African Americans, and it exceeds the income-defined rate among Hispanics only when weighted. The discrepancy probably arises because the income-defined rate picks up a higher proportion of the part-time and marginal self-employed than does the class of worker definition. Therefore, the two most disadvantaged categories, African Americans and Hispanics, have relatively stronger representation in the income definition than in the class of worker definition.

Class of worker rates also maximized the difference between whites and other groups. The income-defined Asian rates were 98.7% of white rates and unweighted Asian rates were 101.3% of white rates. In contrast, utilizing the class of worker definition, the weighted mean Asian self-employment rates were 96.3% of the white rate and the unweighted rates were 102.5%. Similarly, the weighted and unweighted African-American means were 31.2% of white means using the class of worker definition, but 33.3% of white means using the income definition. The Hispanic mean was 52.5% of the white mean when self-employment rates are based on the income definition, but the Hispanic mean reaches 55.2% of the white rate when we substitute the class of worker definition of self-employment. In general then, the income definition minimizes intergroup differences in self-employment rates, whereas the class of worker definition maximizes those differences. Therefore, in stressing the income definition, we minimize intergroup differences.

However, the two definitions of self-employment did not influence much the rank order of the five ethnoracial categories. Whichever definition is used, and for weighted and unweighted measures alike, the foreign whites always rank first in mean self-employment, the Hispanics always rank fourth, and the African Americans always rank fifth or last. The operational definition of self-employment affects the rank of only Asians and native whites. However self-employment is defined, unweighted measures of self-employment put Asians narrowly in second place ahead of native whites. The weighted income-defined measure shows a tie for second place between Asians and native whites. Only the weighted class of worker definition puts the native whites ahead of the Asians for second place in mean self-employment rates. Admittedly, native white/Asian differences are always small. Nonetheless, the class of worker definition is slightly more favorable to native white standing relative to Asians than is the income definition.

If we disaggregate the Asian and Hispanic categories into national-origin groups, we find that Koreans (13.6%) always have the highest weighted mean income-defined self-employment rate, followed by the Chinese (9.0%). These two Asian groups also have weighted mean work-defined self-employment rates that sometimes exceed the comparable

Table 2.7. Descriptive Statistics of the Two Measures of the Mean Self-Employment Rate (MSER),[1] for Categories and Groups,[2] in 272 Metropolitan Areas (Percentages)

| | No. of SMSAs (1)[3] | Income-Defined MSER | | | | | | Work-Defined MSER | | | | |
| | | Weighted Mean (2) | Unweighted | | | | Weighted Mean (7) | Unweighted | | | |
			Mean (3)	SD (4)	Min (5)[4]	Range (6)		Mean (8)	SD (9)	Min (10)[4]	Range (11)
Total	272	6.7	6.9	1.7	4.1	9.4	7.1	7.2	1.8	4.6	9.7
Native born	272	6.6	6.9	1.7	3.6	9.9	7.0	7.2	1.8	3.9	10.3
Foreign Born	270	7.2	8.1	3.2	0.0	22.7	8.5	9.1	3.8	0.0	26.7
White	272	7.5	7.6	1.9	4.2	10.4	8.0	8.0	2.1	4.7	12.5
Native born	272	7.4	7.5	1.9	3.8	10.8	7.8	7.9	2.1	4.5	12.8
Foreign Born	245	9.9	9.7	3.8	0.0	22.2	12.0	11.0	4.7	0.0	29.6
Black	245	2.5	2.6	1.3	0.0	7.9	2.5	2.5	1.3	0.0	8.3
Asian	180	7.4	7.7	4.8	0.0	34.8	7.7	8.2	4.7	0.0	30.4
Japanese	51	8.4	7.8	4.3	0.0	22.7	8.2	7.1	4.5	0.0	22.7

Chinese	72	9.0	10.0	6.0	0.0	30.0	9.8	11.6	7.2	0.0	36.4
Filipino	51	3.7	4.2	3.5	0.0	18.2	3.2	4.3	4.1	0.0	19.5
Korean	46	13.6	11.7	6.4	0.0	25.0	16.5	12.7	7.2	0.0	29.2
Vietnamese	35	3.1	3.1	3.4	0.0	11.5	3.4	2.8	3.1	0.0	12.0
Asian Indian	54	7.2	7.1	3.7	0.0	16.1	7.3	7.6	4.9	0.0	23.3
Pacific Islander	36	4.1	4.4	3.8	0.0	20.0	3.7	4.2	4.8	0.0	20.0
Hispanic	230	3.9	4.2	2.8	0.0	20.4	4.4	4.2	2.9	0.0	18.6
Mexican	161	3.5	3.9	3.0	0.0	22.6	3.7	4.1	3.3	0.0	22.6
Puerto Rican	84	2.3	3.0	2.8	0.0	13.3	2.7	2.8	2.4	0.0	10.0
Cuban	44	6.8	7.3	4.8	0.0	21.7	9.0	8.0	4.8	0.0	20.7
Other Spanish	159	4.7	5.5	3.8	0.0	20.0	5.2	5.6	3.6	0.0	15.6

[1] The income definition is based only upon the number of respondents who reported income from self-employment and the work definition is based upon the number of respondents who reported that they were self-employed workers. Each respective type of self-employment was percentaged on the *total number* of each respective category or group who were in the civilian labor force, irrespective of whether or not they engaged in either income-defined or work-defined self-employment.

[2] Not included in the table are statistics for native-born and foreign-born blacks or the Asian and Hispanic categories and groups.

[3] Excludes metropolitan areas in which any category or group did not have at least 400 persons in the civilian labor force.

[4] The unweighted maximum MSER can be obtained by adding the range to the minimum MSER for each category and group.

rates of foreign-born whites. Chinese and Koreans are the only two minority groups that ever exceed the foreign white self-employment rate. At the low end, only Puerto Ricans ever have a lower weighted mean income-defined self-employment rate than African Americans. Vietnamese also have low rates for both weighted and unweighted, income-defined and work-defined self-employment, but Vietnamese are nonetheless above the comparable rates for African Americans. In all conditions, the range of difference in rates among the seven Asian groups exceeds the range among the four Hispanic groups. Comparing means (weighted and unweighted, income-defined and work-defined), although Asians as a category rank above Hispanics as a category, Vietnamese and Filipinos sometimes rank below the Hispanic average and Cubans above the Asian average.

Intracategory Rates

It is hazardous to rely exclusively upon means to assess intergroup differences in entrepreneurial performance. If, for example, one compares the mean self-employment rate of ethnoracial categories or groups in various metropolitan areas, one overlooks variation around the mean. Alas, exclusive reliance on means fully characterizes the existing entrepreneurship literature. Moreover, researchers have selected the weighted mean self-employment rate and mean self-employment income as most representative of group performances, further concealing intermetropolitan variation. Weighted means have, therefore, become the evidentiary linchpin of entrepreneurship research.

Relying upon means, analysts overlooked intragroup dispersion around the mean. The range and standard deviation of mean self-employment rates and incomes expose this dispersion. These measures of dispersion are theoretically important in a resources-based theory. After all, if intergroup disparities in self-employment rates depend upon group resources, then intragroup dispersion around the mean should be modest and/or related to variations in those resources. Possibly the group's people have roughly the same resources, whether in Las Vegas or in Jersey City, and, to the extent that their own resources determine performance, a group's people should display roughly the same entrepreneurial performance in all metropolitan areas.

In actuality, ethnoracial categories and groups display great intermetropolitan variation in mean self-employment rates just as in mean self-employment incomes. We find much puzzling, intragroup variation (Table 2.7). Taking the 272 metropolitan areas together, the unweighted, income-defined mean self-employment rates (column 3) show that Asians and whites tended to have higher rates of self-employment than Hispanics, and that Hispanics tended to have higher rates than African Americans.[36] One may suppose that class and ethnic resources explain this central tendency: those with more resources outperformed those with less. However, the four categories also displayed very unequal ranges and standard deviations. For example, the ranges (column 6) of the four categories are blacks, 7.9; whites, 10.4; Hispanics, 20.4; and Asians, 34.8. Similarly, among three minority categories, the minimum mean self-employment rate (column 5) was zero, whereas the minimum mean self-employment rate of whites was 4.2% Finally, the maxima of some low-ranking groups and categories exceeded the minima of some high-ranking groups, a result possibly inconsistent with resources theory. Thus, African Americans had the lowest mean self-employment rate of any group, but the maximum African-American income-defined rate was 7.9%, whereas the minimum Asian or Hispanic rate was zero, and the minimum native-white rate was 3.8%. This overlap suggests that African Americans had higher self-employment rates than whites *in at least some metropolitan areas*, a result hard to explain in terms of low resources.

RESOURCES AND PERFORMANCE

Means, Standard Deviations, and Correlations

Table 2.8 presents the means and standard deviations of three resources that have affected self-employment in others' research: education, age, and percentage male. Of these, age and percentage male represent demographic resources, a kind of ethnic resource. Education is a class resource. Table 2.8 also presents the correlations of these resources with both income-defined and work-defined self-employment.

The first resource is education. Mean years of education measures a group's human capital investment. Human capital is money sunk into personal productivity. Although the relationship between education and self-employment is not linear, the mean education of the self-employed routinely exceeds that of wage and salary workers (Boyd, 1991:414, 420–421; Bearse, 1985:5; Borjas, 1986:494). Ethnoracial categories varied greatly in their educational level. Asians had the highest mean years of education (14.2 years), and Hispanics had the lowest (11.5 years). Native whites had the second highest mean level of education, 12.9 years. Foreign whites ranked third in mean level of education. But standard

Table 2.8. Means, Standard Deviations, and Correlations of the Two Measures of Mean Self-Employment Rates,[1] with Three Resource Variables, for Five Categories

Independent Variables	Categories				
	Native-born White	Foreign-born White	Black	Asian	Hispanic
Mean education (years)					
Mean	12.87	12.70	11.88	14.16	11.51
Standard deviation	.53	1.29	.70	1.44	1.23
Correlations with					
Income-defined MSER	.42****	.15*	.37****	.11	.26****
Work-defined MSER	.32****	.08	.21***	.12	.28****
Mean age (years)					
Mean	36.97	41.69	35.55	34.90	33.52
Standard deviation	1.30	3.70	1.84	2.03	2.19
Correlation with					
Income-defined MSER	.08	.22***	−.10	.20**	.25****
Work-defined MSER	.12	.24****	.07	.29****	.33****
Mean percentage male					
Mean	57.18	53.24	50.41	52.42	57.92
Standard deviation	2.05	7.93	4.42	10.16	5.76
Correlation with					
Income-defined MSER	−.13*	.17**	.13*	.11	.03
Work-defined MSER	−.11	.19**	.02	.09	−.04
N	272	245	245	180	230

[1] See Table 2.7, note 1.
**** LE .0001.
*** LE .001.
** LE .01.
* LE .05.

deviations also differed. Asians had the highest standard deviation, almost a year and a half, and native whites the lowest, about half a year.

Age measures work experience and also years available to save the wherewithal to capitalize a business. The more experience and the more the savings, the greater the class resource. Therefore, the average age of self-employed workers exceeds that of wage and salary workers (Fuchs, 1982:347; Borjas, 1986:494; Sullivan and McCracken, 1988:173; Reynolds, 1989; Butler and Herring, 1991:82; Boyd, 1991:420-21).[37] In terms of age, foreign-born whites were the oldest (41.7 years), and Hispanics were the youngest (33.5 years old). Standard deviations also ranged from a low of 1.3 years for native-born whites, to a high of 3.7 years for foreign-born whites. Clearly, the Hispanic labor force was almost always appreciably younger than the native white labor force, a youthfulness that presumably reduced Hispanic entrepreneurship.

Males were three times more likely to be self-employed than females (Bates, 1987:546). Although this gender discrepancy was diminishing even then, and subsequently diminished even more (Becker, 1984:16), a big gender gap in self-employment still existed in 1980 (Loscocco and Robinson, 1991). Whatever the causes of this gap, groups and categories that had high proportions of males in their labor force ought to have had higher rates of self-employment than others. African Americans had the lowest average percentage of males in the labor force[38]—only 50.4%. This circumstance should have reduced African-American entrepreneurship. At the other end, the mean percentage of males among Hispanic workers was about 58%, a favorable ratio, comparable to that of native-born whites. Standard deviations for this demographic variable range from a low of about 2% for native-born whites to a high of almost 11% for Asians.

Groups had different resource profiles. True, the resources of African Americans were less than those of native-born whites, but native-born whites were not the most advantaged in terms of every resource. Rather, Asians had the most education, foreign-born whites were the oldest, and Hispanics had a higher percentage of males in the labor force. Of the four minorities, three ranked number one in respect to at least one resource. Entrepreneurship resources resembled a bridge game in which each player has strength in one suit.

We expected a positive zero-order correlation between each resource and the mean self-employment rates of all five categories for both measures of self-employment. This expectation proved basically correct, but the relationships were smaller and less consistent than anticipated. Table 2.8 shows that the correlations for mean years of education and both measures of self-employment are positive and significant for all groups but Asians. The class of worker definition yields positive correlations for native-born whites, blacks, and Hispanics, but not for foreign-born whites or Asians.

Age correlates positively with mean self-employment rates for foreign-born whites, Asians, and Hispanics. This relationship appears whether we use the income definition or the class of worker definition. However, we find no relationship between age and mean self-employment rates for native-born whites or blacks, for either definition.

Percentage male of the category's civilian labor force has the expected positive significant relationship with the income definition of self-employment for only foreign-born whites and blacks. However, contrary to our expectations, for the income-defined self-employed, the percentage male in the labor force has a significant *negative* effect for

native-born whites.[39] Possibly native white women were more entrepreneurial than other women. Percentage male had no correlation with the
self-employment of Asians or Hispanics, nor for the class of worker self-
employment rates of native whites or blacks.

Resource Underpinnings

Next we modeled the simultaneous effects of these resources in
regression equations using both definitions of self-employment. Table
2.9 lists the variables used, their definitions, and operational descriptions. The continuous variables have been "centered,"[40] because these
variables do not include a meaningful zero. For example, no ethnoracial
group has zero mean years of education. Aiken and West (1991:37,
119–138, and Ch. 7, n. 3) recommend that continuous variables be "centered." The mean for the total (in this case, pooled) sample is subtracted
from each raw data score so that the y axis is moved from a meaning-
less zero to the mean for each of the centered independent variables.
Table 2.9 indicates the pooled sample mean that was subtracted from
each respective variable in order to create the centered variables. A prefix "C" has been added to the name of each variable to indicate that it
has been centered.

Table 2.10 shows a separate regression model for each of the five categories for the income (A) and class of worker (B) definitions of self-
employment. The model measures how much combined resources
change mean self-employment rates. In general, the within-groups effect
of resources is positive but small. However, each category has a unique
configuration of resources that explains within-group variation in self-
employment rates among the localities. Comparing the adjusted R^2s
in A and B for each of the five categories, we find that the resource
model for native whites explains income-defined self-employment
and work-defined self-employment rates equally well (i.e., 18 vs. 16%,
respectively). The same is true for foreign whites (i.e., 11 and 10%,
respectively). However, for African Americans, the model better explains
their income self-employment than their class of worker self-
employment (14 vs. 7%, respectively). For the other two minority groups
the model accounts for more variation in class of worker than in income
self-employment rates (i.e., 9 vs. 4% for Asians and 19 vs. 14% for
Hispanics). Overall, these three resources explain an average of only
12.2% of self-employment within the five categories.

Education significantly increases the income and class of worker self-
employment of all groups except Asians. Increasing average age, and
therefore work experience, increases class of worker self-employment of

Table 2.9. Variables Used in the Analyses

Variables	Name and Operational Description of Variables
Dependent variables	
BRODMSER	Income-defined mean self-employment rate[1]
NAROMSER	Work-defined mean self-employment rate[2]
Independent variables[3]	
Human capital	
CCATED1	Category mean years of education centered on the means of each respective category[4]
CCATED2	Category mean years of education centered on the mean of the pooled sample[5]
Demographic	
CCATAGE1	Category mean years of age centered on the means of each respective category[4]
CCATAGE2	Category mean years of age centered on the mean of the pooled sample[5]
CCATPCTM1	Category percentage males centered on the means of each respective category[4]
CCATPCTM2	Category percentage males centered on the mean of the pooled sample[5]

[1] Respondents were defined as self-employed (= 1) if they had reported any income gains or losses from self-employment (INCOME2). We calculated the self-employment rate by dividing the number of persons who reported self-employment income (NINCOME2) by the total number of persons in the civilian labor force for each category.

[2] Respondents were defined as self-employed (=1) if they had reported self-employment work in a business that was not incorporated or as an employee of their own corporation (SETOT).

[3] These continuous independent variables were centered, as recommended by Aiken and West (1991:37, 119–138, and n.3), because the range of values for none of these variables encompassed a meaningful zero (where the linear regression line or plane transects the axis of the dependent variable for "raw" or metric coefficients). Centered variables were created by subtracting either the means from the "raw" data for each respective variable for each of the respective five categories (Table 2.10), or the means for the total pooled sample for each of the categories (Table 2.11).

[4] See Table 2.8 for the means for each respective variable for each of the respective five categories.

[5] Means for the total pooled sample for each of the categories were Mean years of education, 12.56; Mean years of age, 36.67; Percentage males, .54.

all categories and the income self-employment of three. Percentage male has the least effect upon self-employment rates. It increases only the income self-employment of Hispanics and the class of worker self-employment of African Americans.

Next, we pool these five categories, rerunning the model that we tested for the two definitions of mean self-employment rates for each category separately in Table 2.10. In Table 2.11, pooling the five categories improves the explanatory power of the model from the 12%

Table 2.10. Regression of Mean Income-Defined and Work-Defined Self-Employment Rates on Resource Variables[1] (Standardized Coefficients)

	Categories				
	Native-born White	Foreign-born White	Black	Asian	Hispanic
A. Dependent variable Income-defined self-employment rate Independent variables[2]					
Mean years of education	.443****	.278****	.411****	.065	.300****
Mean years of age	.077	.299****	.106	.196**	.279****
Mean percent male	−.035	.108	.060	.073	.133*
Adjusted R^2	.18	.11	.14	.04	.14
B. Dependent variable Work-defined self-employment rate Independent variables:[2]					
Mean years of education	.403****	.202**	.316****	.090	.305****
Mean years of age	.262****	.284****	.218**	.292****	.347****
Mean percentage male	−.046	.126*	−.005	.040	.077
Adjusted R^2	.16	.10	.07	.09	.19
N	272	245	245	180	230

[1] See Table 2.9 for operational definitions of variables.
[2] All three continuous independent variables have been centered on the means of each respective category (see Table 2.9, note 3).
**** LE .0001.
*** LE .001.
** LE .01.
* LE .05.

average for the five separate groups to around 40%. All resource variables are significant and positive.

CONCLUSION AND SUMMARY

Self-employment is more problematic than researchers have realized. The size and composition of the self-employed population depend importantly upon how one defines self-employment. The class of worker definition produces a larger population of self-employed than does an income definition, but a smaller population than the combined income/work definition we identified as the maximum self-employed population. Although the income definition and the class of worker definition do not

Table 2.11. Mean Income-Defined and Work-Defined Self-Employment Rates[1] Regressed on Resource Variables, for Five Categories Pooled, N = 1,172 (Standardized Coefficients)

	Income-Defined	Work-Defined
Independent variables[2]		
Mean years of education	.387****	.362****
Mean years of age	.453****	.517****
Mean percent male	.111****	.096****
Adjusted R^2	.36	.40

[1] See Table 2.9 for operational definitions of variables.
[2] All three continuous independent variables have been centered on the means of the pooled sample (see Table 2.9, note 3).
**** LE .0001.
*** LE .001.
** LE .01.
* LE .05.

differ much in the size of the self-employed population they define, the two definitions achieve only about 58% overlap. The class of worker self-employed consistently earned more money than did the income self-employed. We have elected to stress the income definition rather than the more commonly utilized class of worker definition. This choice permits us to look lower down the self-employment hierarchy than other studies, getting closer to the vanishing point where measured self-employment disappears into the informal economy, an unmeasured zone.

Resources theory has stressed weighted means that smooth out intra-category and intragroup differences in entrepreneurial performance. This emphasis has led to two difficulties. First, weighted means conceal locality effects that appear in unweighted means. Second, all means conceal variation around the mean. This variation is often extreme, and resources theory has trouble explaining it. We found no evidence that high entrepreneurship in metropolitan areas differed from low entrepreneurship in metropolitan areas in respect to the effects of the group and category resources they contained.

NOTES

1. Of course, without this prior case study research, the whole subject would not exist because case studies and selective comparisons created the evidence that validated the need for further research—including this research. For a discussion of case studies' utility, see Orum (1990).

2. This observation reflects no disparagement of case study methods. On the contrary, research traditions are successful when, outgrowing themselves, they encounter as limitations the very methods that once promoted their growth.

3. For a discussion of this concept, see Light (1983:199–204).

4. Creation of the dataset and all statistical work for this research has been done using SAS (1985a, 1985b).

5. Based upon the variables AGE, DISABIL2, LABOR, and INDUSTRY. LABOR excludes those who were "not in the labor force," that is, the unemployed, housewives, and students. The primary industries excluded are "Agriculture, Forestry, and Fisheries."

6. Appendix Table 2A indicates how we made these assignments.

7. Other Mixed Asians comprised about 18,790 persons or 0.5% of the selected sample from the 5% 1980 Census PUM data.

8. We disaggregated each category and group by nativity (U.S. Bureau of the Census, 1983:77). The "foreign born" were either "naturalized citizens" or noncitizens. The "native born" were either "born in the United States or outlying areas" or "born abroad of American parents." In addition, for each metropolitan area, we created a "total native born" category, a "total foreign born" category, and a "total persons" category for the civilian nonagricultural labor force population, age 16 and over. These three categories *do* include the otherwise deleted "Other Mixed Asians" group.

9. Twenty persons in the original 5% 1980 Census PUM sample.

10. For each ethnoracial category and group, Table 3.1 shows the number of metropolitan areas whose civilian labor force, aged 16 or older, met our threshold criterion of 400 persons or more.

11. Using SAS's PROC SUMMARY NWAY program.

12. This procedure was applied to the variables AGE, Weeks Unemployed in 1979 (WEEKSU79), and 1979 Income from Wages and Salaries (INCOME1), and from Nonfarm Self-employment (INCOME2).

13. This was the case for Number of Years in the U.S. (LENGTHR), and Number of Years of Education Completed (YRSED).

14. This procedure was used to create the following variables: Percentage Male (MSEX), Percentage Unemployed (UNTOT), Percentage in each of 12 industrial categories (from INDUSTRY), and Percentage Self-Employed (SETOT).

15. Appendix 2A lists and briefly describes the new variables and the notes for Appendix 2A describe how these variables were created in more detail.

16. This includes many variables that we created, but did not use.

17. The seven classes of workers are private wage and salary employee of a private company, federal government worker, state government worker, local government worker, self-employed worker—business not incorporated, employee of own corporation, and unpaid family worker (U.S. Bureau of the Census, 1983:89).

18. In this narrow definition, the number who are self-employed workers is percentaged on the total number in the civilian labor force, which includes the self-employed, wage and salary workers, and all government workers, but excludes two classes of worker categories—unpaid family workers and those for whom the question was not applicable (i.e., those who were under 16 years

of age, in the Armed Forces, last worked before 1975 and were not in the labor force, and those who have never worked). This variable is indicated as SETOT in Appendix 2A.

19. In this broad definition, the number who reported nonfarm self-employment income (gains or losses) is percentaged on the total number in the civilian labor force (see note 18), to calculate the mean self-employment rate (MSER) for each respective category and group. This variable is indicated as SEITOT in Appendix 2A.

20. Individual respondents also indicated their income gains or losses from one or more other sources, such as wages and salaries, interest, dividends, or net rental income, social security, public assistance, and all other sources (U.S. Bureau of the Census, 1983:90–91).

21. Excluding Native-Born Vietnamese, because no metropolitan areas had a minimum of 400 Native-Born Vietnamese in the labor force.

22. For the Total population: $(18.9\% + 23.6\%)/57.6\% = 73.8\%$ or 74%.

23. That is, no income gains or losses.

24. Given the prohibitive expense in time and money to add these variables, we reluctantly leave to future investigators exploration of what would result if one defined the self-employed as those who receive self-employment income *and/or* primarily worked as self-employed, thus maximizing the entrepreneur population.

25. See explanation for this limitation in the previous paragraph and in note 24.

26. Note that this definition differs from "SE Income Only" in Table 2.4. In Table 2.4, it was defined as just a, whereas, in Table 2.5, "Total # SE Income" is defined as $a + c$.

27. Note that this definition differs from "SE Work Only" in Table 2.4. In Table 2.4, it was defined as just b, whereas, in Table 2.5, "Total # SE Work" is defined as $b + c$.

28. That is, it is equal to the sum of the core and two marginal self-employed in Table 2.4, i.e., $a + b + c$.

29. The weighted, population-level mean self-employment rates are the mean of the total numbers of persons in the civilian labor force in a category or group, in all metropolitan areas, which met the threshold criterion. Weighted means weight metropolitan areas in proportion to their population, that is, the denominator is the total number in each category or group, which includes those with or without self-employment income or losses, as well as those with or without self-employment class of work. (A more extensive discussion of the distinction between weighted and unweighted statistics follows below in the text.)

30. For Total population (see Table 2.5, columns 1 and 2): $[(7.1/6.7) - 1.0] \times 100 = 5.97\%$ or 6%.

31. The greater differences found for the Total percentage "self-employed income only" and "work only" for Koreans and Cubans are due to these two groups being primarily comprised of the foreign born.

32. The "Total Maximum SE" populations are *both* the core self-employed and the two marginal income-only and work-only self-employed, i.e., $a + b + c$.

33.   For Total population: $[(8.8/7.1) - 1] \times 100 = 24\%$ (from Table 2.5, columns 3 and 2) and $[(8.8/6.7) - 1] \times 100 = 31\%$ (from Table 2.5, columns 3 and 1), respectively.

34.   As represented by $a + c$ in Figure 2.1.

35.   Nevertheless, for continuity with the self-employment literature, we include and comment upon the corresponding weighted and unweighted means where appropriate.

36.   The findings are similar for the weighted population-level means, except that whites (7.5) have 0.1% more self-employment than do Asians (7.4).

37.   Evans and Leighton (1989:532) report that age and education do not begin to increase an individual's probability of self-employment for the first 20 years of employment. They attribute this lagged increase to the necessity to "accumulate assets in order to start viable businesses."

38.   This percentage represents the number of males, age 16 and over, as a percentage of the total number of males and females in a category or group working in the civilian labor force.

39.   A higher than average rate of female self-employment would make sense for native whites among whom married women more frequently can afford the luxury of part-time self-employment rather than full-time wage labor outside the home.

40.   See Aiken and West (1991).

APPENDIX

Appendix 2A. Variables Created for the Mean Characteristics of 47 Categories and Groups[1] in 272 Metropolitan Areas

New Variable	Original Variable	Type of Variable	Description[1]
MSEX	SEX	Dummy; 1 = Male[2]	Percent male
AGE	AGE	Interval	Mean years of age; 0 to 89; 90 = 90/more
47 Categories and groups	RACE, OTHER SPANISH, AND CITIZEN	Dummy; 1 = Yes	Category or group as percent of total civilian labor force in each SMSA
LENGTHR[3]	IMMIGR	Interval	Mean number of years in United States; foreign-born only
YRSED[4]	GRADE AND FINGRADE	Interval	Mean years of school completed
UNTOT	LABOR	Dummy; 1 = unemployed	Percent unemployed
12 industrial categories[5]	INDUSTRY	Dummy	Percent in each respective industrial category
SETOT[6]	CLASS	Dummy; 1 = self-employed	Percent self-employed (class of worker definition)
SEITOT	NINCOME2[7]	Dummy; 1 = had nonfarm self-employment income	Percent self-employed (income definition)
WEEKSU79	WEEKSU79	Interval	Mean number of weeks unemployed, looking for work or on layoff; 1–52
INCOME1[8]	INCOME1	Interval	Mean dollar wage and salary income; $5 to $75,000 (no zero $)
INCOME2[9]	INCOME2	Interval	Mean dollar nonfarm self-employment income or losses of all who reported it; $–9,995 to $75,000 (no zero $) (income definition)
INC2[10]	INCOME2 AND SETOT	Interval	Mean dollar nonfarm self-employment income or losses of only the self-employed; $–9,995 to $75,000 (no zero $) (class of worker definition)

[1] Means are for each of the 47 categories and groups in each metropolitan area, unless otherwise stated.

[2] This variable was changed to represent the mean percentage male of categories and groups rather than the mean percent female represented by the original PUMs variable.

[3] The original variable, IMMIGR (Year of Immigration) was converted to an interval-level variable, by assigning the value for the mean number of years in the United States for each original code, as follows:

IMMIGR Codes	Description	LENGTHR Mean Number of Years
0	N/A (born in United States or outlying areas or born abroad of American parents)	Missing value
1	1975–1980	2.5
2	1970–1974	8.0
3	1965–1969	13.0
4	1960–1964	18.0
5	1950–1959	25.5
6	Before 1950	31.0*

* Based upon the conservative assumption of immigration in 1949, just after World War II.

[4] First, the original categorical-level variable, GRADE (Highest Year of School Attended) was adjusted to correspond to actual years of school, by creating an interim variable EDUC that ranged from 1 = first grade to 20 = eighth year or more college, by (1) recoding "never attended school or N/A," "nursery school," and "kindergarten" to 0, and (2) subtracting 2 years from all of the other codes. Second, to calculate the number of years of school *completed*, (1) YRSED was set equal to EDUC, if FINGRADE (Finished Highest Grade) was either "now attending this grade" or "finished this grade." (2) One year was subtracted from EDUC if the respondent "did not finish this grade." (3) Finally, if the respondent had "never attended school or N/A," then YRSED = 0.

[5] Dummy variables were created to correspond to 12 broad 1980 Census industrial categories (U.S. Bureau of the Census, 1983, Appendix H, pp. 142–148) as follows:

Dummy Variables	Description	1980 Census Industry Codes
MININD	Mining	040–050
CONIND	Construction	060
MANUIND	Manufacturing (nondurable and durable)	100–392
TRANIND	Transportation, communication, and other public utilities	400–472
WHOLIND	Wholesale trade (durable and nondurable goods)	500–571
RETIND	Retail trade	580–691
FININD	Finance, insurance, and real estate	700–712
BUSRIND	Business and repair services	721–760
PERSIND	Personal services	761–791
ENTIND	Entertainment and recreation services	800–802
PROFIND	Professional and related	812–892
PUBIND	Public administration	900–932

[6] Respondents were defined as self-employed (= 1) if they were a "self-employed worker—business not incorporated" or an "employee of own corporation."

[7] Respondents were defined as self-employed (=1) if they had reported any income gains or losses from self-employment (INCOME2). The self-employment rate was calculated by dividing the number of persons who reported self-employment income (NINCOME2) by the total number of persons in the civilian labor force for each respective category and group.

[8] According to the codebook (U.S. Bureau of the Census, 1983:90), no income (= 0) is not a valid code, but rather indicated "N/A—under 16 years of age or no income from this source," therefore, it was recoded to the missing value. "75,000" is equivalent to "income of $75,000 or more.")

[9] According to the codebook (U.S. Bureau of the Census, 1983:90), no income (= 0) is not a valid code, but rather indicated "N/A—under 16 years of age or no income/loss from this source," therefore, it was recoded to the missing value. "–9,995" is equivalent to a "loss of $9,990 or more" and "75,000" is equivalent to "income of $75,000 or more.")

[10] See note 10 concerning the income values for this variable. See note 6 for how "self-employed" was defined.

CHAPTER

3

Demand Effects

Max Weber declared that economic sociology must start from the desire for utilities and the provision to furnish them (Swedberg, 1987:29). Adhering to this tradition, textbooks have long hewed to the claim that both supply and demand require attention in a complete explanation of entrepreneurship (Kilby, 1971:19–26). Smelser (1976:126) writes that "like all markets, the market for entrepreneurial services has a demand and a supply side," underscoring this issue. This point would need no restatement but for disciplinary traditions that equip researchers with conceptual tools that better fit one side or the other, thus laying the groundwork for competition between adherents of demand and adherents of supply.[1] Although the competition is hard to avoid, it is misleading to stress features that fit one's disciplinary paradigm while ignoring others.

Supply-side explanations stress inequality in people's entrepreneurial resources and their unequal responsiveness to the attractions and rewards of entrepreneurship, whether material or psychological. For example, if people believe that entrepreneurs are prestigious, and wish to bask in that prestige, then prestige needs caused them to pursue the entrepreneur's role. Money was not their motive. Supply-derived explanations direct attention to the base populations from which entrepreneurs are recruited rather than to the money available to pay them. In this view, the rate of self-employment depends at least partially upon the population's underlying inclination and capacity for the entrepreneur's role, not just upon the role's money rewards. Naturally that inclination depends in part on money rewards, but it also depends upon the availability of people who have the skills, the resources, and the desire to undertake self-employment at various levels of money return (Szelenyi, 1988:211). The presumption is that sociocultural influences affect the responsiveness of people to money rewards and that money is not the only motivator. Personal prestige, self-fulfillment, independence, power, and ethnic or gender honor are frequently encountered nonmonetary motivators (Cochran, 1965:93, 100). In this chapter, we postpone our attention to supply issues, concentrating wholly upon demand. Supply is the subject of the next chapter.

Demand effects are quantitative and qualitative changes in the entrepreneur population that result from changes in the volume of aggregate demand, its industrial distribution, or both. The demand for entrepreneurs refers to the money rewards of entrepreneurship relative to wage or salary employment. Explanations that stress demand direct attention to the money entrepreneurs earn or to rewards that are ultimately translatable into money and wanted for this reason.[2] In this view, the rate of entrepreneurs increases when the role's money rewards increase and decreases when its money rewards decrease. If, for example, technological change renders small firms more competitive with big ones, as Piore and Sabel (1984) have claimed, then owners of small firms earn more money, more workers become small and medium business owners, and the rate of entrepreneurship increases in the economy.

The economist's term "demand" corresponds to "market opportunity," a virtual synonym common in sociology. We somewhat prefer the term demand to market opportunity in this context. Opportunity has a valid and autonomous meaning in status attainment studies (Featherman and Hauser, 1978) where it stands for a vacant prestige niche. Weber (1968) meant by market opportunity the privilege of trading where the right is not routinely available to all. However, in the context of entrepreneurship research, "market opportunity" means demand.[3] Thus, Waldinger, Aldrich, and Ward (1990:21) stress the importance of "opportunity structures" and then define "opportunity structures" as "market conditions." In the last analysis, market conditions offer "opportunity" because of money rewards. Limitless opportunities to perform unpaid services do not create an opportunity structure for housewives.

Sometimes opportunity is defined ostensively. Ostensive definitions list the conditions under which a phenomenon appears. Waldinger (1986b:25) means by opportunity an industry in which entrepreneurs thrive. He lists three characteristics of such industries: low returns to economies of scale, flux and uncertainty, and small and differentiated markets. Expanding the idea, Waldinger, Aldrich, and Ward (1990:25) offer an ostensive definition of "the types of economic environments" that facilitate entrepreneurial opportunity: coethnic consumer products, underserved or abandoned markets, markets with low returns to economies of scale, markets with unstable or uncertain demand, and markets for exotic goods. In the same spirit, Waldinger (1986a:278) earlier declares demand for small firms a product of "markets whose small size, heterogeneity, or susceptibility to flux and instability limit the potential for mass distribution and mass production."

Ostensive definitions suffer two problems. First, explaining from precursors, they remain too low on the abstraction ladder to isolate causality. Thus, knowing that Coca-Cola, candy, doughnuts, and pop tarts encourage tooth decay, one still does not know that sugar causes tooth decay. Additionally, ostensive definitions are subject to reappraisal whenever someone revises the list. If the new lists are added to the existing list, the list of precursors becomes embarrassingly long with no guarantee that additional categories will not shortly appear. Waldinger's (1984) early list resembles, but is shorter than Waldinger, Aldrich, and Ward's (1990) list, so the expansion of the list has already begun. Meanwhile, others have compiled different but equally good lists (White, 1982; Bearse, 1987). White (1982) reasons that small business firms will be viable in industries in which their gross sales represent a big share of total earnings. He found that such industries showed little vertical integration, low capital-to-labor ratios, and sales mainly to other industries. Additionally, industries friendly to small business were likely to be growing rapidly and to enjoy local markets.

Admittedly, these lists identify conditions that encourage small business. But there is no closure possible in compiling such lists, which can be multiplied forever without reaching a level of abstraction that acknowledges money. Money is the key to economic opportunity. In the last analysis, any industry offers "opportunity" because of money rewards. If money returns are abundant, opportunity is abundant. If money rewards are nil, opportunity is nil. In the context of entrepreneurship research, opportunity is a useless circumlocution for demand.

RESEARCH DESIGN

Although demand and supply contribute jointly to entrepreneurial performance, research designs sometimes suppress one in the interest of highlighting the other, a valid application of J. S. Mills' method of difference (Ragin, 1987:36–42). Designs that focus on the same group in different locations hold resources roughly constant while varying demand environments.[4] This design deliberately excludes resources from the explanation. For example, Patterson (1975:347) compared Chinese migrants in Guyana and Jamaica. He found that only the Jamaica Chinese became entrepreneurs, a result he attributed to uneven economic conditions in the two countries, a demand-side explanation. However, within the limits of his evidence, Patterson's design could not disclose supply influences on Chinese entrepreneurship even if any were present. Patterson treated the Chinese in Jamaica and the Chinese in Guyana as if identical in resource endowments but confronting different demand environments. Therefore, Patterson's results do not disprove the existence of supply-side influences that his design rendered invisible, nor, of course, were they intended to do so.

Studies that focus on different groups in the same location have the opposite blind spot. For example, Kallen and Kelner (1983) compared the entrepreneurship of Italians, Jews, and white Protestants in Toronto; Kim, Hurh, and Fernandez (1989) compared the entrepreneurship of Chinese, Gujerati Indians, and non-Gujerati Indians in Chicago. Here the same location means an analytically constant location, whether that location be the same county, the same city, the same state, or even the same society. In such cases, location encompasses all the demand variables. Because a constant cannot explain a change, and location is constant, the only possible explanation of intergroup differences in entrepreneurship lies on the supply side. An example is Light's (1972) comparative analysis of Japanese, Chinese, and African Americans in entrepreneurship before World War II. Treating the location as invariant, a handful of northern cities in a half century, this research had to find cultural explanations for differences in rates of entrepreneurship among the three groups. Even if demand-side explanations existed, the research design rendered it impossible to observe them. This research did not prove that no demand-side influences existed. The results showed only that when demand-side influences were held constant, supply-side influences emerged.

In reaction to these uses of Mills' method of difference, some current researchers have recommended balanced explanations that do simultaneous justice to both supply and demand factors, a position compatible with the textbook view. Thus, Waldinger, Ward, and Aldrich (1985:589) observe that a "common objection to cultural analysis" is its lack of attention to "the economic environment in which immigrant entrepreneurs function." They recommend "an interactive approach" that looks at the "congruence between the demands of the economic environment and the informal resources of the ethnic population." Since they wrote, this reaction has achieved the strength of a movement of thought in the entrepreneurship literature (see Waldinger, Morokvasic, and Phizacklea, 1990; Curran and Burrows, 1987) within which it is now axiomatic that entrepreneurs emerge from the interaction of supply and demand.

At first, this interactionist conclusion sounds like Weber's orthodoxy rewarmed. However, the interaction approach does not represent a return to the older textbook generalization that supply and demand coproduce entrepreneurs. That older view makes no reference to the articulation of the two elements, only insisting that both participate in a complete explanation. In contrast the interaction hypothesis specifies just how supply and demand codetermine entrepreneurship—not just that they do so. Specifically, interaction theory claims that the entrepreneurial performance of groups depends upon the fit between what they have to offer and what the market requires.[5] The better the fit, the more entrepreneurs; and the same group can experience a good fit in some places and a poor fit in others. Thus, the Chinese can operate more restaurants in New York City, whose consumers like Chinese food, than they can in cities whose consumers do not (Tuchman and Levine, 1993:397). The number of Chinese restaurants in a place is a joint product of the number of Chinese in the place and the local public's appetite for Chinese food. The ability to cook Chinese food is an ethnic resource of the Chinese, the public's appetite for Chinese cuisine is a demand characteristic of localities, and the actual number of Chinese restaurants will be a joint product of public tastes and Chinese resources. In fact, every group's entrepreneurship depends upon the fit between what they can do and what the local market demands. This interactionist generalization refines the older view, which merely specified that supply and demand must figure in a complete explanation without explaining just how they must relate.

Since the truth is, as Hegel averred, the whole, the goal of full explanation appropriately returns research to its vocation. However, that vocation imposes design constraints. Interactionist research can utilize three research designs: cases that simultaneously vary both supply and demand conditions, cases that vary demand or supply but not the other, and cases that vary neither. Of these, the simplest is the last, a case study of one group in one demand environment. Enjoying detailed access to all the local evidence, one group/one locality studies permit intensive investigation of theoretically interesting cases. In the context of a larger literature, this design can turn up detailed explanations of how this unusual case occurred.

An example is Light and Bonacich's (1988) case study of Koreans in Los Angeles. Attempting to treat both supply-side and demand-side causes, the authors examined both the resources of the Korean immigrants and the characteristics of their economic niche in Los Angeles. With regard to the Koreans' niche, they stressed the absence of competition from big retail chains in the inner city, a product of economic disincentives arising from low income consumers and high-crime business sites. More broadly, they called attention to the selective effects of the "investor's exemption" provision of the U.S. immigration law, the tax advantages of independent contractors, the timely elimination of fair trade laws in liquor retailing, and lax enforcement of wage and sanitary provisions of the labor code. These external influences created an economic niche in which Korean entrepreneurs could exploit their class and ethnic resources. With respect to resources, they mentioned the Koreans' Protestant religion, patriarchal families, high education levels, social networks, and rotating credit associations.

Strictly speaking, this one group/one locality design offers no variation on either the supply or demand side. Such variation required comparison of groups and/or of localities. In case study designs, both supply and demand are fixed, and the problem is to explain what happened. Therefore, it is impossible formally to induct causal conclusions on the strength of case study designs.

Nonetheless, this one case/one locality was important because of the high entrepreneurship of Koreans in Los Angeles. This extraordinary level rendered the case of interest in itself, as well as for the light it threw upon general theory. But this case study could not explain why non-Koreans in Los Angeles did not take more advantage of the same demand conditions that attracted Koreans to the retail liquor industry, dry cleaning, garment manufacturing, and to the African-American community. Nor, on the other hand, could it explain why Koreans ignored entrepreneurial niches that attracted Chinese and Iranians. Nor, most importantly, could it formally induct the relative importance of supply and demand in Korean entrepreneurship.

The second type of interaction-seeking research permits simultaneous variation of supply and demand conditions. This simultaneous covariation is formally indispensable to the research goal. To expose supply and demand factors, interactionist research designs must permit simultaneous variation in supplier groups and in economic environments. Some interactionist research has met this design requirement; most has not.[6] For example, in their research on Asian entrepreneurs in three British cities, Aldrich, Jones, and McEvoy (1984) compared the Asians with a sample of white entrepreneurs with respect to directly measured practices thought to reflect ethnic business style. They found few differences between Asians and whites with respect to resource endowment, but important differences in business environment among the three cities, with all groups demonstrating higher rates in some cities than in others. Reviewing the evidence, they concluded that "immigrant business activity" was more shaped by internal than by external forces. "The opportunity structure of the receiving society outweighs any cultural predisposition towards entrepreneurship" (Aldrich, Jones, and McEvoy, 1984:205). Without simultaneous variation in both supply and demand conditions, this judgment would not have been permissible.[7]

However, other interaction-seeking research has stumbled over this methodological requirement. For example, in his study of New York City's garment industry, Waldinger (1986b:10) stressed the advantages of a balanced treatment that acknowledges "opportunity structures" as well as cultural influences. In this regard, Waldinger (1986b, Chs. 1, 4) mentioned the economic advantages that lured immigrant Dominican and Chinese entrepreneurs into this industry. These economic advantages included low returns on economies of scale, instability and uncertainty of product demand, small and differentiated product markets, agglomeration advantages, access to cheap labor, and vacant niches caused by the exodus of ethnic white predecessors. These demand-side attractions did not negate what Waldinger (1986b:31) called the "predispositions toward entrepreneurship" of the immigrants, and Waldinger acknowledged the predispositions as well as the economic incentives. Waldinger regarded this conclusion as a balanced one that did justice to supply as well as demand influences.

However, Waldinger's research varied only groups. It did not simultaneously vary demand environments. His multiple groups/one industry design permitted inductive generalizations only about the influence of supply-side resources upon entrepreneurship. It did not permit generalizations about the influence of demand environment, a constant. From a formal point of view, therefore, Waldinger's "balanced" conclusions were of unequal value. On the one hand, the comparison of Chinese and Dominicans permitted conclusions about the influence of different resource profiles in the groups' entrepreneurship. On the other hand, Waldinger's design did not authorize his conclusions about demand.[8] Useful as they were, those conclusions had the same exploratory status as did the observations of Min (1989) or of Light and Bonacich (1988) about the economy of Los Angeles.

Bailey's (1987:22) study of New York City's restaurant industry encountered the same problem. Acknowledging the importance of cultural predisposition and ethnic solidarity in restaurant entrepreneurship, Bailey (1987:53–55) looked for "important causes" that previous studies had "neglected" in the interest of a balanced explanation. These neglected causes turned out to be "market and technological conditions," privileged access to the cheap labor of coethnics, and lack of entrepreneurial interest among native-born workers. Bailey's catalog included supply-side and demand-side factors, and represented, in this sense, a balanced explanation of restaurant industry entrepreneurship. This balance represented an intellectual achievement insofar as previous studies had neglected demand-side explanations. However, Bailey's multiple groups/one industry research design could not offer generalizations about demand effects that had the same inductive power as did his generalizations about differences between immigrants and natives, the groups he compared.

DEFINING SUPPLY AND DEMAND

Since our dataset simultaneously varies groups and localities, we are in a position to induct generalizations about supply and demand. However, building toward that objective, which will be discussed in successive chapters, this chapter examines only demand's independent effects. This enterprise is entirely novel, and sociological treatments of demand are few.[9] Neither Stinchcombe (1983) nor Martinelli and Smelser (1990) index demand, yet these are leading texts in economic sociology. Parsons and Smelser (1956:9) define demand as "the disposition to pay" for goods and services "in a process of market exchange."[10] Demand requires customers with disposable income. The more customers and the more income each has, the more entrepreneurs can thrive in this environment. Aggregate demand is the sum of the demand for all the products and services in the economy.[11] However, aggregate demand does not create entrepreneurs directly. That is, given a million dollars of new spending power, we cannot move directly to how many entrepreneurs that million dollars will generate without considering how consumers spend their money. Consumers may hire butchers, bakers, or candlestick-makers. Aggregate demand for entrepreneurs is the sum of the demand for entrepreneurs in all industries. Therefore, an increase in aggregate demand need not produce equal increases in the demand for all commodities. For example, when the Federal government orders poison gas and smart bombs, ordinance manufacturers increase in number. The same federal expenditure has no direct impact upon the number of taco and tortilla manufacturers.

DEMAND EFFECTS

The interactive approach teaches that the entrepreneur population of every group emerges from the interaction of its resources and demand. Although this proposition improves earlier formulations, it is now possible to go beyond the interaction hypothesis by distinguishing two dissimilar demand effects whose interactions with supply produce quite different results on entrepreneurial performance. We call them *general demand effects* and *specific demand effects*.[12] When changes in aggregate demand expand or contract the entrepreneurial performance of all ethnoracial groups in approximate parity, then we call this demand effect general. As a rising tide raises all boats in the harbor, the ocean liner

and the tugboat alike, so a general demand effect enhances the entrepreneurship of all ethnoracial categories and groups.

An example of a generally favorable change in demand is an emerging, postrecessionary, full employment, high-wage local economy in a
cheap money environment. Putting money in everyone's pockets, this
environment creates consumer demand for a full spectrum of services
and products, thus improving every group's entrepreneurial performance. Asian, African-American, Hispanic, and white entrepreneurs all
benefit from cheap money and full employment. In response to
improved demand conditions, the numbers of each group's entrepreneurs increase in equal proportion. For example, if increased demand
doubles the aggregate population of entrepreneurs, and group A had
10% of entrepreneurs before the change, then, after the change, group A
will continue to have 10% of all entrepreneurs, but it will have twice as
many entrepreneurs.

General demand effects are incompatible with the interaction theory
of entrepreneurship. That is, the interaction theory claims that a group's
entrepreneurship is a joint product of its resources and local demand,
whereas, when general demand effects occur, demand has apparently
exerted a direct influence upon entrepreneurship unmediated by interaction with group resources. We hypothesize that general demand
effects exist, in which case the interaction theory would be wrong.
General demand effects define many researchers' intuitive model of
how demand operates. Advancing this view, Swinton and Handy
(1983:32–33) declare that "In a general sense, all business enterprises
compete for the same market demand." Therefore, the "rate of growth
of opportunities for business expansion in general" constrains the "rate
of expansion of black business ownership." This view assumes that
when business in general expands, black-owned firms expand; and
when business in general stagnates, black business stagnates. Swinton
and Handy assume a tight linkage between aggregate demand and
industrial demand such that all industries benefit equally from
enhanced aggregate demand. If the linkage is tight, then general
demand effect is present, and African Americans will obtain a proportional share of the additional entrepreneurs generated by additional
aggregate demand.

But linkages are not always tight. When Yuppies move into a gentri-
fying neighborhood, aggregate consumer demand rises, but most of the
increase flows into wine bars and nouvelle cuisine restaurants, enterprises in which white entrepreneurs predominate. Mexican owners of
taco stands and neighborhood taverns obtain no share of Yuppie
demand. When enhanced aggregate demand results in unequal
improvement of the entrepreneurial performance of ethnoracial groups,

in this case an improvement of white rates relative to Mexican, then the demand's effect is specific. Specific demand effects mean that some groups appropriate all or much of the demand, some little and some none.[13] Therefore, specific demand changes the share of a metropolitan area's total demand that entrepreneurs of various ethnoracial categories supply. For example, if Koreans in Los Angeles monopolize the janitorial industry, when industrial demand for janitors grows, increasing aggregate demand in the process, Koreans may appropriate the whole increase in aggregate demand, with none of the other ethnic groups obtaining any share. This appropriation would increase the absolute and relative number of Korean entrepreneurs, thus improving the Koreans' self-employment rate.[14]

In real economic environments, specific demand and general demand effects appear simultaneously.[15] However, in textbook illustrations like this one, general and specific demand effects are ideal types. As such, general demand effects are proportional changes in the entrepreneurial performance of each ethnoracial category in a metropolitan area. At a minimum, general demand effects require unequal changes in the same direction among all the groups in the entrepreneur population. When changes in demand cause some groups to gain many entrepreneurs and other groups to gain none, or even to lose them, then the demand effects are not general.

Conversely, specific demand effects arise when changes in demand affect the performance of one group while leaving others unaffected. To illustrate, if French Canadians in Newburyport appropriate the whole demand for widgets, leaving none for the Irish, then the demand effect for widgets is specific, not general. Specific demand effects arise when, confronting changed demand, only one or some entrepreneur groups respond to price incentives as a possible consequence of institutional, legal, class, or cultural barriers that inhibit other groups from responding. Whatever the cause, the demand's effect is unequal. Specific demand effects mean that a beneficiary group increased its rate of entrepreneurship relative to nonfavored groups;[16] therefore, at a minimum, *specific demand* effects require that at least one ethnoracial category obtains no share.

SPECIFIC DEMAND EFFECTS

We distinguish demand effects, not causes. For the theoretical purpose at hand, we need not examine the processes that yield these demand effects even were we in a position to do so, which we are not.

Nonetheless, we can outline the probable process from the existing literature, thus indicating how demand can have specific effects. In so doing, we are enumerating the ways in which supply and demand interact, and thus illustrating what processes the interaction hypothesis explains. Specific demand arises in six ways: discrimination, law, self-exclusion, unique resources, ethnic channeling, and economic closure. Of these, old-fashioned ethnoracial discrimination is the simplest. If prejudiced purchasers discriminate, they demand suppliers of a particular ethnoracial type, not just qualified suppliers. This case is not just hypothetical. Borjas and Bronars (1989:581, 592) argue that consumer racism reduces the self-employment of African Americans.[17] Thus, discriminating housewives want a white plumber, not just a competent plumber; expressed negatively, a purchaser asks for a plumber who is not black. Whether the discrimination is negative or positive, it qualifies a purchaser's job description, thus limiting the chances of African-American entrepreneurs.[18] This is a discriminatory intent whose effect is to depress the number of African-American entrepreneurs. Since the effect of discriminatory demand is unequal, the demand effect is specific.

Legal Constraints

Sometimes unintentionally, laws influence the ability of groups to respond to market demand for entrepreneurs, thus creating specific demand effects. In the Netherlands, formally egalitarian laws raise obstacles to entrepreneurship that, in effect, reduce the chances of immigrant entrepreneurs relative to Dutch entrepreneurs (Boissevain and Grotenbreg, 1987; Ward, 1987:92). In the United States, set-aside laws mandate preference for women, African-American, Hispanic, and Asian entrepreneurs (Bates, 1987:540). In the American marketplace, federal, state, and municipal governments were the principal agencies of affirmative action in the 1970s and 1980s. Setting quotas for ethnic minority and women entrepreneurs, governments "set aside" some portion of their procurement for these entrepreneurs. The policy sought to improve the entrepreneurial performance of benefited categories and groups. Insofar as they achieved these goals,[19] affirmative action policies did so by redistributing government purchasing unequally among ethnoracial groups, a specific demand effect. Even if they failed to achieve their objective, as Green and Pryde (1990:40–41) maintain, a specific demand effect was what the policies intended.

Self-Exclusion

Specific demand effects arise when ethnoracial groups exclude themselves from the supplier pool. Common reasons are ethical, religious, or financial. Some industries are morally controversial, such as prostitution, weapons manufacture, pornography, birth control devices, abortions, nuclear power plants, gambling, tobacco, and narcotic drugs. Religious groups evaluate entrepreneurial opportunities from an ethical or religious perspective. Thus, sincere and consistent Quakers refuse to manufacture and sell weapons, thereby excluding themselves from the Pentagon's lucrative cost-plus contracts. Similarly, pious and observant Roman Catholics refuse to operate abortion clinics or condom factories. Because of Quaker scruples, Roman Catholics enjoy enhanced earning opportunities in poison gas and nuclear weapons manufacture; conversely, Quaker-operated abortion clinics enjoy enhanced profits, because Catholics cannot in conscience participate in this industry.

Price also produces self-exclusion. First, stratified ethnoracial groups do not share the same financial definition of what constitutes a satisfactory money return. Rich groups demand higher returns than do poor ones. What represents an entrepreneurial opportunity for the poor need not represent it for the rich. The causes of this discrepancy are most obviously the quite different financial frame of reference of individuals in different groups. Since groups do not earn the same money returns in wage and salary employment, their opportunity costs of entrepreneurship are likewise different (Bearse, 1985).[20] Wall Street Yuppies have no financial incentive to open pizza parlors on 29th Street, but working-class Puerto Ricans do.

Second, ethnoracial groups have unequal financial resources. Demand for luxury hotels in Atlantic City required entrepreneurs who, in addition to desire for wealth, a general resource, also possessed great personal wealth, banking contacts, and political influence. Donald Trump (1987) had these resources, but African-American and Puerto Rican entrepreneurs did not. The Marxist distinction between the big and little bourgeoisies turns on unequal access to generalized class resources, especially money and credit (Bechofer and Elliott, 1985:188). The small bourgeoisie lacks the financial and political resources to compete with the big bourgeoisie in big projects.

When ethnoreligious groups move up the social hierarchy in succession, they quit industries that they had dominated to undertake more remunerative and prestigious work (Light, 1981; 1983:317-323). This egress creates vacancies that suck lower ranking groups in as replacement entrepreneurs. Waldinger (1989:222) has particularly stressed the effect of ethnic succession upon entrepreneur replacement. Opportunities for newcomer entrepreneurs arise, he argues, when the supply of native owners runs short. The vacancy chain is a form of self-exclusion that arises when a group that has long occupied an industry voluntarily quits it. Note that self-exclusion creates a vacancy. However, a vacancy does not determine whether one newcomer group will appropriate the whole vacancy or whether all newcomer groups will share the vacancy equally.

Unique Resources

Every market demand carries an implicit list of the resources necessary to respond to it. General demand effects arise when entrepreneurs use universally available resources to obtain their share of the demand. Supply resources are *general* when all entrepreneurs have equal access to them. According to the economists, a desire for wealth is one such general resource. No group monopolizes this desire and all share it equally. As a result, lucrative opportunities energize people of all ethnoracial, demographic, and socioeconomic backgrounds. Again, when entrepreneurs buy the factors of production in competitive markets, they obtain resources on terms of equality.

But some market demand calls for unique resources, whether alone, or, more commonly, in combination with general resources (Wallman, 1979:1, 9). Resources are *unique* when only one or some groups have them at all or the possession of the resource is highly unequal. When market demands *require unique or unequally available resources*, they exclude nonpossessors from competition, thereby enhancing the entrepreneurial performance of possessors. For example, Ward (1985:209) finds Asians in Britain entered business in industries that offered them the opportunity to utilize "resources of labour, capital, and expertise available through the community network," a uniquely Asian capability. Non-Asian entrepreneurs could not access these network resources on the same footing as did Asian members. Again, Southwestern agriculture requires much Mexican labor, thus creating entrepreneurial opportunities for labor contractors, used car vendors, doctors and dentists, curanderos, immigration attorneys, border-crossing "coyotes," saloon and pool hall operators, hoteliers, grocery store owners, and taco stands. German, Japanese, and Mongolian entrepreneurs are at liberty to compete in these industries, but they lack the cultural resources, including Spanish language skill, to perform these roles competently. Therefore, in Southwestern towns and cities, Mexican-origin entrepreneurs enjoy unique resources to satisfy Mexican demand, so the demand becomes specific.[21]

Ethnic Channeling

Aggregate demand rarely affects all industries alike. Even in a general boom condition, some industries expand more than do others. More commonly, even in a boom condition, many industries expand, some are unchanged, and a few contract. General industrial expansion means net expansion, not universal expansion. For example, in the last generation, employment expansion has been the result of employment gains in the service sector, which more than offset employment losses in manufacturing (Birch, 1987: Chs. 1, 2).

If ethnoracial groups were evenly distributed among all industries, the uneven character of market opportunities would not affect the entrepreneurial hierarchy. Each group's participation in each industry would equal its share of the labor force as a whole. But ethnoracial groups cluster in niche industries. Urban economies always contain ethnic economic niches, "and that same niche is either not always available or not always appropriate to the same people" (Wallman, 1979:1). *Ethnic channeling* is the inertial effect of an existing ethnic division of labor (Light and Bonacich, 1988:192). We can imagine an extreme case in which each of 26 equal-sized ethnic groups wholly controlled 1 of the 26 industries in a metropolitan area. In this case, it would be possible for net economic expansion in a metropolitan locality to benefit only one group. If only industry 1 expanded, and group A wholly controlled this industry, no non-As being willing, able, or permitted to engage in it (Weber, 1968:340), then group A would obtain all of the demand growth, enriching itself. In this illustrative case, aggregate expansion of a metropolitan region's entrepreneurial opportunities would benefit only the entrepreneurs of one group.[22]

Economic Closure

Economic closure arises from successful efforts to reduce and restrain competition (Weber, 1968:342). Monopoly is the goal of economic closure, and guilds are a universal strategy for achieving monopoly. Guilds did not exist in the United States in 1980. But it was possible, if difficult, for ethnic merchants to organize their buying power, their political power, their ideological influence, or all three, to monopolize economic demand. East Asians have been particularly successful in economic closure in the past (Light, 1972: Chs. 4,5). Of the Chinese in New York City, Wong (1978:350) writes, that their "economic opportunities" still exist in "ethnic businesses zealously guarded in their various trade associations." Similarly, Korean wig dealers organized a collusive organization in restraint of trade. The Korean Hair Products Association was finally dissolved by court order in 1975 (Light and Bonacich, 1988:197). However, the purpose of the Hair Products Association was to obtain a monopoly of the wig business for the members. When monopolies are successful, demand becomes specific, not general.

ENTREPRENEURIAL PERFORMANCE

Having distinguished general and specific demand effects, and outlined the causes of the latter, we now turn to entrepreneurial performance. Rate and rank are two, independent aspects of entrepreneurial performance. A group's *rate of entrepreneurship* is the number of its members self-employed per 1,000 able-bodied adults in the labor force.[23] A group's *intrametropolitan entrepreneurial rank* is its local self-employment rate relative to other groups in that locality. That is, in every metropolitan area the group with the highest self-employment rate ranks first, the group with the second highest rate ranks second, and so on. Entrepreneurial rank and self-employment rate are independent between, but not within, metropolitan areas, in that a group can rank first in a low-entrepreneurship locality, while manifesting a rate below the lowest-ranking group in a high entrepreneurship locality. In principal, a low-resources group can even display higher mean rates than a high-resource group, provided the low-resources group occupies more favorable demand environments than does the high-resources group (Furino and Bates, 1983:81).

RANK AND RATE

Figure 3.1 illustrates hypothetically the difference between entrepreneurial rank and rate. Groups A, B, C, and D are ethnoracial groups. The vertical axis measures each group's self-employment rate, from low to high. The horizontal axis compares each group's mean rate in all cities of the United States, in New York, in Los Angeles, and in Chicago. The unweighted mean self-employment rate of all four groups is 55 in the United States, 80 in New York, 95 in Los Angeles, and 75 in Chicago. This unweighted mean measures the strength of local demand for self-employment. As we look down columns, we see the groups' entrepreneurial rank. The first column shows the mean self-employment rate and rank of every group in all metropolitan areas. A's mean rate nationally is 70 self-employed per 1,000 in the labor force. This rate is higher than that of any of the other groups, so A's mean national rank is first, B's mean rate nationally is 60, so its mean national rank is second, C's mean rate is 50, so its mean rank is third, and D's mean rate is 40, so its mean rank is fourth.

In the figure, A and B are high resource groups; C and D are low resource groups. Although group A's mean national rank exceeds D's, D's self-employment rate in Los Angeles is higher than group A's mean rate in the United States. This disparity arises because demand for entrepreneurs in Los Angeles is generally stronger than in other metropolitan areas. The proof is the high mean rate of self-employment in Los Angeles, 95 per 1,000 in the labor force, whereas the mean self-employment rate in the United States is only 55. The high demand in Los Angeles buoys the rate of low-resource group D until it exceeds A's national mean rate and equals A's rate in Chicago. Therefore, group D, a low-resource group in a high self-employment locality, can exhibit sporadic self-employment rates superior to a high-resource group's average rate.

When resources interact with aggregate demand, outcomes depend upon whether demand effects are mostly specific or mostly general. If demand effects are general, even extreme interlocal variations in aggregate demand are compatible with continuity of rank order within localities. That is, in demand-supportive localities, average entrepreneurial performance of all groups increases, but high-resource groups continue to outrank low-resource groups. Conversely, in restricted demand localities, every group's entrepreneurial performance falls, but high-resource groups continue to outrank low resource groups. Aggregate demand effects improve or reduce the entrepreneurial performance of localities and general demand effects improve the entrepreneurial performance of all players without, however, affecting the rank order of groups within metropolitan areas. In sum, general demand effects *do not affect the intrametropolitan rank order* of ethnoracial categories or groups in entrepreneurship. The comparison of New York with the U.S. mean in Figure 3.1 shows how general demand can raise the self-employment levels of all groups without changing the normal rank order of groups in self-employment.

However, specific demand effects could shift upward or downward the normal resource-derived rank of a group. When appropriating a demand, a group would rank higher in a locality than it usually does. Thus, when blacks ranked first in entrepreneurship in Richland, WA, as they did in 1980, they ranked higher than they usually did, possibly

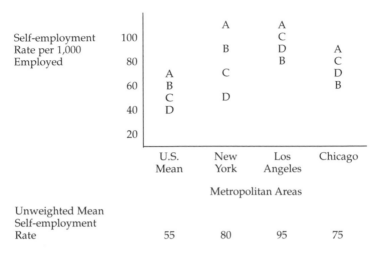

Figure 3.1. Hypothetical rate and rank of Entrepreneurship.

because African Americans benefited from a specific demand in Richland that did not exist elsewhere. Should a group with low resources appropriate a big specific demand, possibly through set-aside laws, that appropriated demand alone might add enough entrepreneurs to its account to improve the group's rank as well as its rate. If the rate alone increased, the group's rank would not change unless the group also appropriated more than its usual share of entrepreneurial demand.

Unlike general demand effects, which affect all groups alike, *specific demand effects may change a group's rank, not just its rate.* The comparison of New York and Chicago in Figure 3.1 illustrates this contingency. The two localities do not differ much in respect to the unweighted mean self-employment rate of all groups, a measure of the strength of demand for self-employment. This mean rate is 80 in New York and 75 in Chicago. However, for some reason, group B ranks second in New York and fourth in Chicago. Presumably group B's resources do not connect so successfully to demand in Chicago as in New York. Comparing these two metropolitan areas, one explains the difference in B's rank order in terms of specific demand effects, not general demand effects. The same strength of general demand had quite different effects upon B's rank in the two localities. Since B's mean national rank is second, we say that conditions in Chicago caused B to drop below its normal rank.

If specific demand effects cancel one another, benefiting A in one industry and B in another, we find no aggregate effect upon the entrepreneurial rate or rank of either A or B in a locality. Thus, if A monopolizes contracts for buttons and B for buttonholes, the overall effect on

A's entrepreneurship will be the same as if A and B had shared contracts for buttons and buttonholes rather than each monopolizing half the demand. Similarly, if resources alone simply determine groups' access to demand, each receiving market share in strict proportion to its resources, then demand will not deflect a group's entrepreneurial rank away from its resource-derived level. That is, if specific demand effects never occurred, resources would provide a complete explanation of rank. In reality, specific demand effects may, but need not, influence entrepreneurial rate or rank. Specific demand effects are, however, *the only way* in which demand can influence the entrepreneurial rank of ethnoracial categories. General demand effects cannot influence entrepreneurial rank. General demand effects influence only rate, not rank.

General demand effects and specific demand effects normally appear together. Figure 3.1's metros illustrate the point. Comparing the intermetropolitan mean and the means of the three metropolitan areas, we find that the average level of entrepreneurial performance is higher in New York than in the intermetropolitan average, but lower in Chicago than in New York. These are general demand effects. However, Los Angeles and Chicago also contain some departures of rank order from New York. Specifically, B ranks fourth in Los Angeles and Chicago and second in New York and the intermetropolitan average. These changes in B's rank are specific demand effects. Therefore, both specific and general demand effects are present in Los Angeles and Chicago.

Our distinction between general and specific demand effects is a new one necessitated by a determined effort to find ways in which demand can influence entrepreneurial rank and rate. We do not know a priori the empirical balance of strength between general demand effects and specific demand effects. Obviously, that balance matters. If general demand effects were the only demand effects, and specific demand effects never occurred, then demand could exert no influence upon entrepreneurial rank. Demand would then influence rate only. This convenient situation would render the interaction of supply and demand exceedingly easy to explain: supply would affect both rank and rate; demand would affect rate only. Demand would not affect the rank of groups, and the "interactive hypothesis" would be wrong when applied to rank and rate alike. Conversely, if all demand effects were specific, as the interaction approach hypothesizes, then demand would influence rate and rank alike. The interaction approach would always be confirmed. Possibly, however, the world contains general demand effects *and* specific demand effects rather than only one or the other. Both effects influence rate, but only specific demand effects influence ranks. If the latter is not found, the interaction approach would be correct with respect to rate, but wrong with respect to rank.

COMPOSITION OF METROPOLITAN AREAS

To examine demand effects further, thus passing from theory to evidence, we must statistically ascertain the effects of demand upon entrepreneurial rank and rate. However, entrepreneurial rank is meaningful only in those metropolitan areas that contained all five ethnoracial categories. Unequal ranks would give an unfair advantage to groups that are more commonly present, since, in the absence of other groups, they would rank higher than when the other groups are present. For example, even if group E always ranks last, it would rank third when three groups were present, fourth when four groups were present, and fifth when all five groups were present. This inequality would, therefore, elevate its mean rank.[24] Therefore, we examined the actual structure of ethnoracial pluralism, categorizing metropolitan areas according to the number of ethnoracial categories they contained.

Table 3.1 lists 16 possible types of metropolitan area, an exhaustive list. Each type contains a different profile of effective representation[25] among the five major ethnoracial categories: native whites, foreign whites, blacks, Asians, and Hispanics. We designate types of metropolitan area by acronyms formed from the first letters of each effectively represented ethnoracial category. Thus, an NWFWBAH metropolitan area was one in which each of the five ethnoracial categories was represented above our threshold. In this acronym, NW = native white, FW = foreign white, B = Black, A = Asian, and H = Hispanic. An NWFWBA metropolitan area (SMSA) contained all groups except Hispanics; an NWFW metropolitan area contained only native and foreign whites, and so forth. Three of the logical types had no empirical representatives, so the 272 metropolitan areas are actually represented by only 13 empirical types.

All five ethnoracial categories enjoyed effective representation in only 167 of the 272 metropolitan areas. We designate these 167 the "matched" areas. In the other 105 metropolitan areas, one or more of the minority groups were missing.[26] Minority groups are all ethnoracial categories except native white. Table 3.1 shows 50 metropolitan areas in which four of the five categories were represented, 30 with three categories, 22 with two categories, and three with only 1 category above the threshold of effective representation. In these three monoethnic metropolitan areas, native whites were the only ethnoracial group represented above threshold levels. For the record, these three metropolitan areas were Altoona, Pennsylvania, St. Cloud, Minnesota, and Wausau, Wisconsin.[27] In addition to the 167 matched areas, blacks and foreign whites were effectively represented in another 78 areas, Hispanics in an additional 63

Demand Effects

Table 3.1 Ethnoracial Composition of 167 Metropolitan Areas[1]

Metropolitan Area Type	Ethnoracial Categories Represented[2]					
	NB White (NW)	FB White (FW)	Black (B)	Asian (A)	Hispanic (H)	Number of This Type
5 categories						
NWFWBAH	X	X	X	X	X	167
4 categories						50
NWFWBA	X	X	X	X		3
NWFWBH	X	X	X		X	40
NWFWAH	X	X		X	X	6
NWBAH	X		X	X	X	1
3 categories						30
NWFWB	X	X	X			11
NWFWA	X	X		X		1
NWFWH	X	X			X	10
NWBA	X		X	X		2
NWBH	X		X		X	6
NWAH	X			X	X	0
2 categories						22
NWB	X		X			15
NWA	X			X		0
NWFW	X	X				7
NWH	X				X	0
1 category						3
NW	X					3
Total						272

[1] Threshold level = minimum of 400 persons in the category in the metropolitan areas (20 in the original 5% PUMS sample).
[2] NB, native born; FB, Foreign born.

metropolitan areas, and Asians in only another 13. Oddly, the smallest category, Asians, most closely approximated the same settlement pattern as the matched configuration. There were no metropolitan areas comprised only of foreign whites, blacks, Asians, or Hispanics.

We compared the 167 metropolitan areas with the larger list of 272 from which they were culled to ascertain whether the smaller list showed different self-employment rates than the larger. Mean self-employment rates for each group were virtually identical on the large list of 272 metropolitan areas and the culled list of 167. This result suggests that the smaller list of 167 metropolitan areas was virtually identical to the larger list with respect to the demand environment of entrepreneurship.

Self-employment rates are the percentage of each category's labor force that received income from self-employment (INCOME2). This income definition is broader than the class of worker definition because it includes part-time self-employment as well as fulltime.[28] Self-employment *rank* is a category's ordinal position relative to the other four categories within each metropolitan area. For example, in Abilene, Texas, foreign whites ranked first in self-employment rate, Asians ranked second, native whites ranked third, blacks ranked fourth, and Hispanics ranked fifth.

Utilizing only the 167 matched metropolitan areas, we now ascertain how much agreement the five ethnoracial categories display with respect to within-category self-employment ranks and self-employment incomes. For this purpose, each of the five ethnoracial categories was ranked separately across all 167 metropolitan areas. That is, we computed the *intra*group ranks of each metropolitan area, ranking 1 the metropolitan area in which each respective category had the highest self-employment rate. We ranked the area in which each had the lowest 167. Other metropolitan areas ranked between these extremes. If general demand effects predominated, we would expect very close agreement among the groups because all would prosper in the same high-demand environments and decline in the same low-demand environments. In other words, ranking each ethnoracial category across all 167 metropolitan areas, we would find that all five ranked highest in the same metropolitan area. To illustrate this point, Table 3.2 lists the metropolitan area that ranked number one with respect to the income-defined self-employment rate and mean self-employment income for each category. We also show the ranks of each of the other four ethnoracial categories for comparison. For example, Chico, California ranked 1 in self-employment rate for Asians and native whites, 3 for Hispanics, 13 for blacks, and 35 for foreign-born whites. Similarly, Cedar Rapids, Iowa ranked 1 in mean self-employment income for blacks, 42 for foreign whites, 141 for Asians, 125 for native whites, and 94 for Hispanics.

To the extent that general demand predominated, we expect agreement of the intermetropolitan rank orders[29] among the five categories. Such agreement would show that all categories benefited equally from local demand conditions. In an extreme case, only one metropolitan area should be listed in Table 3.2 as all five ethnoracial categories would share that area's top-market opportunities. Although perfect agreement is missing, Table 3.2 shows some agreement. Chico, California was the first ranking city for two ethnoracial categories, and that central California city also ranked high for the other three. This coincidence suggests a favorable demand environment in Chico that encouraged every group's entrepreneurship. Daytona, Florida also provided a favorable demand

Table 3.2. Where[1] the Categories Rank[2] First[3] in Self-
Employment Rates[4] and Incomes[4]

	Categories				
Metropolitan Areas[2]	NB White	FB White	Black	Asian	Hispanic
A. Self-Employment Rank of Metropolitan Areas					
Chico, CA	1	35	13	1	3
Daytona, FL	7	1	8	9	5
Knoxville, TN	118	4	149	53	1
Santa Cruz, CA	2	12	1.5	24	35
Northeast PA	84	16	1.5	100	11
B. Self-Employment Income of Metropolitan Areas					
Cedar Rapids, IA	125	42	1	141	94
Columbus, OH	91	75	107	87	1
Lansing-East Lansing, MI	151	143	132	1	124
Norwalk, CT	1	58	23	148	144
Wichita Falls, TX	20	1	138	94.5	104

[1] Among the 167 metropolitan areas in which all five ethnoracial categories are present at or above the threshold level.
[2] Intermetropolitan ranks for each category, i.e., 1 = the highest mean self-employment rate or income and 167 = the lowest. Metropolitan areas are listed in alphabetical order.
[3] The ranks of the other four ethnoracial categories are also listed for each of the metropolitan areas in which one of the categories ranks first.
[4] Income definition of self-employment.

environment for all. But Table 3.2 also displays some rank disagreements incompatible with a general demand explanation. For example, Knoxville, Tennessee provided the number one economic environment of Hispanics, and foreign whites clearly benefited from the same economic environment. Knoxville provided the fourth most favorable environment for foreign whites. However, for blacks, the Knoxville metropolitan area ranked only 149, for Asians 53, and for native whites, 118. If the Knoxville demand environment were generally positive, why did African Americans, Asians, and native whites not benefit from it?

Mean self-employment income offers another measure of demand environment for entrepreneurs. Other things being equal, demand environments are positive where self-employment incomes are high. Therefore, to the extent that demand effects were general, the rank order of groups ought to coincide with respect to mean self-employment income, as well as with respect to mean self-employment rate. Table 3.2B shows the rank orders with respect to mean self-employment income. Thus, Cedar Rapids, Iowa ranked number one in self-employment income among blacks. That result signifies that the mean black self-employment income was higher in Cedar Rapids than in any other of the 167 matched metropolitan areas. If Cedar Rapids simply rewarded entrepreneurs well, all groups should have basked in its economic sunshine. In fact, only blacks found Cedar Rapids the most rewarding economic environment. For some reason, Cedar Rapids was relatively better for blacks than for nonblacks. Whatever this was, it was not a general demand effect.

Spearman correlation coefficients measure the extent to which category rank orders agreed, so that higher ranking metropolitan areas for one group tended to be higher ranking areas for another, and vice versa (Blalock, 1960:317–319). Therefore, we computed the simple rank order correlation for each pair of ethnoracial categories with respect to both self-employment rate and self-employment income. Table 3.3 shows the Spearman rank correlations above the diagonal, summarizing general demand effects. The rank order coefficients are significant in 7 of 10

Table 3.3. Spearman[1] and Pearson Correlations[2] of Intermetropolitan Ranks[3] of Mean Self-Employment Rates[4] and Incomes[4] of Five Ethnoracial Categories

| | Categories | | | | |
Categories	NB White	FB White	Black	Asian	Hispanic
A. For Ranks of Mean Self-Employment Rates					
NB white	1.00	.41**	.52**	.13	.27**
FB white	.38**	1.00	.25**	.27**	.30*
Black	.43**	.28*	1.00	.06	.17*
Asian	.17*	.22**	.04	1.00	.14
Hispanic	.37**	.33**	.19*	.17*	1.00
Mean correlation with native-born whites	.34				
B. For Ranks of Mean Self-Employment Income					
NB white	1.00	.33**	.33**	.14	.03
FB white	.33**	1.00	.20*	.11	.08
Black	.33**	.20**	1.00	.13	.23**
Asian	.14	.11	.13	1.00	.25**
Hispanic	.03	.08	.23**	.25**	1.00
Mean correlation with native-born whites	.21				

[1] Spearman rank correlations are above the diagonal.
[2] Pearson correlations are below the diagonal.
[3] See Table 3.2, note 2.
[4] Income definition of self-employment.
* $p < .05$.
** $p < .01$.

paired comparisons with respect to self-employment rate, and in 5 of 10 paired comparisons with respect to self-employment income. The mean rank order correlation of the four minorities with native whites is .34 for self-employment rate and .21 for self-employment income. We repeated this analysis using Pearson correlation coefficients. Results, displayed below the diagonal in Table 3.3, are similar to those obtained with rank order correlation.

MEASURES OF DEMAND

Investigating general and specific demand effects, we next utilize regression analysis to evaluate the simultaneous effects of several measures of demand. Table 3.4 lists the variables, their definitions, and operational descriptions. We centered continuous variables as in Chapter 2.[30] Table 3.4 indicates the pooled sample mean that was subtracted from each respective variable to create the centered variables. A prefix "C" has been added to the name of each variable to indicate that it has been centered.

Following Razin (1988, 1993), Rekers, Dijest, and Van Kempen (1990), and Boyd (1990, 1991), we measure demand for entrepreneurs in terms of local demand environments. The 272 metropolitan areas encompass

Table 3.4. Variables Used in the Analyses[1]

Variables	Name and Operational Description of Variables
Dependent variables	
CATMSER	Income-defined mean self-employment rate[2]
CATRANK	Rank of category mean income-defined self-employment rate[3]
Demand variables[4]	
Category demand	
CCATSIZE	(Category mean labor force size/10,000)—.30552[5]
Metropolitan demand[6]	
Local economic market	
CSMSAI1	(Mean wage and salary income/10,000)—1.22563
SMSA industrial structure[7]	
CCONIND	Mean % in construction industry—.07
CMANUIND	Mean % in manufacturing industry—.23
CRETIND	Mean % in retail industry—.18
CFININD	Mean % in financial industry—.06
CBUSIND	Mean % in business services industry—.04
CPERSIND	Mean % in personal services industry—.03
CPROFIND	Mean % in professional industry—.21
CPUBIND	Mean % in public administration industry—.06

Table 3.4. (Continued)

Variables	Name and Operational Description of Variables
Regional economy[8]	
NYNJPA	Dummy variable (SMSA in NY, NJ, or PA = 1; else = 0)
ECENTRAL	Dummy variable (SMSA in East Central = 1; else = 0)
WCENTRAL	Dummy variable (SMSA in West Central = 1; else = 0)
SATLANTIC	Dummy variable (SMSA in South Atlantic = 1; else = 0)
MIDSOUTH	Dummy variable (SMSA in Mid-South = 1; else = 0)
CENTRLSO	Dummy variable (SMSA in Central South = 1; else = 0)
WESTMTNS	Dummy variable (SMSA in Western Mountains = 1; else = 0)
PACIFIC	Dummy variable (SMSA in Pacific = 1; else = 0)
Independent variables for augmented Models	
Ethnic identity intercept variables[9]	
FBW	Dummy variable (foreign-born white = 1; else = 0)
BLACK	Dummy variable (black = 1; else = 0)
ASIAN	Dummy variable (Asian = 1; else = 0)
HISPANIC	Dummy variable (Hispanic = 1; else = 0)
Interaction Variables[10]	
4 ethnic identity intercept variables × 18 general demand variables	

[1] See Chapter 2, Appendix 2A, for detailed descriptions.

[2] This variable is the same as "BRODMSER" used in Chapter 2. Respondents were defined as self-employed (= 1) if they had reported any income gains or losses from self-employment (INCOME2). We calculated the self-employment rate by dividing the number of persons who reported self-employment income (NINCOME2) by the total number of persons in the civilian labor force for each category in each respective metropolitan area.

[3] Groups were rank ordered *within* each metropolitan area (1 = highest rank; 5 = lowest rank for lowest CATMSER in each metropolitan area).

[4] These continuous independent variables were centered, as recommended by Aiken and West (1991:37, 119–138, and n. 3), because the range of values for none of these variables encompassed a meaningful zero (where the linear regression line or plane transects the axis of the dependent variable for "raw" or metric coefficients). Centered variables were created by subtracting either the means from the "raw" data for each respective variable for each of the respective five categories for CCATSIZE, or the means for the total pooled sample for each of the categories for all the demand variables.

[5] Centered on the pooled sample for the regressions in Tables 3.6 and 3.8. However, in Tables 3.5 and 3.7, for the individual category regressions, the means for CCATSIZE for each of the respective five categories was centered on the means of each respective category. These means were native whites 1.00, foreign whites .05, blacks .17, Asians .04, and Hispanics .10. Since these original category means were divided by 10,000, they really represent, for example, an average of 10,000 native whites, 500 foreign whites, 1,700 blacks, 400 Asians and 1,000 Hispanics, in each metropolitan area.

[6] Centered on the means of the pooled sample. These means are given in this table for all of the metropolitan demand variables.

[7] The reference group deleted was the percentage in the following industries: mining, transportation, wholesale, and entertainment and recreation services.

[8] New England is the omitted region.

[9] Native-born white is the omitted reference category. See "Categories and Groups," in Chapter 2, for a detailed description. Aiken and West (1991:116, 130) advise that dummy coded variables *not* be centered.

[10] There are no native-born white interaction variables because native-born white is the omitted reference group. The demand variables were first centered, but not the dummy variables.

all of the largest metropolitan areas in the United States, and each area offers a unique demand environment. Baton Rouge does not have a demand environment identical to Boston. Eighteen demand variables measure the economic characteristics of metropolitan areas that govern the local economy's self-employment. We distinguished four components of metropolitan demand. The first is the absolute size of an ethnoracial category's labor force. Portes and Bach (1985) argued that "ethnic enclave economies" mobilize demand most effectively in support of coethnic entrepreneurs. Ethnic enclave economies arise where ethnoracial groups are sufficiently numerous to benefit from agglomeration. If so, then the larger a category's absolute labor force, the higher might be its self-employment rate.

Total size of the labor force of each metropolitan area could provide another measure of aggregate demand. Some international research has found that larger metropolitan regions have higher aggregate self-employment rates than do smaller ones (Razin, 1988:286). Although the causes of this result are unclear, the empirical generalization offers a demand variable that merits examination. However, we found no association between size of a metropolitan area's labor force and its self-employment rate.[31] Furthermore, metropolitan area labor force size was also significantly correlated with the size of categories in each metropolitan area.[32] For both of these reasons, we deleted this variable from the model, but retained category size.

The second demand component is the aggregate consumer demand of the metropolitan area itself. We assigned this component one measure: the metropolitan area's mean wage and salary income (CSMSAI1) in ten thousands. This measure ought to promote self-employment in that, when there is higher income, entrepreneurs can tap a wealthy constituency, thus buoying the self-employment rate of all ethnoracial categories.

The third component is metropolitan industrial structure. We defined industrial structure as the percentage of the locality's labor force employed in eight industries. Five of these eight industries contain heavy proportions of self-employed workers (retail trade, business and repair services, personal services, finance, insurance, and real estate, professional and related services), so metropolitan areas heavy on these industries ought to have heavy demand for entrepreneurs too. For example, percentage in retail is the percentage of the metropolitan area's labor force that worked in retail trade. Since retail trade is a small business industry, self-employment rates ought to be higher in metropolitan areas that contain much retail trade. The same considerations apply to the other industrial measures we selected, except for public administration, which Boyd (1991:413) has found to depress the self-employment of African Americans. Four industries are deleted as the reference group:

%Mining, %Transportation, %Wholesale, and %Entertainment and Recreation Services.

We employ eight dummy variables to measure the fourth demand component, regional economy. The omitted region is New England, which has the lowest mean self-employment rate.[33] This measure permits us to establish the effects of supply variables upon category self-employment rates net of regional differences in settlement patterns. Mean self-employment rates differ among regions of the United States (Bearse, 1987; Haber 1985a:17). In 1983, the South and the West had the most self-employment, and the Northeast and North Central had the least. In the metropolitan areas of the Pacific Region, an overall self-employment rate of 9.3% prevailed, whereas among those of the Northeast region, the overall self-employment rate was only 6.4%, fully one-third lower.[34] Part-time, income-defined self-employment rates manifest more extreme regional differences than do full-time, work-defined rates. Ethnoracial categories and groups were unequally distributed among regions. In general, Asians and Hispanics settled disproportionately in the West; blacks were overrepresented in the South. Conceivably the regional differences in mean self-employment rates could inflate or depress the mean self-employment rates of the various ethnoracial groups and categories in complex ways.

Our regression analyses extend the procedures followed in Chapter 2. First, we test the demand model for each of the five categories separately. Second, we test this baseline model for the pooled sample of these five categories. In addition, however, we also test whether there are significant general and/or specific demand effects, by analyzing an augmented model in which we add ethnoracial dummy variables, omitting native whites as the reference group. We also add dummy slope interaction variables created by multiplying the ethnoracial dummy variables by each of the demand variables for each category, again deleting such variables for native-born whites.[35]

Next, we apply the Chow Test (Hanushek and Jackson, 1977:124–129) to ascertain if the dummy intercept and dummy slope variables significantly increase the variation explained in the augmented model compared to the baseline model. If the gain is significant, we check for commonalities and differences between native-born whites and the other four categories that we found in the tables in which the models were run for each ethnoracial group separately. Effects are general if a main effect is significant and no interactions show a significant difference with native whites; otherwise, effects are specific. These specific effects are tested by first adding intercept dummy variables to represent each of the four minority categories and the maximum 72 interaction slope dummy variables. The latter are created by the interaction of each of the 4 intercept dummy variables by each of the 18 demand variables. However, if an interaction variable has no significant coefficients for any of the four minority groups, we delete it from the model. We take these steps first, to model the effects of demand variables on mean income-defined self-employment rates; and then to model the effects on mean income-defined self-employment ranks.

SELF-EMPLOYMENT RATES

Table 3.5 shows the effects of the 18 demand variables upon the self-employment rates of each category. The demand model is unequally successful in explaining the self-employment rates of each of the five categories. Examining Table 3.5, we find that demand factors explain 66% of variation in the mean self-employment rate of native-born whites, but they explain much less variation among the minorities. This result does not betoken general demand effects. If demand effects were general, demand variables should affect all groups alike.

The baseline model in Table 3.6 examines these same demand variables' effects upon the self-employment rates of the pooled sample of the five categories where $N = 1,172$. Only two of the 18 demand variables demonstrate a significant main effect. These are %Retail and Pacific Region. These main effects are weak. They explain only 6% of variation in self-employment rates. The augmented model adds ethnic category intercept and interaction slope dummy variables to the demand variables whose main effects represent general demand effects. The intercepts and interactions are specific demand effects. The augmented model includes four intercept variables and eight interaction variables that reach significance. Their addition raises the adjusted R^2 from .06 to a hefty .50.

Interaction variables expose significant differences between the minorities and native-whites, the omitted category. The augmented model tests whether or not these differences are significant in size or direction. If so, they represent specific demand effects. %Retail and Pacific Region showed significant main effects in the baseline model, and these main effects remain significant in the augmented model. Although self-employment rates generally increase for all categories in metropolitan areas with higher percentages in retail trade and in the Pacific region, a general demand effect, the augmented model shows specific demand effects too. When interacted with the ethnoracial dummy variables, both %Retail and Pacific Region affect one or more of the four minority groups differently than they affect native whites. For

Table 3.5. Regression of Mean Income-Defined Self-Employment Rates[1] on Demand Variables,[2] Five Separate Categories (Unstandardized Coefficients)

Independent Variables[2]	Categories				
	NB White	FB White	Black	Asian	Hispanic
Category demand:					
Category size[3]	−.000	−.001	−.002	−.011	−.001
Local market SMSA mean wage and salary income[3]	−.021**	.024	.000	.027	.004
SMSA industrial structure					
Construction	.043	−.104	.128*	−.475	.304
%Manufacturing	.062*	−.235**	.062*	−.183	.019
%Retail	.293****	.201	.134*	.368	.146
%Finance	.167**	−.044	.140*	−.128	.095
%Business	.322****	−.467	.421****	−.690	−.007
%Personal services	.107	−.230	.066	−.202	.066
%Professional	.098***	−.215*	.071*	−.134	.093
%Public administration	.032	−.307**	.046	−.335*	−.002
Regional economy					
NY, NJ, and PA	.005	.031**	−.003	−.010	−.000
East Central	.002	.021	.002	−.003	−.009
West Central	.009*	−.003	.006	−.033	−.008
South Atlantic	.007	.024*	−.002	.005	.000
Mid-South	.010*	.011	.001	.030	.010
Central South	.029****	.011	.005	−.020	−.001
Western Mountains	.023****	.019	−.005	−.018	.009
Pacific	.034****	.045***	.008	.004	.002
Intercept	.063****	.077****	.025****	.082****	.043****
Adjusted R^2	.66	.13	.28	.06	.06
N	272	245	245	180	230

[1] See Table 3.4, note 2.
[2] See Table 3.4, notes 4–8 for definition of variables.
[3] Reported coefficients in 10,000 metric.
**** LE .0001.
*** LE .001.
** LE .01.
* LE .05.

example, a 1% increase in %Retail increases general self-employment rates by 30.4%, but *decreases* the mean self-employment rates of foreign whites by 16.5%.[36] The negative effect of %Retail on foreign whites coexists with its generally positive effect on the other groups.

Similarly, Pacific region produces a 3.2% increase in mean self-employment rates of all the groups (augmented model, Table 3.6), a

Table 3.6. Regression of Mean Income-Defined Self-Employment Rates[1] on Baseline[2] and Augmented[3] Demand Models,[4] Five Categories Pooled, in 272 Metropolitan Areas, $N = 1,172$

Independent Variables[4]	Baseline Model Unstandardized	Augmented Model Unstandardized	Augmented Model Standardized
Category demand			
Size of category[5]	.001	−.001	−.024
Local market			
SMSA mean wage and salary income[5]	.005	.004	.016
SMSA industrial structure			
%Construction	.028	.011	.006
%Manufacturing	−.059	.014	.035
%Retail	.192*	.304**	.172
%Finance	.041	.060	.026
%Business	−.081	.219	.068
%Personal service	−.054	−.027	−.012
%Professional	−.005	.069	.073
%Public administration	−.105	.002	.001
Regional economy			
NY, NJ, and PA	.004	.006	.045
East Central	.001	.003	.035
West Central	−.007	.008	.052
South Atlantic	.001	.007	.073
Mid-South	.006	.011*	.065
Central South	.001	.028***	.224
Western Mountains	.002	.024*	.133
Pacific	.016*	.032****	.276
Ethnic identities			
Foreign-Born White	—	.023****	.230
Black	—	−.047****	−.473
Asian	—	.014***	.130
Hispanic	—	−.029****	−.289
Interactions			
%Manufacturing × FB white	—	−.166**	−.183
%Manufacturing × Black	—	.024	.027
%Manufacturing × Asian	—	−.095	−.082
%Manufacturing × Hispanic	—	−.070	−.076
%Retail × FB white	—	−.469**	−.121
%Retail × Black	—	−.147	−.038
%Retail × Asian	—	.027	.006
%Retail × Hispanic	—	−.184	−.049
%Business × FB white	—	−.592*	−.084
%Business × Black	—	.183	.026
%Business × Asian	—	−.814**	−.102
%Business × Hispanic	—	−.266	−.036
%Professional × FB white	—	−.219**	−.106
%Professional × Black	—	−.018	−.009

Table 3.6.   (Continued)

Independent Variables[4]	Baseline Model Unstandardized	Augmented Unstandardized	Augmented Standardized
%Professional × Asian	—	−.117	−.051
%Professional × Hispanic	—	−.057	−.026
%Public admin × FB white	—	−.244*	−.093
%Public admin × Black	—	.010	.004
%Public admin × Asian	—	−.270*	−.090
%Public admin × Hispanic	—	−.049	−.018
West Central × FB white	—	−.023*	−.068
West Central × Black	—	.003	.009
West Central × Asian	—	−.035**	−.084
West Central × Hispanic	—	−.012	−.034
Central South × FB white	—	−.030***	−.112
Central South × Black	—	−.016	−.062
Central South × Asian	—	−.047****	−.155
Central South × Hispanic	—	−.020*	−.078
West Mountains × FB white	—	−.021	−.056
West Mountains × Black	—	−.020	−.043
West Mountains × Asian	—	−.046***	−.110
West Mountains × Hispanic	—	−.024	−.064
Pacific × FB white	—	.001	.004
Pacific × Black	—	−.017*	−.067
Pacific × Asian	—	−.026**	−.109
Pacific × Hispanic	—	−.022**	−.090
Intercept	.061****	.066****	
Adjusted R^2	.06	.50	

Significance test[6] for the addition of the intercept and slope dummy variables to the baseline model: F for df: 40, 1113: 25.28 sig. at .01 level

[1] See Table 3.4, note 2.
[2] Demand variables only.
[3] Demand, intercept, and slope dummy variables.
[4] See Table 3.4, notes 4–10 for definition of variables.
[5] Reported coefficients in 10,000 metric.
[6] Chow Test (see Hanushek and Jackson, 1977:124–129).
**** LE .0001.
*** LE .001.
** LE .01.
* LE .05.

general demand effect. However, examining the interaction effects, we find that the rate of increase for blacks, Asians, and Hispanics is significantly less than for native whites.[37] If %Retail and Pacific Region showed no significant interaction terms, we could declare their effects general demand. The significant interaction terms mean that even these two variables had specific demand effects.

Of the eight measures of industrial demand, seven have no significant main effects. However, %Manufacturing has a negative interaction with foreign white; %Business has a negative interaction with foreign white and Asian; %Professional has a negative effect on foreign white; and %Public Administration has a negative interaction with foreign white and Asian. These negative interactions are specific demand effects of variables that show no general demand effect.

Of the eight measures of regional demand for the self-employed, four have significant main effects. These four regions are the Mid-South, Central South, Western Mountains, and Pacific region. That is, compared to those who work in New England, all groups in these four regions experienced increased self-employment rates. Looking further, we find no significant interactions between Mid-South and the four ethnoracial minorities. This result means that none of the minorities differed from the native whites in the positive effect that Mid-South had upon their self-employment rate. Therefore, Mid-South produced the *only* general demand effect in these data.[38] In contrast, Central South, Western Mountains, and Pacific all exhibited significant interactions with ethnoracial categories. For example, in addition to its positive main effect on general entrepreneurship, Pacific region negatively interacted with Hispanics, blacks, and Asians. Therefore, unlike Mid-South, the effects of Pacific region, Central South, and Western Mountains were specific, not general.

In summary, we find that demand's main effects cannot explain self-employment in the pooled samples. Demand's explanation hugely improves when we examine its interactions with the ethnoracial categories. The interactions even bring up to significance main effects of demand that had previously been insignificant. Although our data show both main effects and interactions, Mid-South is the only variable whose effects are truly general. Our data unmistakably record the preponderant impact upon self-employment rates of specific demand effects. General demand effects exist, but their importance is negligible.

SELF-EMPLOYMENT RANKS

Turning to Tables 3.7 and 3.8, we again alternate the baseline and augmented models, this time attempting to explain intrametropolitan self-employment rank rather than rate. Table 3.7 presents the general demand model for each of the separate five categories, and Table 3.8 presents the baseline and augmented models for the pooled sample. Since we are explaining rank, and 1 is the highest rank and 5 the lowest, negative signs indicate *improved* performance.

Table 3.7. Regression of Mean Income-Defined Intrametropolitan Self-Employment Ranks[1] on Demand Variables,[2] Five Separate Categories (Unstandardized Coefficients)

Independent Variables[2]	Categories				
	NB White	FB White	Black	Asian	Hispanic
Category demand:					
Category size[3]	.041	−.042	.118	.211	.213
Local market SMSA mean wage and salary income[3]	.139	−.779	.616	.063	.016
SMSA industrial structure					
%Construction	.881	2.466	−14.401***	13.575	.850
%Manufacturing	−5.152**	7.063**	−2.555	1.821	−1.064
%Retail	−4.534	12.459*	−3.725	−7.083	4.522
%Finance	−9.212	6.069	−3.410	.300	3.994
%Business	−6.905	9.693	−18.012***	13.848	−2.336
%Personal services	−9.691*	10.424*	−1.877	2.926	-2.201
%Professional	−5.312*	9.024**	−1.912	.964	−2.488
%Public administration	−8.197***	5.630	−3.266	7.412	−1.096
Regional economy					
NY, NJ, and PA	.042	−.598	−.467	.725	−.803*
East Central	.072	−.327	.105	.531	−.569
West Central	−.521	−.270	−.041	1.346*	−.639
South Atlantic	−.090	−.103	.696*	.204	−.929*
Mid-South	.488	.459	.661*	−.175	−1.599***
Central South	−1.147**	.305	.737*	.938	−1.101*
Western Mountains	−1.025**	.109	.682*	.833	−.773
Pacific	−.597	−.477	.559*	.818	−.572
Intercept	2.60****	1.890****	4.228****	1.888****	4.637****
Adjusted R²	.28	.19	.17	.11	.08
N	167	167	167	167	167

[1] See Table 3.4, notes 2 and 3.
[2] See Table 3.4, notes 4–8 for definition of variables.
[3] Reported coefficients in 10,000 metric.
**** LE .0001.
*** LE .001.
** LE .01.
* LE .05.

In Table 3.7 we seek demand variables whose effects are of the same size and in the same direction for each of our five ethnoracial categories. That behavior would represent general demand effects. But there are no such variables. None of the demand variables affects more than two groups. Moreover, even in those cases, the demand variable's effects are

Table 3.8. Regression of Mean Income-Defined Intrametropolitan Self-Employment Ranks[1] on Baseline[2] and Augmented[3] Demand Models,[4] Five Categories Pooled, in 167 Metropolitan Areas, $N = 835$

Independent Variables[4]	Baseline Model Unstandardized	Augmented Model Unstandardized	Augmented Model Standardized
Category demand			
Size of category[5]	−.077	.048	.035
Local economic market			
SMSA mean wage			
and salary income[5]	.031	−.019	−.002
SMSA industrial structure			
%Construction	−.889	.552	.008
%Manufacturing	−.056	−2.799	−.174
%Retail	−.309	−2.467	−.036
%Finance	.702	−.436	−.005
%Business	.878	−6.138	−.054
%Personal service	−.101	−7.094	−.097
%Professional	−.097	−3.507	−.104
%Public administration	−.156	−6.673*	−.148
Regional economy			
NY, NJ, and PA	.052	−.032	−.008
East Central	.054	−.033	−.009
West Central	.037	−.576	−.101
South Atlantic	.059	−.037	−.010
Mid-South	.044	.542	.082
Central South	.063	−.999***	−.234
Western Mountains	.050	−.943*	−.142
Pacific	.057	−.537*	−.146
Ethnic identities			
Foreign-born white	—	−.873****	−.247
Black	—	2.207****	.624
Asian	—	−.289*	−.082
Hispanic	—	1.422****	.402
Interactions			
%Manufacturing × FB white	—	7.845**	.221
%Manufacturing × Black	—	1.369	.039
%Manufacturing × Asian	—	3.338	.094
%Manufacturing × Hispanic	—	1.617	.046
%Retail × FB white	—	17.977**	.121
%Retail × Black	—	−4.860	−.033
%Retail × Asian	—	−4.246	−.028
%Retail × Hispanic	—	4.424	.030
%Business × FB white	—	12.756	.053
%Business × Black	—	−12.478	−.052
%Business × Asian	—	20.034*	.083
%Business × Hispanic	—	7.655	.032

Table 3.8. (Continued)

Independent Variables[4]	Baseline Model Unstandardized	Augmented Unstandardized	Augmented Standardized
%Personal service × FB white	—	16.830*	.105
%Personal service × Black	—	6.689	.042
%Personal service × Asian	—	8.305	.052
%Personal service × Hispanic	—	3.960	.025
%Professional × FB white	—	11.719****	.155
%Professional × Black	—	2.200	.029
%Professional × Asian	—	2.476	.033
%Professional × Hispanic	—	1.443	.019
%Public admin × FB white	—	11.382**	.113
%Public admin × Black	—	5.390	.054
%Public admin × Asian	—	13.079***	.130
%Public admin × Hispanic	—	3.996	.040
West Central × FB white	—	.569	.046
West Central × Black	—	.106	.009
West Central × Asian	—	1.444***	.116
West Central × Hispanic	—	.646	.052
Mid-South × FB white	—	.191	.013
Mid-South × Black	—	−.417	−.029
Mid-South × Asian	—	−1.130**	−.078
Mid-South × Hispanic	—	−1.492***	−.103
Central South × FB white	—	1.467****	.162
Central South × Black	—	1.041**	.115
Central South × Asian	—	1.683****	.186
Central South × Hispanic	—	.609	.067
West Mountains × FB white	—	1.209*	.083
West Mountains × Black	—	.931	.064
West Mountains × Asian	—	1.491**	.103
West Mountains × Hispanic	—	.930	.064
Pacific × FB white	—	.189	.025
Pacific × Black	—	.537*	.071
Pacific × Asian	—	1.072****	.141
Pacific × Hispanic	—	.709**	.093
Intercept	2.942****	2.542****	
Adjusted R^2	−.02	.67	

Significance test[6] for the addition of the intercept and slope dummy variables to the base-line model: F for df: 48, 768: 33.63 sig. at .01 level

[1] See Table 3.4, notes 2 and 3.
[2] Demand variables only.
[3] Demand, intercept, and slope dummy variables.
[4] See Table 3.4, notes 4–10 for definition of variables.
[5] Reported coefficients in 10,000 metric.
[6] Chow Test (see Hanushek and Jackson, 1977:124–129).
**** LE .0001.
*** LE .001.
** LE .01.
* LE .05.

in opposite directions. For example, %Manufacturing has a significant negative effect on native whites, but it has a significant positive effect on foreign whites. Moreover, the demand variables explain precious little variation in the self-employment ranks of the five ethnoracial categories. The range varies from .08 for Hispanics to .28 for native whites. This disaggregation by ethnoracial category shows no general demand effects and little explanatory power on the demand side.

These lackluster results continue in Table 3.8. First, we find no main effects of demand on self-employment ranks in the pooled sample baseline model and an adjusted R^2 of −.02! Second, as before, the explanation improves when we drop in the interaction terms. This addition raises the explained variation from nil to a mighty .67. Moreover, The interaction terms bring up to significance four main effects that had previously been below the threshold of significance. These are %Public Administration, Central South, Western Mountains, and Pacific regions.

However, all four main effects also show significant interactions with ethnoracial categories. First, %Public Administration reduces Asian self-employment rank relative to native whites' self-employment rank. Second, Central South, Western Mountains, and Pacific reduce the self-employment ranks of two or three categories relative to native whites. These interactions mean that the same demand variables have only specific effects. They tend to raise or reduce some groups while at the same time not affecting other groups.

Several industrial variables obtain significance only when interacted with ethnoracial categories. These are %Manufacturing, %Retail, %Business, %Personal Service, and %Professional. None of these demand variables exerts a significant main effect upon self-employment rank of the pooled samples, but each has significant interactions with one or more ethnoracial categories. For example, %Professional drastically reduces the foreign white self-employment rank below the native white rank. In summary, the main effects of demand on rank are nil in the baseline model. Furthermore, when we drop in the intercept and slope dummies in the augmented model, we still do not find any purely general demand effects.

DISCUSSION

The interaction theory of entrepreneurship predicts that the effects of demand will appear as specific demand, not general. Our evidence supports this inference. Whether we are discussing rate or rank, general demand effects are few. We found only one regional variable that produced general demand effects. Demand's effect is almost wholly derived from interaction with the ethnoracial categories. These category labels stand for supply features of the categories. Without further examining the meaning of these category labels, a task reserved for the next chapter, we cannot further interpret the substantive significance of the interactions. We do not, for example, know what it is about African Americans that causes their self-employment rates to flourish when in the presence of a demand environment heavy in business services. Nonetheless, the tables show that the interaction of supply and demand variables yields about the same explanation of self-employment rate and rank. As this result is just what the interaction theory proposes, the tables give that theory strong empirical support.

SUMMARY AND CONCLUSION

In this chapter, we addressed demand effects upon self-employment, introducing a distinction between specific and general effects. When demand equally encourages the entrepreneurship of all ethnoracial categories in a locality, we term the effect general. When demand encourages some groups more than others, we call the effect specific. From the literature, we explained six ways in which specific demand effects arise. These are discrimination, law, self-exclusion, unique resources, ethnic channeling, and economic closure. Specific demand effects can coexist with general demand effects but we expect one or the other to predominate.

Entrepreneurial performance has three components: rate, intrametropolitan rank, and intermetropolitan rank. Intermetropolitan rank is the rank of an area's self-employment rate for each category, among the 167 matched communities. To the extent that general demand predominate, we expect complete agreement between the intermetropolitan ranks of the five ethnoracial categories. That is, the same metropolitan region ought to prove equally beneficial to each and every group. Each group would, therefore, have the same ranks (1 to 167) in each metropolitan area. To test the intermetropolitan rank order agreements, we culled from our list of 272 metropolitan areas the 167 in which representatives of all five ethnoracial categories were found above a threshold minimum. Both Spearman rank correlations and Pearsonian correlations detected significant agreement among the ranks of the rates and income of the five ethnoracial groups. Nonetheless, visual inspection of the data and the moderate size of the correlations suggest that the agreement is partial.

Regression analysis also shows negligible general demand effects on self-employment rates. General demand effects do not appear in connection with intrametropolitan ranks at all; their influence upon rates is slight. Almost the entire effect of demand upon self-employment rate depends upon interaction with ethnoracial categories. These categories stand for supply features of the provider groups. The interactions arise when ethnoracial categories register results quite different from those obtained for the native whites from the same demand values. These unequal results amount to specific demand. The preponderance of specific demand indicates that the interaction theory has successfully understood the manner in which demand affects supply. Substantive interpretation of these results waits until the next chapter. This chapter has demonstrated only that the form of a statistical explanation of demand effects conforms to what interaction theory predicts.

NOTES

1. In general, economists, geographers, human ecologists, and Marxists have emphasized demand-side explanations of entrepreneurship (Nafziger, 1977:14–17). Demand-derived explanations fit their disciplinary paradigms. On the other hand, anthropologists, psychologists, and sociologists have stressed supply-side explanations (Wilken, 1979:7; McClelland and Winter, 1971:6; Alexander, 1967), which fit their paradigms.

2. When desired for its own sake, the perceived prestige of the role represents a supply-side influence upon a worker's disposition to select the entrepreneur's role. When prestige is desired because of the money one can squeeze out of it, as a movie star desires prestige in order to wrest a higher paying contract from Paramount Studios, then the influence of prestige is reducible to money rewards. In that case, prestige is a demand-side influence. In actuality, alas, movie stars want prestige for both reasons; the distinction between supply and demand collapses in these complex cases.

3. Opportunity is the right concept when one is discussing opportunities for someone to achieve social equality, upward mobility, or prestige. These are frequent and valid uses of the concept because the existence of opportunities depends upon social conditions broader than the capacity to obtain income.

4. See for example, Swinton and Handy's (1983) examination of African-American entrepreneurship in 155 metropolitan areas. This research disclosed "conditions in the local economy" that were "major determinants of the overall level of demand" for African-American business. This is a worthy goal. The study did not, and was not intended to examine variation in the ability of African Americans to take advantage of market demand. See also Johannisson's (1988) study of Swedish entrepreneurs in different economic regions of Sweden.

5. "We emphasize the fit between immigrant firms and the environments in which they function, including not only economic and social conditions but also the unique historical conditions encountered at the time of immigration" (Waldinger, Aldrich, and Ward, 1990:32).

6. See Razin (1988, 1993), Reynolds (1989), Bearse (1987), and Ong (1981).

7. Of course, one might dispute the sweeping conclusion on other grounds. First, it is incompatible with the textbook claim that supply and demand resources always interact to produce entrepreneurship. Second, the researchers did not examine demographic or class resources on the supply side, nor did they look into intermetropolitan continuities of rank, a condition we discuss in this chapter. These supply issues might have required a modification of their lop-sided conclusion, a contradiction to the textbook model, that only demand side influences affected entrepreneurship in the British cities. However, within the realistic limits of this research, the design permitted no conclusion other than the one these researchers drew.

8. Given his design, Waldinger could not explain why, on the supply side, immigrant groups other than Dominicans and Chinese were not drawn into the garment industry, nor, on the demand side, whether other New York City industries did not offer more or equally favorable demand opportunities to Dominicans and Chinese.

9. Berg (1981:3–6) discusses demand, but does not define the term. Granovetter (1981:32) mentions the reluctance of sociologists and economists to utilize one another's concepts. The reluctance probably applies particularly well to this case because, as Bearse (1981) has observed, the concept of market "demand for entrepreneurs" is cloudy because "the conventional concept of market demand may not apply to more than a minor part of the phenomenon."

10. An influential economist declares that "the demand curve of a particular group for a particular commodity" consists of "the locus of points, each of which shows the maximum quantity of the commodity that will be purchased by the group per unit time at a particular price" (Friedman, 1976:13).

11. "Total demand is determined by determining each component and adding them up to get the total. This is loosely called aggregate demand" (Klein, 1983:2).

12. This distinction parallels one drawn by economists who study human capital. "Two types of education and training investments may be distinguished: general and specific. Investment in the first type is broadly applicable to all occupations; the applicability of the latter is limited to specific jobs. Formal education is commonly viewed as a general training investment. Experience accumulated in working for a given employer (job tenure) may be regarded as a specific training investment, although obviously this training is not always no narrowly focused. Much human capital investment falls between these extremes, being partly general and partly specific, or having applicability limited to an occupation or group of occupations" (Fredland and Little, 1981:316).

13. In Weber's (1968) terms, some groups appropriate more than their share of the enhanced "market opportunities" that a local economy now affords.

14. If the number of janitorial service firms triples among the Koreans, and nothing else changes in the local economy, then the Koreans will have increased their share of the total entrepreneur population.

15. General demand and specific demand are analytic distinctions that combine in empirical economies and firms. For example, before Turkish restaurants

existed in Germany, Germans had no interest in Turkish cuisine. From Dusseldorf to Berlin, immigrant Turks monopolized the supply of Turkish culinary knowledge as well as the demand for this product. When Turkish restaurants at last began to appear, they serviced at first a strictly coethnic clientele. Thereafter, however, Turkish restaurants in Germany developed a clientele of younger Germans who had learned to appreciate Turkish cuisine. In this sense, Turkish restaurants enhanced demand for Turkish food, ultimately producing more Turkish restaurant entrepreneurs than the Turkish community in Germany could have supported. A decade later, Germany's numerous Turkish restaurants simultaneously reflect a specific demand for Turkish-style restaurant meals, the de facto monopoly by Turks of the requisite cooking skill, and a prosperous general demand environment that put disposable income in the pockets of Germans and immigrant Turks alike.

16. What Light (1972:10–15) has earlier labeled a "special consumer demand" is a special case of specific demand. A special consumer demand benefits coethnic entrepreneurs who are uniquely qualified to offer what coethnics want to buy. Special consumer demands link coethnic consumers and coethnic suppliers. For example, Chinese are best qualified to cook meals that other Chinese want to eat. No law prohibits Persians, Parisians, and Indonesians from selling Chinese meals to Chinese consumers, but Chinese have an obvious advantage in this coethnic market: they know how to cook Chinese meals.

17. The truth of this claim remains in contention. Borjas and Bronars infer consumer discrimination from pricing outcomes. They have no direct evidence of discrimination. But the justice of their claim is immaterial here. We entirely agree that if, and to the extent, consumers discriminate against African Americans, black self-employment will suffer relative to nonblacks, a specific demand effect.

18. As a secondary disadvantage, those subject to discrimination in self-employment are compelled to depend for demand upon coethnics, who are usually subject to discrimination in wage and salary employment. This vicious circle is the origin of the "limited market" demand for black entrepreneurs to which Swinton and Handy (1983:10–12) refer. Without discrimination, black entrepreneurs would enjoy exactly the same market demand as do white entrepreneurs.

19. Evidence does not indicate that government set-asides were very effective in achieving these goals (Waldinger et al., 1990: Ch. 7). Only 32 metropolitan areas had municipal set-asides programs.

20. That is, if group A's mean wage and salary income is $25,000 yearly, whereas that of group B is only $15,000, the average members of these two groups will react differently to new opportunities that offer money returns of $20,000 a year. The average member of group A will find this return too skimpy; the average member of group B will see the same return as handsome. By implication, this expansion would most benefit group B workers.

21. We are just arguing that the ability to produce certain services is unevenly distributed in populations. But we also believe, but do not stress, that the economist's concept of "physical productivity" cannot be used here, because

consumers expect competence only from people of particular ethnic backgrounds (cf. Cain, 1986:695–696).

22.   Granted, one rarely finds in industrialized societies total correspondence between ethnic groups and industries such that one ethnic group wholly controls particular industries (Light, 1983: Ch. 12; Cohen, 1969). Nonetheless, clustering is typical, and any tendency toward occupational and industrial clustering weakens the possibility of general demand (Timms, 1975). In the example of 26 industries above, even if group A monopolized only one, the other 25 industries being shared equally by groups A through Z, expansion of those 26 industries would still benefit group A more than the others.

23.   Otherwise, normally referred to as a percentage.

24.   For the same reason, we can study the rank of only five major ethnoracial categories. If we expanded the rank study to all 13 national origin groups in our dataset, we would find only a handful of metropolitan areas that contained all 13 groups. In that case, our N would be too small to permit statistical evaluation of the results.

25.   Effective representation was defined as a minimum of 20 adults in the labor force in the 1980 U.S. Census 5% PUMs sample. Such a criterion implies a true labor force of 400 persons. Below that criterion we declared groups too small for accurate study.

26.   Native-born whites were present above the threshold level in all 272 metropolitan areas.

27.   This useful information would be of obvious value for additional research, but, to minimize the cost of this book, it could not be included in an Appendix. Persons desiring a complete list of the metropolitan areas (SMSAs) of each type, plus the size of the category labor force of each in 1980, should write to Professor Ivan Light, Department of Sociology, University of California, 405 Hilgard Avenue, Los Angeles CA 90024 USA.

28.   See Chapter 2 for a more detailed accounting of the similarities and differences between these two definitions.

29.   Inter-SMSA ranks for each category, i.e., 1 = the highest mean self-employment rate or mean self-employment income to 167 = the lowest (among the metropolitan areas in which native whites, foreign whites, blacks, Asians, and Hispanics are all present).

30.   See Aiken and West (1991).

31.   We computed the Pearson correlation coefficient between the size of a metropolitan area's labor force and the self-employment rate (SER) of each of the five ethnoreligious categories. Correlational results indicated no positive effect of metropolitan size on the entrepreneurial performance of ethnoracial categories. Using the full list of 272 metropolitan areas (SMSAs), we found no statistically significant correlations for any of the categories. Deeming the subject worthy of further exploration, we compared metropolitan areas above and below the mean population size with respect to MSER. Big metropolitan areas did not exhibit higher MSERs than small ones. On the contrary, in the 167 areas, smaller metropolitan areas had significantly higher SERs than did the larger ones. However, differences were slight, and existed only for all persons and the

native born. No significant differences affected the native whites or any of the four minorities. The reasons for this curious dualism probably reflect what Lieberson (1980) has called a "compositional effect." That is, the effect of metropolitan size operated at the aggregate without constraining smaller subgroups. In most metropolitan areas, native whites were 85% or more of the total population so constraints affecting the aggregate affected them the most.

We also tested for a curvilinear relationship between labor force size and entrepreneurial performance, regressing the size of the labor force of each metropolitan area and its square on MSER for each ethnoracial category. The only significant results showed a curvilinear relationship with work-defined MSEI for the total labor force, native-born labor force, and native-born white labor force of the 272 areas. We found no curvilinear relationship for any of the minority categories. The curvilinear relationship between labor force size and income-defined MSEI was significant only for the total aggregate labor force.

In summary, from contingency tables, size of metropolitan labor force evidenced some effect upon aggregate self-employment rate but none upon the rate of the four minorities. Moreover, even the aggregate effects were small. These results do not suggest that size of labor force affects entrepreneurial performance.

32. The absolute size of the metropolitan area's labor force was highly correlated with the variable CCATSIZE (the absolute size of each category in a metropolitan area). For the pooled sample, the $r = .56$, but was as high as .98 for native whites.

33. The following are the mean self-employment rates of all nine regions (listed from low to high): New England 5.7%; East Central 6.0%; NY, NJ, PA 6.1%; Mid-South 6.3%; South Atlantic 6.4%; West Central 7.1%; Central South 7.7%; Western Mountains 8.3%; and Pacific 9.3%.

34. Similarly, in metropolitan areas of the Central South Region, MSEIs were $12,917, whereas among East Central metropolitan areas, MSEIs were $11,162, 86% of the leading region's income.

35. This procedure is described by Gujarati (1970).

36. This is the net effect, which is calculated as follows: the metric coefficient for %RETAIL (for native whites) is 30.4% minus the metric coefficient for the interaction of foreign whites and %RETAIL (46.9%), which equals −16.5% (see Table 3.6).

37. Net rates of increase for blacks, Asians, and Hispanics are 1.5, 0.6, and 1.0%, respectively. Foreign whites are essentially the same as native whites, i.e., 3.3%.

38. The four interaction variables of ethnic identity and this region were deleted from the model.

4

Supply Effects

Parsons and Smelser (1956:9–10) define supply as "the production of utility or economic value." Entrepreneurs are of use because of the goods and services they produce or cause to be produced. Consumers do not buy entrepreneurs. They buy their products and services. Therefore, entrepreneurs are a producer good, not a consumer good. For this reason, many economists treat entrepreneurs as a fourth factor of production along with land, labor, and capital. Alternatively, Light and Bonacich (1988: pt. 4) treat entrepreneurship as a special form of labor service. Either way, the supply of entrepreneurs is a factor of production. Economic theory treats all factors of production as commodities.

Yet, as Polanyi (1957: Ch. 6) long ago observed, factors of production are only "fictitious commodities." Fictitious commodities are noncommodities treated for convenience as though real. Real commodities originate in someone's plan to obtain exchange value. Thus, a farmer raises wheat intending to sell it. Therefore, wheat is a real commodity. In contrast, fictitious commodities, even when sold, do not originate in a plan to resell them for gain. As Polanyi observed, land is just nature, the long-term product of the Big Bang. If the Big Bang had an author at all, the author's intent was presumably not financial gain, so land cannot be a real commodity.

Human labor is another fictitious commodity. Except in extreme and degrading situations, as when slave owners breed their chattel for sale, human beings are neither produced nor nurtured for sale.[1] Moreover, even under those extreme conditions, the slave owners' intention is not the immediate cause of the human being's production. Rather, the immediate cause is the gleam in the father's eye and the mother's sexual receptivity, both long-term products of nature, a nonprofit operation. Since entrepreneurs are human beings, their production as able-bodied, competent, motivated working-age adults precedes any decision they make to offer their entrepreneurship to the market. This offer of entrepreneurial labor services transforms an adult into an entrepreneur, and one may conceptualize the adult's offer and subsequent work as a real labor commodity produced for sale and sold for gain. However, one may not so characterize the prior production of the adult who makes the offer. Therefore, entrepreneurship too is a fictitious commodity.

Supply effects are changes in the entrepreneur population that result from changes in their supply. The supply of entrepreneurs depends upon how many adults have the motive and capability to become entrepreneurs. The production of entrepreneurial adults requires parents who bear and socialize offspring with the motives, abilities, and other resources entrepreneurs need. Naturally, families do not have exclusive responsibility for socialization. They are assisted by the communities in which they exist, the media they consume, the educational, health care, and religious institutions in which they participate, and the kinship and value systems of their group. All these feed into entrepreneur socialization in ways that we need not analyze further. We refer to all these feeder systems as *social causation*. In general, social causation underpins the supply of entrepreneurs, and responds slowly to market demand, if at all.

Except for social causation, the number of work-age adults would measure the supply of entrepreneurs. In fact, the correlation between number of workers and number of entrepreneurs is high, leading to the impression that all workers have an equal proclivity for entrepreneurship. However, this high correlation masks social causation whose effects are unequal. After all, gender roles, health care, birth rates, and immigration are social causes that affect the number of workers potentially available for entrepreneurship. If any of these social causes change, the supply of entrepreneurs changes too. Moreover, sheer size of labor force overlooks qualitative differences that affect the motivation and capability of adult workers to undertake entrepreneurship. These include all the ethnocultural heterogeneity in the labor force. For example, as a result of their historic trading traditions, middleman minorities are better prepared for entrepreneurship, and possess more motivational and practical resources for it than do nonmiddlemen (Zenner, 1991). To the extent that they are culturally different, human groups have different and often unequal motives and resources for entrepreneurship, so group size is only a rough measure of entrepreneurial supply.

VARIANT AND INVARIANT RESOURCES

Even in a pluralistic society such as the United States, many elements of social causation are similar or the same everywhere. For example, the media, the national welfare state, and primary education homogenize groups and regions. Relative to the historic past, these homogenizing influences are stronger than before. The Middle Ages are definitely over.

To that extent, cultural trends have validated Max Weber's expectation that advanced capitalism would cease to depend upon exogenous and eccentric cultural sources (like religion) for its entrepreneurs. As we also indicated in Chapter 1, cultural homogenization underlies the modern tendency to ignore and dismiss entrepreneurship. After all, even if social causation is acknowledged, to the extent that all regions and groups experience identical social causation, all will produce identical supplies of entrepreneurs. Moreover, to the extent that modernization has reshaped socialization broadly conceived to suit the needs of the advanced economy, and all groups and regions share in this reshaped socialization, society engenders no residual cultural differences between groups or regions in their proclivity for entrepreneurship.

As indicated in Chapter 1, this classical view is oversimple. Conceding that cultural homogenization has occurred, we reject the supposition that the United States is so culturally homogeneous that localities do not differ in their supply of entrepreneurs. Quite to the contrary, local labor forces are mosaics of groups whose entrepreneurial resources are unequal. One might urge against this position that apparent differences in supply are really products of differences in demand. Specifically, the same group performs quite differently in entrepreneurship under different conditions of local demand. Arguably, if Chinese are more entrepreneurial in Syracuse than in Albany, then higher demand in Syracuse must explain the discrepancy. Although this answer appears persuasive, we reject its unexamined assumption that intermetropolitan variations in an ethnoracial group's entrepreneurial performance *must* result from variable demand conditions, supply having been ruled out. That assumption is at stake when Patterson (1975) assumes that the Chinese in Jamaica and the Chinese in Tobago are the "same" group, so demand must explain the difference in their entrepreneurship.

In point of fact, the same cultural groups normally have different resources in different localities. Demand explains all interlocal differences in group entrepreneurship only if resource endowments are invariant, never departing in one locality from the level obtained in others. That is exactly how researchers have conceptualized interlocal comparisons of the same group. This conceptualization is oversimplified because intragroup variation in entrepreneurial performance may result from interlocal variation in resource endowment as well as from interlocal variation in demand conditions.

Take Mexicans as an example. On the average, Mexicans are less educated than native whites, but Mexican/white differences vary among metropolitan areas. In some, the white/Mexican educational gap is large; in others it is small. Since education is a class resource, supportive of entrepreneurship, Mexicans demonstrate higher entrepreneurial performance in those metropolitan areas in which their mean education is higher. In the same sense, since men generally owned more businesses than did women in 1980, Mexicans demonstrate superior entrepreneurship where Mexican labor forces contain a higher proportion of men. In general, one expects Mexican rates most closely to approximate native white rates of self-employment in those metropolitan areas in which Mexican resources are strongest. Therefore, interlocal variation in Mexican rates *supports* the resources theory to the extent that Mexicans demonstrate superior entrepreneurship where their resources are superior.

Interlocal variation in group resources does not require us to jettison the common-sense assumption that ethnic groups differ one from another. Indeed, it is hard to jettison that assumption without surrendering the idea that groups are real. If the Chinese in Jamaica and the Chinese in Tobago have nothing in common, then a Chinese group does not exist. Instead, we would have one group in Tobago, another in Jamaica, and they would be two separate and independent groups, sharing only a misleading label.[2] We rather maintain that in addition to their class and ethnic dimensions, ethnic resources also have a more and less variant dimension. Although some resource endowments of the same group or category vary synchronically among localities, others vary little. In particular, socioeconomic and demographic resources of ethnoracial categories vary from locality to locality more than do culturally derived resources such as language, religion, values, networks, and kinship. Additionally, self-identification with the named group, associational habits and patterns, leadership, and even external designation as a group are change-resistant properties of the same group in different localities. Mexicans in Chicago might display above average education and a higher than average proportion of men in their 40s without ceasing to share change-resistant cultural characteristics with Mexicans in Laredo.[3]

To treat any group as an invariant resource stock is to assume away interlocal variation in resources. At the other extreme, to treat any group as a bundle of interlocally varying class, ethnic, and demographic resources ignores the change-resistant substratum that gives it coherence. Acknowledging that Mexican resources vary interlocally, we still distinguish Mexicans from Chinese, another group whose resources vary interlocally. Yet, if Mexicans are only a bundle of variant resources, as are Chinese, Germans, and everyone else, then nothing gives interlocal continuity and identity to any group. Continuity means group coherence *above and beyond* local variation in resource endowments. What gives continuity to a group may be independent of the class and demographic resources that also promote its self-employment. However, possibly change-resistant cultural characteristics are also resources that influence entrepreneurship. That question is empirical, not definitional.

Accordingly, the best way to conceptualize entrepreneurial supply at any moment is to distinguish *variant and invariant resources* of ethnoracial groups and categories.[4] Variant resources routinely change strength, size, or intensity from locality to locality. They include the mean size, percentage male, mean education, and mean age of the labor force of each group in each locality. In contrast, when viewed synchronically, invariant resources do not vary among localities, and it is this invariance that gives coherence to the group. Invariant resources include culturally derived beliefs and values, kinship, endogamy, religion, language, institutions, and art. Normally, such profound cultural characteristics define a group's identity, conferring coherence despite interlocal disparities in class or demographic composition.

The census data do not permit direct measurement of these invariant resources. However, the census does measure ethnic self-identification, an invariant property of each group that can proxy other invariant resources. That is, each ethnoracial category consists of respondents who assigned themselves to this ethnoracial category when asked with what category they identified. Even if they differ in every other respect, respondents in every locality share identification with the same ethnic label. Therefore, ethnic self-identification is an interlocally *invariant* property of these ethnoracial categories and groups. Ethnic self-identification residually measures ethnic and class resources that the literature has found important but into which the census does not inquire. Since the measurement is residual, it is also inexact. That is, ethnic self-identification stands for every feature of the group or category that is not separately measured. These features surely include variant properties of the categories that could, in principle, be separated from ethnic identity, thus improving the direct measurement of the local category's invariant attributes.

SUPPLY EFFECTS

According to the interaction theory, supply affects entrepreneurship in interaction with the demand environment as when Chinese restaurateurs in New York City benefit from the Jewish appetite for Chinese food (Tuchman and Levine, 1993). Thus construed, groups and categories respond only to local demands whose requirements match their resources. Therefore, groups with scant resources cannot respond to demands that require vast resources. Older groups cannot respond to demands that require youth. Predominantly male groups cannot respond effectively to demand that favors women. Small groups cannot respond to demands that require big groups.

However, some demands require resources nearly everyone has, such as the ability to add and subtract. Conversely, some ethnic resources are of specific rather than general utility. *Specific utility* refers to provider characteristics that confer a special advantage in a particular demand context but are not of general use. Conversely, *general utility* refers to resources that permit versatile response to multiple demands, possibly to all. For example, in the restaurant industry, wine connoisseurship confers an advantage in French restaurants, but it does not confer the same advantage in Persian restaurants, because Muslims do not serve alcohol. Therefore, wine connoisseurship is a less versatile business resource than the willingness to work long hours, a useful characteristic in any business. When a demand meets the provider populations from which entrepreneurs emerge, specific resource endowments can produce specific demand effects. This alteration does not arise only because groups have different levels of class resources, some rich and others poor. It also arises because some resources are specific and some are general.

Although the interaction theory illuminates the restaurant industry, and others like it that call for special skills, such as the ability to cook Chinese food, it does not illuminate industries that require general resources. General resources confer a capability to do any kind of business. Following Sway (1984), who linked the concept to Gypsies, we call that generalized capacity *entrepreneurial versatility*. Versatile groups prosper in the flower business, where that is in demand, and they prosper in construction, where that is in demand. Universally versatile groups prosper everywhere. Of course, universal versatility is an unrealistic extrapolation in the interest of illustration. No group's versatility is universal. However, some resources are more versatile than others.

If every resource were universal, and every group had universal versatility, then the interaction theory would be useless. Every group could do everything equally well as every other. Mexicans could prepare won ton soup as well as the Chinese, and the Chinese could brew beer as well as the Germans, who could make caviar as well as the Russians, etc. In that circumstance, one could not very well explain entrepreneurship in terms of "a congruence between the demands of the economic environment and the informal resources of the ethnic population," since all groups would have identical informal resources (Waldinger, Ward, and Aldrich, 1985:591). The interaction theory cannot explain entrepreneurial versatility because the interaction theory requires specific resources, not general ones. Even though no resources are really universal, to the extent that resources approach universality, an interaction explanation proves inadequate.

Class resources are more universal than ethnic resources. Money to invest and human capital are general resources that support entrepreneurship in any demand environment. Rich people can invest in hotels when that industry in profitable, and later redirect their capital to nuclear weapons when they become profitable. Educated people can learn forestry, then turn their minds to highway construction. When groups enjoy generalized resources, aggregate demand matters because entrepreneurs can switch into any industry in which demand expands. The superior educational level of Korean entrepreneurs offers an illustration. Korean entrepreneurs have, on average, more years of education than do non-Korean entrepreneurs. Therefore, in whatever city they reside, Korean immigrant entrepreneurs have a human capital advantage that supports their entrepreneurial success. Possibly as a result, Koreans in New York City enjoyed their biggest commercial success in the greengrocer business where they introduced ready to eat fruits and vegetables in bite-size pieces. Koreans in Los Angeles never specialized in the greengrocer business, nor did Koreans have any resource affinity for greengroceries. Korean immigrants in Los Angeles operated gasoline service stations, dry cleaning, and liquor stores—not greengroceries. Yet none of these Los Angeles specialties reflected any unique aptitude either. Rather, the Korean Americans adapted to whatever demand environment they inhabited, New York or Los Angeles, nimbly switching versatile resources from industry to industry as demand warranted. Had the Koreans lacked entrepreneurial versatility, being greengrocers, they would have lacked the ability to run gas stations, or vice versa.

SPECIFIC SUPPLY EFFECTS

Paralleling demand effects, discussed in the preceding chapter, supply effects are specific or general. *Specific supply effects* arise when ethnic identity exerts unequal effects upon the entrepreneurship of various groups, changing some more than others or increasing some while decreasing others. Specific supply effects arise as the main effect of ethnoracial self-identification, an interlocally invariant supply characteristic.[5] Since invariant supply refers to residual properties of groups not reducible to universal variables, the effects of invariant characteristics are unequal where groups' change-resistant cultural endowments differ in entrepreneurial versatility. The proverbial business acumen of middleman minorities is of this type. Middlemen minorities enjoy versatile ethnic resources that permit them to accommodate a wide range of demand environments.

General supply effects occur when supply characteristics raise or lower the entrepreneurship of all ethnoracial groups equally. General supply effects can involve invariant or variant supply characteristics such as age or education. Invariant supply effects are general when each ethnic identity has the same effect upon demand. Variant supply effects are general when each affects the entrepreneurship of all groups in comparable ways. For example, education improves the entrepreneurial performance of all groups albeit nonlinearly (Boyd, 1991:414; Bates, 1985b). Therefore, education's supply effect is general. Naturally, localities in which the general level of education is high ought to experience high entrepreneurship as a result, and wherever ethnoracial categories have more education, their entrepreneurship should also improve.[6]

Human capital is an individual's investment in personal productivity. Human capital theories explain entrepreneurship on the basis of the work experience and education of individuals. Human capital theories require general supply effects, and cannot explain specific supply effects. Since groups differ in respect to average human capital, human capital theories offer some potential for explaining intergroup differences in entrepreneurship rate and rank. Groups with high human capital ought to demonstrate higher rates of self-employment and higher entrepreneurial rank than do groups with low human capital. The more human capital groups have, the higher their predicted rates and ranks of entrepreneurship. Human capital being the same, groups ought to have the same entrepreneurial performance in the same economic environment, and, when they do, their effect is general.

However, although they exemplify it, human capital theories do not exhaust the manner in which general supply effects occur. Health status, gender ratio, knowledge of English, and nativity are supply variables in terms of which one may characterize all ethnoracial groups. That is, all groups have some level of general health, they have a sex ratio, they enjoy some level of English language ability, and they have a proportion of adults who are foreign born. Healthy groups outperform unhealthy ones in entrepreneurship, male-preponderant groups outperform female-preponderant ones, and so forth. When these universal effects are present, then supply effects are general. Yet, gender and nativity are not forms of human capital, and health status and language competence are only partially such. After all, to possess human capital, a worker must have invested in his or her work capacity, if only through the opportunity cost of skill acquisition. Workers do not invest in gender other than through sex change operations. Workers do invest in health, and reap economic rewards for it. But many diseases are hereditary, and costless life styles (not smoking, not drinking, not drugging) are the most healthful. To that extent, a population's health status is not a human capital variable. The same arguments apply to language competence and nativity. Therefore, although human capital illustrates general supply effects, it does not exhaust the category.

TYPES OF DEMAND/SUPPLY INTERACTION

As we explained in the preceding chapter, general demand effects arise when features of the demand environment have the same effect upon the entrepreneurship of all ethnoracial categories and groups. In this case, a rising tide raises all boats equally. In contrast, specific demand effects arise when supply characteristics combine with the demand environment to yield irregular consequences. Since irregular combination is precisely what the interaction theory expects, specific demand is the empirical form that the interaction theory takes.

However, one can extend the interaction theory to specify more exactly the ways in which demand and supply interact. To this end, we distinguish general and specific interactions and within the latter a demand-led and a supply-led specific interaction of demand characteristics and ethnic identity. Specific, demand-led interaction arises when demand itself favors or disfavors specific ethnic identities. Prejudiced buyers create specific demand-led interaction since they ask for entrepreneurs of a certain age, sex, or color rather than just for qualified entrepreneurs. In this way, as noted earlier, prejudiced buyers influence the entrepreneur population. Conversely, specific supply-led interaction occurs when resources permit some groups to respond to a universalistic demand better than others. When we find, for example, that consumer demand for Chinese food benefits Chinese more than non-Chinese, we infer that Chinese are normally better qualified to produce their own cuisine than are non-Chinese. If non-Chinese could cook Chinese food as well as the Chinese, then consumers would buy it. In fact, they cannot—so consumers prefer Chinese suppliers. However, our census data do not permit us to decide whether customers prefer Chinese-owned Chinese restaurants because they are prejudiced against non-Chinese or because Chinese cook Chinese food better. The former is a demand-led explanation; the latter a supply-led explanation.

General interaction is another type of demand/supply interaction. Unlike specific interaction, which requires ethnic identities, general interaction utilizes variant supply. This interaction arises, for example, when mean education of all groups increases all groups' self-employment rates more in some regions than in others. General interaction is universal. It exists when the copresence of supply and demand affects self-employment rates and ranks in a multiplicative way in addition to an additive way. Thus, for example, we ask whether age and industrial structure interact to increase or decrease self-employment of all of the groups in particular localities. If so, the interaction may be considered a legitimate extrapolation of human capital theory since regional economies have distinct entrepreneurship needs. Some need older and some need younger entrepreneurs; some need more educated and some need less educated entrepreneurs.

MEASUREMENT

To clarify the conceptual issues, the rest of this chapter uses regression analysis to evaluate the joint effects of supply and demand upon self-employment rates and ranks. The names and operational definitions of variables appear in Table 4.1. Our description of lower order terms precedes the description of higher order interaction terms for supply and demand variables. We test the effects of the supply and demand on two alternative dependent variables. These dependent variables are the mean income-defined self-employment rates for 272 metropolitan areas, and the mean income-defined self-employment ranks for 167 metropolitan areas. Both are analyzed using the pooled samples of the five

Table 4.1. Variables Used in the Analyses[1]

Variables	Name and Operational Description of Variables
Dependent variables	
CATMSER	Income-defined mean self-employment rate[2]
CATRANK	Rank of category mean income-defined self-employment rate[3]
Supply variables	
Invariant supply (intercept variables)[4]	
FBW	Dummy variable (Foreign-born whites = 1; else = 0)
BLACK	Dummy variable (Blacks = 1; else = 0)
ASIAN	Dummy variable (Asians = 1; else = 0)
HISPANIC	Dummy variable (Hispanics = 1; else = 0)
Variant supply[5]	
CPCTCAT[6]	Relative size of category — .23022
CCATPCTM	Category mean percentage male — .54
CCATED	Category mean years of education — 12.56
CCATAGE	Mean years of age — 36.67
Demand variables[5]	
Metropolitan demand	
SMSA local economic market	
CSMSAI1	(Mean wage and salary income/10,000 — 1.22563

Table 4.1. (continued)

SMSA industrial structure[7]

CCONIND	Mean % in construction industry — .07
CMANUIND	Mean % in manufacturing industry — .23
CRETIND	Mean % in retail industry — .18
CFININD	Mean % in finance industry — .06
CBUSIND	Mean % in business services industry — .04
CPERSIND	Mean % in personal services industry — .03
CPROFIND	Mean % in professional industry — .21
CPUBIND	Mean % in public administration industry — .06

Regional economy[8]

NYNJPA	Dummy variable (SMSA in NY, NJ, or PA = 1; else = 0)
ECENTRAL	Dummy variable (SMSA in East Central = 1; else = 0)
WCENTRAL	Dummy variable (SMSA in West Central = 1; else = 0)
SATLANTC	Dummy variable (SMSA in South Atlantic = 1; else = 0)
MIDSOUTH	Dummy variable (SMSA in Mid-South = 1; else = 0)
CENTRLSO	Dummy variable (SMSA in Central South = 1; else = 0)
WESTMTNS	Dummy variable (SMSA in Western Mountains = 1; else = 0)
PACIFIC	Dummy variable (SMSA in Pacific = 1; else = 0)

Interaction independent variables
  17 Demand × 4 invariant supply[9]
  17 Demand × 4 variant supply[10]

---

[1] See Chapter 2, Appendix 2A, for detailed descriptions.

[2] Respondents were defined as self-employed (= 1) if they had reported any income gains or losses from self-employment (INCOME2). We calculated the self-employment rate by dividing the number of persons who reported self-employment income (NINCOME2) by the total number of persons in the civilian labor force for each category in each respective metropolitan area.

[3] Groups were rank ordered *within* each metropolitan area (1 = highest rank; 5 = lowest rank for lowest CATMSER in each metropolitan area).

[4] Native-born white is the omitted reference category. See "Categories and Groups,' in' Chapter 2, for a detailed description. Aiken and West (1991:116, 130) advise that dummy coded variables *not* be centered.

[5] These continuous independent variables were centered, as recommended by Aiken and West (1991:37, 119–138, and n. 3), because the range of values for none of these variables encompassed a meaningful zero (where the linear regression line or plane transects the axis of the dependent variable for "raw" or metric coefficients). Centered variables were created by subtracting the means for the total pooled sample from the "raw" data for each of the categories for each respective variable. These means are indicated in each of the operationalizations described in Table 4.1. These variables are identical to those used in Chapter 2, as described in Table 2.9, "centered" on the means of the total pooled samples for rates (N = 1,172). For the regression equations on mean self-employment ranks in Table 4.3, these same variables were centered on the means for the pooled sample for the 167 metropolitan areas, N = 835. The following are the only six means used that differ from those indicated in Table 4.1 for the mean self-employment rates (N = 1,172): CPCTCAT .19874, CCATED 12.73, CCATAGE 36.52, CSMSAI1 1.25, CMANUIND .21, and CRETIND .17.

[6] CPCTCAT is the category's percentage of a metropolitan area's labor force.

[7] The reference group deleted was the percentage in the following industries: mining, transportation, wholesale, and entertainment and recreation services.

[8] Each region is a dummy variable. New England is the omitted region.

[9] There are no native-born white interaction variables because native-born white is the omitted reference group. The metropolitan area mean wage and salary income and industrial structure variables were first centered, but not the dummy variables.

[10] The continuous general demand and variant supply variables were first centered, but not the dummy variables.

ethnoracial groups.[7] As before, to model the rank order of a category's self-employment rate, we had to restrict the analysis of rank orders to the 167 metropolitan areas.[8] Only in this manner could we assure that every metropolitan area in the model would contain all five ethnoracial categories. However, this constraint did not apply to self-employment rate as a dependent variable.

SUPPLY VARIABLES

Invariant supply means ethnoracial self-identification. Self-identification proxies unmeasured entrepreneurial resources. Examples include culturally derived beliefs and values, kinship, endogamy, religion, language, institutions, art, and what Coleman (1988:S103) has labeled "social capital." Admittedly, it would be preferable to measure these variables directly. However, census data do not treat these topics. Therefore, we resort to residual measurement, treating invariant supply as the ethnoracial category expressed as a dummy variable (0,1) for each of four categories: foreign whites (FBW), blacks, Asians, and Hispanics, omitting native whites as the reference group.[9] Since we have separately expressed the ethnoracial category's local profile of human capital and demographic advantage, the ethnoracial dummy variables include any and all features of the category unexpressed in the variant supply. Naturally, that residual will include variant features of each category that were not separately measured. However, it ought principally to measure invariant features of the ethnoracial category that influence the category's self-employment rate—if there be any such features. Native whites are the selected reference group because they are the most advantaged in the American economy. Presumably they have more freedom to choose between wage and salary or self-employment work. Furthermore, they have easier access to, and fairer compensation from, wage and salary work.

Variant supply means resource-related characteristics of ethnoracial categories that vary among metropolitan areas. We distinguished demographic advantage and human capital.[10] All variant supply variables and many demand variables are continuous. They have therefore been "centered," as described in the previous chapters,[11] because their ranges do not include a substantively meaningful zero. Table 4.1 indicates the pooled sample mean[12] that was subtracted from each respective variable in order to create the centered variables. A prefix "C" has been added to the name of each variable to indicate that it has been centered.

Our models test two measures of demographic advantage: the relative size of each category (CPCTCAT) and the percentage male of each category's labor force (CCATPCTM).[13] CPCTCAT tests the effects of the labor supply of coethnics.[14] Possibly, the higher a category's percentage of a metropolitan area's labor force, the higher their self-employment rate, by virtue of ethnic enclave demand. Since men were more frequently self-employed than women in 1980 (Fuchs, 1982), we supposed that in metropolitan areas where categories had a higher proportion of men in the labor force, their self-employment rate might be higher.

We also tested two human capital measures: a group's mean years of education in the metropolitan area (CCATED)[15] and the mean age of the category's labor force (CCATAGE).[16] Since more educated persons are more likely to be self-employed, we expected a comparable relationship between the mean years of education of a group and that group's mean self-employment rate and rank. Similarly, since the self-employed are generally older than other workers, we supposed that in metropolitan areas where a category's labor force was somewhat older, the category's self-employment rate and rank might be somewhat higher as well.

DEMAND VARIABLES

As before, we measure local demand for entrepreneurs in terms of local demand environments. The 272 metropolitan areas in our data set encompass all of the largest metropolitan areas in the United States. Each metropolitan area offers a unique demand environment. Some localities encouraged entrepreneurship more than others. For example, those well endowed with industries conducive to small and medium business had higher rates of self-employment.

The 17 demand variables[17] measure the economic characteristics of metropolitan areas and regions that govern the local economy's need for self-employment. We distinguished three components of demand. The first is the aggregate consumer demand of the metropolitan area itself as measured by the metropolitan area's mean wage and salary income (CSMSAI1) in ten thousands. Arguably, aggregate demand promotes self-employment in that when there is higher income, an economy supports more entrepreneurs.

The second component of general demand is each metropolitan area's industrial structure. We measured industrial structure in terms of the percentage of the locality's labor force that was employed in eight industries.[18] Five of these eight industries contain heavy proportions of self-employed workers: retail trade, business and repair services, personal services, finance, insurance, and real estate, and professional and related services. Therefore, when these five are strong, a metropolitan economy ought to support more entrepreneurs.

The third component of demand is the geographic region in which a metropolitan area is located. Some regions have higher entrepreneurship than others. Region also permits us to establish the effects of supply variables upon category self-employment rates net of regional differences in settlement patterns. We defined eight regional economies with New England the omitted one.

To test the interaction theory, we must examine the interaction of supply and demand. To this end, we interact the four ethnoracial identities, the invariant supply variables, with the 17 metropolitan demand variables. This procedure created 68 new variables. We created another 68 variables by interacting the effects of the 17 demand variables with the four variant supply variables: relative size, gender ratio, education, and age. These two interaction sets created 136 interaction variables from which the interaction theory expects the entrepreneur population to emerge.

TECHNIQUE

To test for interactive effects between these supply and demand variables, we follow Aiken and West (1991: Ch. 7). We analyze a succession of regression models, beginning with the simplest model containing just the four category dummy invariant supply variables. This method tests whether the mean self-employment rates of any of the four ethnoracial groups differ from that of the reference group, native whites. In the second model, we add the four variant supply variables to measure the effects of demographic and human capital characteristics.

Finally, in model three, we add the 17 general metropolitan demand variables, 68 demand by invariant supply interactive variables, and 68 demand by variant supply interactive variables, to model two. We first check whether any of the interaction demand variables are significant. Then we modify the model, retaining only those interaction variables that are significant, to yield a final modified model 3 that will be retested.

To summarize, utilizing the census data, we organize 161 independent variables into lower order and higher order measures of supply and demand. We then regress the broad measure of mean self-employment rate on these independent variables in three successively more complex equations. In the first model, only measures of invariant supply appear as independent variables. In the second, we combine invariant supply and variant supply variables. Finally, we add general demand variables and two types of demand interaction variables for the third model. We check this last model to see whether demand effects (if any) are general or specific. The models will be modified to retain only those variables that significantly explain why 5 different ethnoracial groups, living in 272 metropolitan areas, are engaged in self-employment. Table 4.2 presents the standardized coefficients for mean self-employment rates for these models. Table 4.3 replicates this analysis to generate and test three progressively more complex models to explain the contribution that supply and demand factors make to the mean self-employment ranks of the 5 groups in 167 metropolitan areas.

MEAN SELF-EMPLOYMENT RATES

Our strategy is to identify which effects actually occur in the census data, and how strong each is. We begin by asking whether the mean self-employment rates and ranks of foreign whites, blacks, Asians, and Hispanics differ from those of native whites. In other words, we ask whether ethnoracial self-identification, our measure of invariant supply, affected the rate of entrepreneurship for the pooled sample in the 272 metropolitan areas, because, if it did not, we are barking up the wrong tree. Thus, we begin with a multiple regression analysis appropriate to test this question:[19]

$$Y = b_1D_1 + b_2D_2 + b_3D_3 + b_4D_4 + b_0 \qquad (4.1)$$

where Y = predicted mean income-defined self-employment rate

D_1 = dummy category variable, foreign whites (FBW) = 1, others = 0
D_2 = dummy category variable, blacks = 1, others = 0
D_3 = dummy category variable, Asians = 1, others = 0
D_4 = dummy category variable, Hispanics = 1, others = 0
b_0 = the predicted mean self-employment rate for the reference category, native whites

Model 1 in Table 4.2 tests this regression model, which includes only the four ethnoracial category variables. This model is significant. The ethnoracial categories explain 42% of the variance in the mean self-employment rates of these five groups.

The ethnoracial identity variables indicate each group's difference from the native white self-employment rate, b_0. Since each categorical variable, D, has either the value 1 or 0, we can substitute the values of

Table 4.2. Regression of Mean Income-Defined Self-Employment Rates on Baseline and Augmented Supply and Demand Models,[1] Five Categories Pooled, in 272 Metropolitan Areas, N = 1,172 (Standardized Coefficients)

	Models		
	1	2	3[2]
Independent variables			
Invariant supply			
Foreign-born white	.217****	.049	.056
Black	−.502****	−.434****	−.347****
Asian	.014	−.054	.045
Hispanic	−.334****	−.214*	−.142
Variant supply			
Mean category percent of labor force		−.065	−.019
Mean percent male		.051*	.329**
Mean years of education		.221****	.233****
Mean years of age		.248****	.198*
Metropolitan Demand			
SMSA mean wage and salary income[3]			−.022
SMSA industrial structure			
%Construction			−.028
%Manufacturing			−.033
%Retail			.149****
%Finance			−.012
%Business services			−.021
%Personal services			.008
%Professional			.023
%Public administration			−.062
Regional economy			
NY, NJ, and PA			.001
East Central			−.004
West Central			−.021
South Atlantic			.070
Mid-South			.050
Central South			.117**
Western Mountains			.050
Pacific			.187****
Interactions			
Metropolitan demand × Invariant supply[4]			
SMSA industrial structure × Variant supply[5]			
%Construction × Mean percent male			.093**
%Manufacturing × Mean years of education			−.109***
%Business × Mean years of education			−.081***
%Professional × Mean years of education			−.107***
Regional economy × variant supply[6]			
NY, NJ, and PA × Mean percent male			−.114**
East Central × Mean percent male			.062
West Central × Mean percent male			−.051

Table 4.2.   (continued)

South Atlantic × Mean percent male			−.126
Mid-South × Mean percent male			−.064
Central South × Mean percent male			−.114*
Western Mountains × Mean percent male			−.053
Pacific × Mean percent male			−.000
NY, NJ, and PA × Mean years of age			.079*
East Central × Mean years of age			.055
West Central × Mean years of age			.005
South Atlantic × Mean years of age			.055
Mid-South × Mean years of age			−.009
Central South × Mean years of age			.064
Western Mountains × Mean years of age			.026
Pacific × Mean years of age			.147****
Adjusted R^2	.4223	.4695[7]	.5625[7]

[1] See Table 4.1 for operational definitions of variables.
[2] Modified version in which only interaction variables with one or more significant coefficients were included in the final model, and the others deleted.
[3] In ten thousands.
[4] All possible metropolitan demand × invariant supply interactions were tested, but since none was significant, they were deleted from the final model.
[5] All possible SMSA industrial structure demand × variant supply interactions were tested, but only those variables with significant effects were retained in the final model as reported in this table.
[6] All possible regional economy demand × variant supply interactions were tested, but only those variables with one or more significant coefficients were included in the final model. These interaction variables are interpreted in terms of how each differs from the same effects for CCATPCTM × NEW ENGLAND or CCATAGE × NEW ENGLAND, the respective reference categories.
[7] The variables in this model, which were added to the preceding model, increase the adjusted R^2 significantly ($p = .01$), using Aiken and West's equation 6.5 (1991:106–107).
**** LE .0001.
*** LE .001.
** LE .01.
* LE .05.

the metric coefficients for this model[20] to obtain the predicted mean of each of the five ethnoracial groups:

NBWs: $Y = b_1(0) + b_2(0) + b_3(0) + b_4(0) + .075 = .075$[21]
FBWs: $Y = .021(1) + b_2(0) + b_3(0) + b_4(0) + .075 = .096$[22]
Blacks: $Y = b_1(0) + (−.50)(1) + b_3(0) + b_4(0) + .075 = .025$[23]
Asians: $Y = b_1(0) + b_2(0) + (.002)(1) + b_4(0) + .075 = .077$
Hispanics: $Y = b_1(0) + b_2(0) + b_3(0) + (−.034)(1) + .075 = .041$[24]

Three of the four ethnoracial groups differ from native whites. On the one hand, the mean self-employment rate of foreign whites is much higher than the mean self-employment rate of native whites (9.6 vs. 7.5%). On the other hand, blacks and Hispanics have much lower mean rates of self-employment than native whites (2.5 and 4.1%, respectively). Only Asians have self-employment rates comparable to that of native whites (7.7%).

When we next add the four general variant supply variables to the four invariant supply variables in Eq.(2),[25] the adjusted R^2 increases to 47%, a slight improvement.[26] Three of the four variant supply variables significantly increase self-employment rates. A category's percentage male, its mean years of education, and its mean age all increased its self-employment. Thus, if the percentage of males in all of the categories increased by 1%, their mean self-employment rate would increase by 2.9%; if their mean years of education increased by 1 year, their mean self-employment rate would increase by 0.7%; and, finally, if their mean years of age increased by 1 year, their mean self-employment rate would increase by 0.3%.[27] We find no significant relationship between the relative size of the category's labor force and the mean self-employment rate for the categories, as Lieberson (1980:379) proposed.[28] Therefore, these data yield no support for Lieberson's compositional hypothesis. As expected, higher percentages of males and older workers increase the self-employment rates of all five ethnoracial categories, as does increased educational level.

In the second model, the constant, b_0, represents the predicted mean self-employment rate of native whites (7.6%), at the mean value of each of the four variant supply variables.[29] Only two of the minority groups retain net predicted means, which differ from native whites: 3.3% for blacks and 5.5% for Hispanics. Foreign-born whites and Asian rates remain almost identical to those of native whites, 8.1 and 7.0%, respectively.

Adding Demand Variables

The third model adds measures of metropolitan demand. We begin by adding 17 general demand variables, 68 demand by invariant supply interaction variables, and 68 demand by variant supply interaction variables to model 2. The main demand effects represent aggregate consumer demand in each metropolitan area, the industrial structure of the metropolitan area, and the regional economy.[30] Deleting 116 nonsignificant demand variables reduced the model to just 45 variables.[31] These demand variables increased the explained variance in the mean self-employment rates of the pooled sample by almost 10%, bringing the adjusted R^2 to 56%.

Three demand variables are significant. First, the percentage of a metropolitan area's labor force engaged in retail trade is the only one of eight measures of industrial structure that *increases* categories' mean self-employment rates. A 1% increase in a metropolitan area's retail trade increases self-employment rate by more than 26%. As expected, metropolitan areas with larger sectors of their labor force in retail trade have significantly higher self-employment rates for all ethnoracial categories. Finally, all groups also have higher mean self-employment rates in the metropolitan areas of two regions. That is, working in a metropolitan area in the Central Southern states increases self-employment rates by 1.5% relative to New England; working in the Pacific states increases self-employment by 2.2%.

Net of demand, three of the four variant supply variables continue to explain the variation in mean self-employment rates of all five ethnoracial groups. As in the preceding model, mean percentage male, mean years of education, and mean years of age remain significant. A 1% increase in percentage male increases the predicted mean self-employment rate of all groups by 18.9%, a 1 year increase in mean education increases their self-employment by 0.7%, and a 1 year increase in local mean category age raises self-employment of all groups by 0.2%. The relative size of the categories, however, again does not affect their self-employment rates.

None of the metropolitan demand by invariant supply interaction variables is significant, indicating that the effects of the 17 demand variables are essentially the same for all five ethnoracial categories. However, there are four significant industrial structure demand by variant supply interaction variables. On the one hand, the self-employment rates of all five groups increased, the higher the percentage male of the group and the percentage of the metropolitan area's labor force engaged in construction. On the other hand, the self-employment rates of all five groups decreased from the interaction of their levels of education and the percentage of their labor force working at jobs in manufacturing, business, or professional industries in each metropolitan area.

We find four significant regional demand by variant supply interactions. On the one hand, increasing the percentage of males of all groups and living in New York, New Jersey, and Pennsylvania or the Central Southern states, significantly decreased their mean self-employment rates relative to those who worked in New England. On the other hand, the mean self-employment rates of all groups increased compared to those in New England, the more work experience they had (i.e., years of age), if they lived in New York, New Jersey, or Pennsylvania or in the Pacific states.

Finally, the addition of the demand measures and the general demand/variant supply interactions has reduced, but not eliminated, the significance of ethnoracial self-identification. Native white ethnic identification yields a baseline net mean self-employment rate of 6.6%. Foreign whites, Asians, and Hispanics do not significantly differ. Their respective rates are 7.2, 7.1, and 5.2%. However, blacks continue to lag native whites with 3.2%.

Thus, in the final model, the metropolitan demand variables add significantly to the explanation of the self-employment rates of all five ethnoracial groups. On the one hand, the unique invariant ethnoracial contributions have been eliminated for all the groups except for African Americans, who continue significantly to lag behind native whites. On the other hand, the demand variables do not erase the contributions that sex ratio, education, and age make to variations in mean self-employment rates. None of the invariant supply by metropolitan demand interaction variables was significant, and only a few of the variant supply by metropolitan demand interaction variables were significant.

Discussion

Reviewing the regression results, especially model 4.3, one observes main effects, in addition to the demand/supply interactions. There are main effects of variant supply, of invariant supply, and of several metropolitan demand variables. Since there are no significant metropolitan demand/invariant supply interaction variables, the main effects of both supply and demand have the same effects for all five ethnoracial categories.

These results are not unusual. They resemble those that Fairlie and Meyer (1993) reported. However, on their face, these results do not support the interaction theory, which proposes that supply and demand interact to generate entrepreneurship. If that theory were valid, the interaction terms ought to be all-powerful and the main effects nonexistent. In our final model, the main effects overpower the interaction effects. Because interactions are less important, one might conclude that the data do not support the interaction theory.

However, when interpreted in light of our theoretical discussion above, these regression results do support the interaction theory. After all, dominant main effects need not mean that supply/demand interactions did not occur. The main effects might mean that the interaction of supply and demand is *statistically invisible* because of the versatility of the underlying resources involved. This interpretation hinges on the distinction between general and specific resources introduced above. On the supply side, general resources translate into a broadly positive (or negative) entrepreneurial versatility. Versatility means the ability to respond with self-employment to many demand environments. Thus construed, the main effects of invariant and variant supply variables represent generalized competencies that straddle demand conditions. For example, the positive main effects of age and education imply that better educated and more experienced groups produced more entrepreneurs *whatever the local demand context*. Similarly, the main effects of ethnic self-identification measure each group's entrepreneurial versatility. When positive, a group's versatility is high, endowing it with the capacity to respond to a wide variety of demand environments. When negative, a group's versatility is low, restricting it to a limited range of demands.

On the demand side, similar ideas pertain. Positive main effects of demand variables translate into economic conditions that generate entrepreneurship because all ethnoracial groups have the general resources needed. Thus, the main effect of %Retail suggests that this structural condition is one to which all ethnoracial groups could respond with expanded entrepreneurship because *all groups possessed the general resources necessary*.[32] The census data cannot identify these general resources, but the ability to count is a plausible example. Everyone can count, so if counting is all a response requires, everyone has the necessary resource. Favorable regional climates also benefit everyone's entrepreneurship because sunshine does not discriminate. General demand effects require general resources universally available in every ethnoracial segment of the labor force.

We find significant interactions between metropolitan demand and variant supply. Significant interactions between variant supply and metropolitan demand occur when demand utilizes variant supply's specific resources rather than general ones. That is, the variant supply variables contain specific and general resources. For example, age contains savings and work experience, general resources, but it also contains physical stamina, a resource of unique importance in longshore, truck driving, and comparable occupations. When regions and occupations require specific resources, they interact with variant supply. The presence of specific resources, which lock onto particular demand conditions, results in statistically significant interaction terms. For example, construction trades interact positively with percentage male (Table 4.2). This result means that percentage male in a group's labor force had a stronger than usual effect upon self-employment in construction. Possibly, men are much more interested than women in construction. Alternatively, it is much more difficult for women entrepreneurs to enter construction trades. Either way, and we cannot distinguish these possibilities, the construction/gender interaction represents unique affinities that are not reducible to human capital or generalized competencies.

MEAN SELF-EMPLOYMENT RANKS

Next, we replicate our analysis of supply and demand variables to see if these models can also explain variations in the mean, intrametropolitan self-employment ranks in 167 metropolitan areas. As in Chapter 3, we point out that 1 = the highest ranking mean self-employment rank and 5 = the lowest rank in each metropolitan area. Therefore, the positive coefficients in Table 4.3 *decrease* rank, while negative coefficients *increase* rank.

In Table 4.3's first model, we find that ethnoracial self-identification explains 62% of the variance![33] Foreign whites have the highest mean rank (1.6), native whites have the second highest average rank (2.3), Asians are just slightly lower than native whites (2.5), followed by Hispanics (3.9) and blacks (4.7). All four minority groups significantly differ from native whites.

Model 2 adds the four variant supply variables to the first model.[34] The additional four variables together significantly ($p \leq .05$) increase the adjusted R^2 to .64. Three variant supply variables improve a category's rank. Increasing the category's percentage males by 1% increases its

Table 4.3. Regression of Mean Income-Defined Intrametropolitan Self-Employment Ranks on Supply and Demand Models,[1] Five Categories Pooled, in 167 Metropolitan Areas,[2] N + 835 (Standardized Coefficients)

	Models		
	1	2	3[3]
Independent variables			
Invariant supply			
Foreign-born white	−.202****	−.048	−.049
Black	.671****	.681****	.647****
Asian	.067*	.154	.144
Hispanic	.446****	.447****	.422****
Variant supply			
Mean category percent of labor force		.101	.091
Mean percent male		−.066**	−.100***
Mean years of education		−.104***	−.128***
Mean years of age		−.139****	−.058
Metropolitan Demand			
SMSA mean wage and salary income[4]			.036
SMSA industrial structure			
%Construction			−.006
%Manufacturing			−.040

Table 4.3. (continued)

%Retail			−.025
%Finance			−.001
%Business services			−.000
%Personal services			−.014
%Professional			.010
%Public administration			−.030
Regional economy			
NY, NJ, and PA			.069
East Central			.036
West Central			.006
South Atlantic			.021
Mid-South			.031
Central South			−.013
Western Mountains			.008
Pacific			.009
Interactions			
Metropolitan demand × Invariant supply[5]			
SMSA industrial structure x Variant supply[6]			
Regional economy × Variant supply[7]			
NY, NJ, and PA × Mean years of age			−.098*
East Central × Mean years of age			−.030
West Central × Mean years of age			−.043
South Atlantic × Mean years of age			−.003
Mid-South × Mean years of age			.064 **
Central South × Mean years of age			−.028
Western Mountains × Mean years of age			−.012
Pacific × Mean years of age			−.090*
Adjusted R^2	.6248	.6417[8]	.6482[9]

[1] See Table 4.1 for operational definitions of variables.
[2] The sample is limited to only those 167 metropolitan areas in which each of the five categories has a minimum of 400 persons in the labor force.
[3] Modified version in which only interaction variables with one or more significant coefficients were included in the final model, and the others deleted.
[4] In ten thousands.
[5] All possible metropolitan demand × invariant supply interactions were tested, but since none was significant, they were deleted from the final model.
[6] All possible SMSA industrial structure demand × variant supply interactions were tested, but since none was significant, they were deleted from the final model.
[7] All possible regional economy demand × variant supply interactions were tested, but only those variables with one or more significant coefficients were included in the final model. These interaction variables are interpreted in terms of how each differs from the same effects for CCATAGE × NEW ENGLAND, the respective reference category.
[8] The variables in this model, which were added to the preceding model, increase the adjusted R^2 significantly ($p = .05$), using Aiken and West's equation 6.5 (1991:106–107).
[9] The variables in this model, which were added to the preceding model, do *not* increase the adjusted R^2 significantly, using Aiken and West's equation 6.5 (1991:106–107)·
**** LE .0001.
*** LE .001.
** LE .01.
* LE .05.

rank by 1.4.[35] If a category's mean years of education increases by 1 year, their rank improves by .11. Finally, if they have 1 more year of work experience (i.e., are 1 year older), their mean self-employment ranks rise by .06. However, the relative size of an ethnoracial category in a metropolitan area's labor force is of no consequence for its self-employment rank.

The initial relative ranks of the five categories (the invariant supply variables) change somewhat when compared to the first model. That is, with the addition of the variant supply variables, the net mean rank of foreign whites becomes essentially equal to native whites (2.0 vs. 2.1). Asians continue to have about the same rank as native whites (2.7 vs. 2.1). However, the mean ranks of blacks and Hispanics remain significantly below the mean rank of native whites (4.5 and 3.7, respectively).

Adding Demand Variables

In the third model, we replicate model 3 of Table 4.2, first testing the addition of 17 demand variables, all 68 metropolitan demand by invariant supply interaction variables, and all 68 metropolitan demand by variant supply interaction variables.[36] We then modify the model by retaining only the demand interaction variables that are significant.[37] The less than 1% increase in adjusted R^2 from these additional 25 variables was not significant. As might be expected, *none* of the 17 general demand variables is significant. Additionally, *none* of the metropolitan demand by invariant supply interaction variables is significant, nor are any of the metropolitan industrial structure demand by variant supply interaction variables. Only the interaction of three regions with mean years of age was significant. That is, compared to New England, the mean self-employment ranks of all groups working in New York, New Jersey, and Pennsylvania, and the Pacific states increase with their mean age. However, an increased mean age became a liability to self-employment ranks for all groups working in the Mid-South. The effects of mean age upon the self-employment ranks of all groups in the other five regions did not differ from those found in New England.

These added demand variables, nonetheless, modified the effects of one of the variant supply variables, mean years of age. It no longer affects the rank of any of the five groups. However, education and sex ratio do continue to increase the mean self-employment ranks of all five groups. A 1% increase in the mean percentage males of a group improves its self-employment rank by 2.06. Education has a significant, but modest, effect of increasing a group's rank by .14. Finally, the relative size of a group continues to be nonsignificant.

The effects of the four invariant supply variables remain the same as in the preceding model. From adding these demand and demand interaction variables to the model, foreign whites and Asians continue to have the same initial rank as native whites (1.9 and 2.6, respectively, compared to 2.1). However, the other two groups continue to differ significantly from native whites (blacks 4.4 and Hispanics 3.6).

Discussion

These models explain more variation in rank than in mean self-employment rates. However, the models for rank are less able to explain away the differences in mean ranks of Hispanics compared to native whites. Mean percentage male and mean years of education increase all five groups' self-employment, but relative size and mean age have no significant effects. Demand only has a few feeble interaction effects— between three regions and mean years of age.

The effect of demand upon entrepreneurial performance depends importantly upon whether we measure that performance in self-employment rates or ranks. Demand variables consistently produce a stronger explanation of rate than of rank. This discrepancy does not arise because rank is harder to explain than rate. On the contrary, Table 4.3's augmented model explained rank better than Table 4.2's explained rate. At least some of demand's effect was general. General demand effects raised and lowered ethnoracial categories in tandem, changing their absolute self-employment but leaving their rank order unaffected. Naturally, to the extent that absolute self-employment level is at issue, analysis must take account of the general demand effects. However, when relative entrepreneurial performance is at issue, we find demand's effects are less influential. In effect, resources theory provides a somewhat better explanation of relative performance than it does of absolute performance.

SUMMARY

Although popular and intuitively satisfactory, the interaction theory of entrepreneurship does not sit on a body of evidence wide enough to raise the issues our research design has posed. As one result, the interaction theory has not confronted the distinction between general and specific resources. The interaction theory claims that the interaction of supply and demand links specific competencies and specific demands. That relationship exists, but our theoretical analysis shows that general demand effects and general supply effects exist too, especially the latter. General demand and general supply effects are inexplicable so long as the interaction theory defines the interaction of supply and demand narrowly as the linkage between specific competencies and specific industrial demands.

Statistically interpreted, this theoretical dilemma turns into the problem of how to deal with powerful main effects of demand and supply. The interaction theory predicts that no main effects of demand or supply can occur. If main effects of supply and demand were nil, interactions would explain everything, thus completely vindicating the interaction theory. Conversely, if we find only main effects, and no interactions, then the interaction theory would be wrong. Our data fall between these extremes. However, in our data, the main effects are more powerful than the interaction effects. Since these main effects overpower interactions, a major part of our explanation does not display the requisite interaction, challenging the interaction theory. This situation tempts us to ask whether supply or demand "explains more" of the variation in self-employment. However, since, according to the interaction theory, supply and demand must each explain half the variation, such an imbalance is theoretically uninterpretable. If the entrepreneur population arises from interaction of supply and demand, supply cannot explain more than demand, nor vice versa.

The interaction theory can be salvaged if we distinguish specific and general resources in addition to the existing distinction between ethnic and class resources (Light, 1984). General and specific resources may be class resources, ethnic resources, or both. The examples that best illustrate the interaction theory stress specific resources (e.g., the ability to cook Chinese food), but many overlooked resources are general. Versatile resources enable groups to thrive everywhere, entering whatever industries offer the best local opportunity. As a result, the interaction of resources and environment remains statistically invisible. Similarly, some demand environments require such a low level of resources that all ethnoracial groups always possess them. When this situation exists, general demand effects appear in the regression equations, leaving the puzzling impression that this time, at least, demand did not interact with supply. In actuality, the requisite interaction did occur; however, it was statistically invisible because all groups possessed the resources necessary to hook this demand.

This distinction between general and specific resources is a new one capable of cross-classification with the existing distinction between class and ethnic resources. In our data, education and work experience, both class resources, are general resources too. This result is surprising since lawyers cannot be physicians, or vice versa, yet both are highly educated. However, since our measures are aggregated, these results need not mean that education's effects are invariably general. Similarly, the results need not imply that work experience in a specific trade prepares one for entrepreneurship in general, rather than for entrepreneurship in that trade in which one obtained one's experience. Rather, one concludes that a *group's* high level of education and of work experience are generalized resources that confer upon the *group* a versatile competence in entrepreneurship (Friedland and Little, 1981:334). Individual-level research will be necessary to ascertain the extent to which individual education and experience fit a person for entrepreneurship in a narrow range of trades rather than generally.

The main effects of ethnic identity are particularly interesting. They indicate a generalized resource of the whole group, independent of age, gender composition, or education. When positive, they represent versatility that connects with a broad spectrum of demand environments. When negative, they represent a truncated versatility capable only of connection with a narrow range of demands. Although based on residual measurement, the strong and robust main effects of ethnic identity support the literature's claim that ethnoracial groups have different endowments of social capital, network multiplexity, action orientations, and the like. The principal argument against this position has held that apparent intergroup differences in entrepreneurship are spurious products of unequal human capital endowment (Bates, 1994b). Portes and Zhou (1992) already showed that human capital did not explain away the superior entrepreneurship of four national origin groups (Chinese, Japanese, Koreans, Cubans), and our analysis extends their demonstration for much larger ethnoracial categories among 72 million Americans. True, four of these broad categories are purely nominative. Asians, Hispanics, native-born whites, and foreign-born whites are agglomerations of internally heterogeneous ethnic stocks. If the internal proportions of each category were changed (more high-entrepreneurship and fewer low-entrepreneurship subgroups, or vice versa) the aggregate's performance would change too. Therefore, the concrete meaning of the ethnic identity coefficient is fuzzy even if its general meaning is clear.

But the same objection does not apply to African Americans. Because the number of foreign-born blacks was so modest in 1980, our intermetropolitan data really measure the entrepreneurship of African Americans, a homogeneous and historic ethnic group. Blacks are not a nominal category like the others. The negative main effect of black ethnic identity upon entrepreneurship implies a generalized shortfall of entrepreneurial resources in any and all economic environments. This negative effect is reduced by controls for human capital and percentage male but it is not eliminated. Net of human capital, age, and percentage male, African-American entrepreneurship is still lower than it should be relative to native whites.

Entrepreneurs and Society

Entrepreneurship is an obvious and significant juncture at which society affects economic development and growth. A society's or a group's entrepreneurship is suboptimal when economies do not fully exploit all the opportunities an environment affords. In such cases, opportunities are missed altogether, delayed, or lost to external competitors. For example, when Americans did not develop the solar-powered calculator fast enough, the Japanese seized the opportunity. American entrepreneurship was suboptimal in this case. Here as elsewhere, lost opportunities became economic growth that was slower than it would have been had entrepreneurship been stronger.

If markets generated the entrepreneurs they need by price signals, then shortages of entrepreneurs would rarely or never occur, and real economic growth would rarely or never fall short of the potential immanent in demand. Such a healthy situation could plausibly exist if the supply of entrepreneurs depended only upon the prior supply of investment capital. In that case, markets would unerringly allocate society's limited human and financial capital to entrepreneurship in exactly the right proportion to maximize growth. Odd bed-fellows, Marxists and neoclassical economists once agreed on just this orthodoxy.

However, with all its comforting intellectual consistency, that orthodoxy has collapsed, leaving a puzzle. We now know that markets alone do not guarantee optimal entrepreneurship. This is the point at which immigration makes a theoretical, as well as practical contribution to our understanding (Portes and Sensenbrenner, 1993). Except for immigration, societies would ultimately consist of labor forces whose members are culturally homogeneous. Homogeneity would inhibit attention to internal characteristics of groups that support entrepreneurship. However, immigration creates and recreates a pluralistic society whose labor force consists of initially diverse groups, still unequally assimilated and acculturated. In economic terms, cultural diversity means a mosaic of groups that differ with respect to socially oriented action patterns, embeddedness, social networks, social capital, ethnic resources, and so forth. A now quite impressive array of case studies has documented the contributions that these ethnocultural differences make to entrepreneurship. Studies find that ethnic resources (families, rotating credit associations, enforceable trust, multiplex social networks, ideologies, religion, etc.) encourage and support the founding of new business firms, especially by people short of money and education.

Additionally, quantitative analyses of census data, like ours, now find that money and human capital do not explain intergroup differences in entrepreneurial responsiveness. Therefore, one turns to group characteristics for explanation of persistent intergroup differences in entrepreneurial responsiveness. Some of these differences are cultural; others are not. However, we must avoid the imputation that all intergroup differences in entrepreneurship are cultural in origin. After all, policy differences between Republican administrations and Democratic administrations affect entrepreneurship too, but the differences are not cultural in origin. Unfortunately, Republicans and Democrats are both part of American culture! Similarly, some intergroup differences arise because ethnic leadership has selected one route for policy priority rather than another. Ever since the Niagara Conference of 1905, at which the followers of W. E. B. DuBois (1966) routed the followers of Booker T. Washington, African-American leadership in the mainstream has stressed education and job opportunity over entrepreneurship. That was a policy choice, not a cultural heritage, but that historic choice arguably contributed to the underrepresentation of African Americans in self-employment that our data record.[38] Intergroup differences in entrepreneurship that arise from policy choices are more amenable to change than differences that arise from cultural features.

NOTES

1. Partially for gain, yes, but not for sale. Humans are produced for gain when mom and pop decide to have children to obtain extra help on the farm. This utilitarian objective does not evade the unmistakable contribution of nature to their ability to reproduce so the motive is only partially gain. Moreover, the farm hands thus produced are produced for use, not for sale. Therefore, they cannot be commodities.

2. In the same sense, the same person does not exist since every person changes slightly from minute to minute. Therefore, strictly speaking, Jones at 21 years of age and Jones at 22 are not the same person.

3. Change-resistant does not mean changeless. In the course of two centuries, transplanted Englishmen in the colonies became Americans, a culturally distinct group.

4. We realize that we are, in reality, dealing with more and less variant dimensions since, as Heraclitus long ago knew, nothing remains unchanged.

However, for simplicity's sake, and in the interest of a sociological rather than a philosophical discussion, we will call the less variant dimension invariant. Alternatively, variant and invariant resources can be thought of as distinguishing between measured and unmeasured variables, in that the invariant resources are category identities, which stand for unmeasured characteristics of different ethnoracial groups.

5.   A second specific supply effect arises from the interaction of variant and invariant supply characteristics. If we find, for example, that a preponderance of males in the labor force increases the entrepreneurship of Hispanics, but exerts no effect upon the entrepreneurship of other groups, we might interpret the result as a product of unique gender roles that proscribe entrepreneurship to Hispanic women. Such a result would be wholly the product of supply features, owing nothing to demand conditions.

6.   Net of demand, and other supply features being equal, Chicago ought to produce more entrepreneurs than Biloxi as a result of its educational superiority. That difference would represent a general supply effect to the extent that it held true for all ethnoracial groups.

7.   For the maximum number of metropolitan areas that have threshold numbers of each category, i.e., NBW = 272 areas, FBW = 245, blacks = 245, Asians = 180, and Hispanics = 230, for a total of 1,172 cases.

8.   These are metropolitan areas that have all five ethnoracial groups: NW = native whites, FW = foreign whites, B = black, A = Asians, and H = Hispanics.

9.   See Aiken and West (1991:116–117, 129–130).

10.   Three of these variables were tested in the models in Chapter 2.

11.   See Aiken and West (1991).

12.   That is, the means for the sample size of 1,172.

13.   This variable is identical to CCATPCTM2 in Chapter 2, which was centered on the mean for the pooled sample.

14.   In Chapter 3, we tested the effects of CCATSIZE, the absolute size of a category, as a measure of category demand. Whereas in Chapter 3, the demand aspects of CCATSIZE were emphasized, in this chapter we consider its labor supply potential, testing Lieberson's (1980:379) hypothesis about the effects of the relative size of a group with the variable CPCTCAT. However, we cannot distinguish in our data whether CPCTCAT provides only labor supply or demand or both.

15.   This variable is identical to CCATED2 in Chapter 2, which was centered on the mean for the pooled sample.

16.   This variable is identical to CCATAGE2 in Chapter 2, which was centered on the mean for the pooled sample.

17.   These variables are identical to those tested in Chapter 3.

18.   The reference category deleted from the model was composed of four industries: mining, transportation, wholesale, and entertainment and recreation services.

19.   See Aiken and West (1991:123–125).

20.   Metric coefficients for model 4.1 are not reported in Table 4.2.

21. Predicted mean self-employment rates were calculated for each of the four minority ethnoracial groups. For example, the intercept, or constant, b_0, represents the predicted mean of native whites (7.5%). To obtain the rate for foreign whites, we add their metric coefficient to the intercept, i.e., $7.5 + 1.1 = 9.6\%$.

22. The predicted mean differs only slightly from the actual mean, .097, due to rounding error.

23. The predicted mean differs only slightly from the actual mean, .026, due to rounding error.

24. The predicted mean differs only slightly from the actual mean, .042, due to rounding error.

25. Model 4.2, the regression of mean self-employment rates on four invariant supply category dummy variables and four variant supply continuous variables is

$$Y = \text{Eq. (4.1)} + b_5\text{CPCTCAT} + b_6\text{CCATPCTM} + b_7\text{CCATED} + b_8\text{CCATAGE} + b_0 \tag{4.2}$$

The added four invariant supply variables together were significant at the .01 level.

26. We used Aiken and West's equation 6.5 to test the significance of R^2 change (1991:106–107):

$$F = \frac{(R^2{}_{\text{in}} - R^2{}_{\text{out}})/m}{(1 - R^2{}_{\text{in}})/(n - k - 1)}, \quad df = m, (n - k - 1)$$

27. Changes in the dependent variables predicted by independent variables presented here in the text in metric coefficients are not reported in Table 4.2.

28. "When the migration of a group accelerates, the ability to develop and exploit these special niches is badly handicapped. Such specialties can only absorb a small part of a group's total work force when its population grows rapidly or is a substantial proportion of the total population" (Lieberson, 1980:379).

29. See Aiken and West (1991:119–123, 138:n3) for the advantages of interpreting the constant and dummy variables when the continuous variables have been centered.

30. Original model 4.3, the regression of mean self-employment rates on four invariant supply category dummy variables, four variant supply continuous variables, 17 demand by invariant supply interaction variables, and 17 demand by variant supply interaction variables is

$$\begin{aligned}
Y = \text{Eq. (4.2)} &+ b_9(\text{CSMSAI1}) + b_{10}(\text{CCONIND}) + b_{11}(\text{CMANUIND}) \\
&+ b_{12}(\text{CRETIND}) + b_{13}(\text{CFININD}) + b_{14}(\text{CBUSRIND}) \\
&+ b_{15}(\text{CPERSIND}) + b_{16}(\text{CPROFIND}) + b_{17}(\text{CPUBIND}) \\
&+ b_{18}(\text{NYNJPA}) + b_{19}(\text{ECENTRAL}) + b_{20}(\text{WCENTRAL}) \\
&+ b_{21}(\text{SATLANTC}) + b_{22}(\text{MIDSOUTH}) + b_{23}(\text{CENTRLSO}) \\
&+ b_{24}(\text{WESTMTNS}) + b_{25}(\text{PACIFIC}) + b_{26}(\text{CSMSAI1} \times \text{FBW}) \\
&+ b_{27}(\text{CSMSAI1} \times \text{Black}) + b_{28}(\text{CSMSAI1} \times \text{Asian}) \\
&+ b_{29}(\text{CSMSAI1} \times \text{Hispanic}) + b_{30}(\text{CCONIND} \times \text{FBW})
\end{aligned}$$

$+ b_{31}(\text{CCONIND} \times \text{Black}) + b_{32}(\text{CCONIND} \times \text{Asian})$
$+ b_{33}(\text{CCONIND} \times \text{Hispanic}) + b_{34}(\text{CMANUIND} \times \text{FBW})$
$+ b_{35}(\text{CMANUIND} \times \text{Black}) + b_{36}(\text{CMANUIND} \times \text{Asian})$
$+ b_{37}(\text{CMANUIND} \times \text{Hispanic}) + b_{38}(\text{CRETIND} \times \text{FBW})$
$+ b_{39}(\text{CRETIND} \times \text{Black}) + b_{40}(\text{CRETIND} \times \text{Asian})$
$+ b_{41}(\text{CRETIND} \times \text{Hispanic}) + b_{42}(\text{CFININD} \times \text{FBW})$
$+ b_{43}(\text{CFININD} \times \text{Black}) + b_{44}(\text{CFININD} \times \text{Asian})$
$+ b_{45}(\text{CFININD} \times \text{Hispanic}) + b_{46}(\text{CBUSRIND} \times \text{FBW})$
$+ b_{47}(\text{CBUSRIND} \times \text{Black}) + b_{48}(\text{CBUSRIND} \times \text{Asian})$
$+ b_{49}(\text{CBUSRIND} \times \text{Hispanic}) + b_{50}(\text{CPERSIND} \times \text{FBW})$
$+ b_{51}(\text{CPERSIND} \times \text{Black}) + b_{52}(\text{CPERSIND} \times \text{Asian})$
$+ b_{53}(\text{CPERSIND} \times \text{Hispanic}) + b_{54}(\text{CPROFIND} \times \text{FBW})$
$+ b_{55}(\text{CPROFIND} \times \text{Black}) + b_{56}(\text{CPROFIND} \times \text{Asian})$
$+ b_{57}(\text{CPROFIND} \times \text{Hispanic}) + b_{58}(\text{CPUBIND} \times \text{FBW})$
$+ b_{59}(\text{CPUBIND} \times \text{Black}) + b_{60}(\text{CPUBIND} \times \text{Asian})$
$+ b_{61}(\text{CPUBIND} \times \text{Hispanic}) + b_{62}(\text{NYNJPA} \times \text{FBW})$
$+ b_{63}(\text{NYNJPA} \times \text{Black}) + b_{64}(\text{NYNJPA} \times \text{Asian})$
$+ b_{65}(\text{NYNJPA} \times \text{Hispanic}) + b_{66}(\text{ECENTRAL} \times \text{FBW})$
$+ b_{67}(\text{ECENTRAL} \times \text{Black}) + b_{68}(\text{ECENTRAL} \times \text{Asian})$
$+ b_{69}(\text{ECENTRAL} \times \text{Hispanic}) + b_{70}(\text{WCENTRAL} \times \text{FBW})$
$+ b_{71}(\text{WCENTRAL} \times \text{Black}) + b_{72}(\text{WCENTRAL} \times \text{Asian})$
$+ b_{73}(\text{WCENTRAL} \times \text{Hispanic}) + b_{74}(\text{SATLANTC} \times \text{FBW})$
$+ b_{75}(\text{SATLANTC} \times \text{Black}) + b_{76}(\text{SATLANTC} \times \text{Asian})$
$+ b_{77}(\text{SATLANTC} \times \text{Hispanic}) + b_{78}(\text{MIDSOUTH} \times \text{FBW})$
$+ b_{79}(\text{MIDSOUTH} \times \text{Black}) + b_{80}(\text{MIDSOUTH} \times \text{Asian})$
$+ b_{81}(\text{MIDSOUTH} \times \text{Hispanic}) + b_{82}(\text{CENTRLSO} \times \text{FBW})$
$+ b_{83}(\text{CENTRLSO} \times \text{Black}) + b_{84}(\text{CENTRLSO} \times \text{Asian})$
$+ b_{85}(\text{CENTRLSO} \times \text{Hispanic}) + b_{86}(\text{WESTMTNS} \times \text{FBW})$
$+ b_{87}(\text{WESTMTNS} \times \text{Black}) + b_{88}(\text{WESTMTNS} \times \text{Asian})$
$+ b_{89}(\text{WESTMTNS} \times \text{Hispanic}) + b_{90}(\text{PACIFIC} \times \text{FBW})$
$+ b_{91}(\text{PACIFIC} \times \text{Black}) + b_{92}(\text{PACIFIC} \times \text{Asian})$
$+ b_{93}(\text{PACIFIC} \times \text{Hispanic}) + b_{94}(\text{CSMSAI1} \times \text{CPCTCAT})$
$+ b_{95}(\text{CSMSAI1} \times \text{CCATPCTM}) + b_{96}(\text{CSMSAI1} \times \text{CCATED})$
$+ b_{97}(\text{CSMSAI1} \times \text{CCATAGE}) + b_{98}(\text{CCONIND} \times \text{CPCTCAT})$
$+ b_{99}(\text{CCONIND} \times \text{CCATPCTM}) + b_{100}(\text{CCONIND} \times \text{CCATED})$
$+ b_{101}(\text{CCONIND} \times \text{CCATAGE}) + b_{102}(\text{CMANUIND} \times \text{CPCTCAT})$
$+ b_{103}(\text{CMANUIND} \times \text{CCATPCTM}) + b_{104}(\text{CMANUIND} \times \text{CCATED})$
$+ b_{105}(\text{CMANUIND} \times \text{CCATAGE}) + b_{106}(\text{CRETIND} \times \text{CPCTCAT})$
$+ b_{107}(\text{CRETIND} \times \text{CCATPCTM}) + b_{108}(\text{CRETIND} \times \text{CCATED})$
$+ b_{109}(\text{CRETIND} \times \text{CCATAGE}) + b_{110}(\text{CFININD} \times \text{CPCTCAT})$
$+ b_{111}(\text{CFININD} \times \text{CCATPCTM}) + b_{112}(\text{CFININD} \times \text{CCATED})$
$+ b_{113}(\text{CFININD} \times \text{CCATAGE}) + b_{114}(\text{CBUSRIND} \times \text{CPCTCAT})$
$+ b_{115}(\text{CBUSRIND} \times \text{CCATPCTM}) + b_{116}(\text{CBUSRIND} \times \text{CCATED})$
$+ b_{117}(\text{CBUSRIND} \times \text{CCATAGE}) + b_{118}(\text{CPERSIND} \times \text{CPCTCAT})$
$+ b_{119}(\text{CPERSIND} \times \text{CCATPCTM}) + b_{120}(\text{CPERSIND} \times \text{CCATED})$
$+ b_{121}(\text{CPERSIND} \times \text{CCATAGE}) + b_{122}(\text{CPROFIND} \times \text{CPCTCAT})$

$+ b_{123}(\text{CPROFIND} \times \text{CCATPCTM}) + b_{124}(\text{CPROFIND} \times \text{CCATED})$
$+ b_{125}(\text{CPROFIND} \times \text{CCATAGE}) + b_{126}(\text{CPUBIND} \times \text{CPCTCAT})$
$+ b_{127}(\text{CPUBIND} \times \text{CCATPCTM}) + b_{128}(\text{CPUBIND} \times \text{CCATED})$
$+ b_{129}(\text{CPUBIND} \times \text{CCATAGE}) + b_{130}(\text{NYNJPA} \times \text{CPCTCAT})$
$+ b_{131}(\text{NYNJPA} \times \text{CCATPCTM}) + b_{132}(\text{NYNJPA} \times \text{CCATED})$
$+ b_{133}(\text{NYNJPA} \times \text{CCATAGE}) + b_{134}(\text{ECENTRAL} \times \text{CPCTCAT})$
$+ b_{135}(\text{ECENTRAL} \times \text{CCATPCTM}) + b_{136}(\text{ECENTRAL} \times \text{CCATED})$
$+ b_{137}(\text{ECENTRAL} \times \text{CCATAGE}) + b_{138}(\text{WCENTRAL} \times \text{CPCTCAT})$
$+ b_{139}(\text{WCENTRAL} \times \text{CCATPCTM}) + b_{140}(\text{WCENTRAL} \times \text{CCATED})$
$+ b_{141}(\text{WCENTRAL} \times \text{CCATAGE}) + b_{142}(\text{SATLANTC} \times \text{CPCTCAT})$
$+ b_{143}(\text{SATLANTC} \times \text{CCATPCTM}) + b_{144}(\text{SATLANTC} \times \text{CCATED})$
$+ b_{145}(\text{SATLANTC} \times \text{CCATAGE}) + b_{146}(\text{MIDSOUTH} \times \text{CPCTCAT})$
$+ b_{147}(\text{MIDSOUTH} \times \text{CCATPCTM}) + b_{148}(\text{MIDSOUTH} \times \text{CCATED})$
$+ b_{149}(\text{MIDSOUTH} \times \text{CCATAGE}) + b_{150}(\text{CENTRLSO} \times \text{CPCTCAT})$
$+ b_{151}(\text{CENTRLSO} \times \text{CCATPCTM}) + b_{152}(\text{CENTRLSO} \times \text{CCATED})$
$+ b_{153}(\text{CENTRLSO} \times \text{CCATAGE}) + b_{154}(\text{WESTMTNS} \times \text{CPCTCAT})$
$+ b_{155}(\text{WESTMTNS} \times \text{CCATPCTM}) + b_{156}(\text{WESTMTNS} \times \text{CCATED})$
$+ b_{157}(\text{WESTMTNS} \times \text{CCATAGE}) + b_{158}(\text{PACIFIC} \times \text{CPCTCAT})$
$+ b_{159}(\text{PACIFIC} \times \text{CCATPCTM}) + b_{160}(\text{PACIFIC} \times \text{CCATED})$
$+ b_{161}(\text{PACIFIC} \times \text{CCATAGE}) + b_0$ (Original 4.3)

31. Modified model 4.3, the regression of MSER on four invariant supply category dummy variables, four variant supply continuous variables, zero demand by invariant supply interaction variables, and 20 demand × variant supply interaction variables is

$Y = \text{Eq. (4.2)} + b_9(\text{CSMSAI1}) + b_{10}(\text{CCONIND}) + b_{11}(\text{CMANUIND})$
$+ b_{12}(\text{CRETIND}) + b_{13}(\text{CFININD}) + b_{14}(\text{CBUSRIND})$
$+ b_{15}(\text{CPERSIND}) + b_{16}(\text{CPROFIND}) + b_{17}(\text{CPUBIND})$
$+ b_{18}(\text{NYNJPA}) + b_{19}(\text{ECENTRAL}) + b_{20}(\text{WCENTRAL})$
$+ b_{21}(\text{SATLANTC}) + b_{22}(\text{MIDSOUTH}) + b_{23}(\text{CENTRLSO})$
$+ b_{24}(\text{WESTMTNS}) + b_{25}(\text{PACIFIC})$
$+ b_{99}(\text{CCONIND} \times \text{CCATPCTM}) + b_{104}(\text{CMANUIND} \times \text{CCATED})$
$+ b_{116}(\text{CBUSRIND} \times \text{CCATED}) + b_{131}(\text{NYNJPA} \times \text{CCATPCTM})$
$+ b_{133}(\text{NYNJPA} \times \text{CCATAGE}) + b_{135}(\text{ECENTRAL} \times \text{CCATPCTM})$
$+ b_{137}(\text{ECENTRAL} \times \text{CCATAGE}) + b_{139}(\text{WCENTRAL} \times \text{CCATPCTM})$
$+ b_{141}(\text{WCENTRAL} \times \text{CCATAGE}) + b_{143}(\text{SATLANTC} \times \text{CCATPCTM})$
$+ b_{145}(\text{SATLANTC} \times \text{CCATAGE}) + b_{147}(\text{MIDSOUTH} \times \text{CCATPCTM})$
$+ b_{149}(\text{MIDSOUTH} \times \text{CCATAGE}) + b_{151}(\text{CENTRLSO} \times \text{CCATPCTM})$

$+ b_{153}(\text{CENTRLSO} \times \text{CCATAGE}) + b_{155}(\text{WESTMTNS} \times$
$\text{CCATPCTM})$
$+ b_{157}(\text{WESTMTNS} \times \text{CCATAGE}) + b_{159}(\text{PACIFIC} \times \text{CCATPCTM})$
$+ b_{161}(\text{PACIFIC} \times \text{CCATAGE}) + b_0$ (Modified 4.3)

These 37 added demand and demand interaction variables together were significant at the .01 level.

32. Similarly all groups may also react negatively, e.g., avoiding self-employment when opportunities for government employment exist. (However, this variable was not significant.)

33. This model has the same independent variables as Eq. (4.1) in Table 4.2.

34. The model has the same independent variables as Eq. (4.2) in Table 4.2.

35. The metric effects noted in the text are not presented in Table 4.3.

36. See note 30 for the original model 4.3.

37. Modified model 4.3 for mean self-employment ranks is

$Y = \text{Eq. (4.2)} + b_9(\text{CSMSAI1}) + b_{10}(\text{CCONIND}) + b_{11}(\text{CMANUIND})$
$+ b_{12}(\text{CRETIND}) + b_{13}(\text{CFININD}) + b_{14}(\text{CBUSRIND})$
$+ b_{15}(\text{CPERSIND}) + b_{16}(\text{CPROFIND}) + b_{17}(\text{CPUBIND})$
$+ b_{18}(\text{NYNJPA}) + b_{19}(\text{ECENTRAL}) + b_{20}(\text{WCENTRAL})$
$+ b_{21}(\text{SATLANTC}) + b_{22}(\text{MIDSOUTH}) + b_{23}(\text{CENTRLSO})$
$+ b_{24}(\text{WESTMTNS}) + b_{25}(\text{PACIFIC})$
$+ b_{133}(\text{NYNJPA} \times \text{CCATAGE}) + b_{137}(\text{ECENTRAL} \times \text{CCATAGE})$
$+ b_{141}(\text{WCENTRAL} \times \text{CCATAGE}) + b_{145}(\text{SATLANTC} \times$
$\text{CCATAGE})$
$+ b_{149}(\text{MIDSOUTH} \times \text{CCATAGE}) + b_{153}(\text{CENTRLSO} \times \text{CCATAGE})$
$+ b_{157}(\text{WESTMTNS} \times \text{CCATAGE}) + b_{161}(\text{PACIFIC} \times \text{CCATAGE})$
$+ b_0$ (Modified 4.3)

38. On policy disputes with African-American leadership, see Conti and Stetson (1993: Ch. 1).

5

Labor Market Disadvantage

Disadvantage is the oldest explanation of superior entrepreneurship. This idea has played a serious role in the history of sociology. Weber maintained that the religious ethic of sectarian Protestants encouraged the universalistic business behavior characteristic of true bourgeois capitalism. But even Weber (1958:37–39) acknowledged that Protestant sectarians also selected entrepreneurship because tests of religious conformity excluded them from the civil service and the armed forces. This exclusion amounted to a labor force disadvantage arising from religious discrimination. Subjected to religious discrimination, Protestant sectarians turned to entrepreneurship. Therefore, Weber thought that labor force disadvantage supplemented the religious affinity of sectarian Protestantism in the production of entrepreneurs.

Disputing Weber in a historic debate, Werner Sombart returned to the problem of capitalism's origin, attributing it to Jews, not Protestants (Parsons, 1928). Sombart (1951) described the rationalism of the Jews as a cultural resource that had fitted them for entrepreneurship and stressed this cultural resource. However, Sombart (1951:300–301) also mentioned the Jews' exclusion from medieval trade guilds, membership in which was open only to Christians. In consequence of this disadvantage, Jews were compelled to start their own firms and to operate them competitively, thereby creating capitalism. Thus, like Weber, Sombart split his explanation of entrepreneurship into a component of religious affinity and a component of labor force disadvantage born of religious discrimination. Both Weber and Sombart stressed the contribution of religious affinity to entrepreneurship, but both also mentioned the contribution of labor force disadvantage.

In the recent revival of interest in immigrant and ethnic entrepreneurship that classic formula (affinities + disadvantage) at first persisted. Cultural influences initially received the most emphasis, but labor market disadvantage received secondary recognition. Light (1972:43–44) stressed the "cultural repertoires" that influenced minority entrepreneurship in the United States before World War II. But he also declared (1972:8) prewar Chinese business firms "monuments to the discrimination that had created them." In a later publication, that represented an important maturation of this literature, Light (1979) formally distinguished disadvantage explanations from cultural ones, and pointed out the inadequacy of purely cultural explanations.

In the 1980s, cultural explanations went out of fashion in social science. Research stressed labor market disadvantage to the point that this idea dominated the discourse, sometimes to the exclusion of affinities. This position revised classic theory. Unlike Weber and Sombart, both of whom understood that disadvantage explanations complemented affinities explanations, the main explanation, many contemporary writers treated disadvantage as a way of not having to examine affinities at all. Indeed, Jones, McEvoy, and Barrett (1994:190) declare it a "form of racist discrimination" even to discuss ethnocultural affinities in entrepreneurship when discrimination, a labor force disadvantage, also compels people to chance entrepreneurship. Other writers, less extreme, simply ignore affinities, advancing disadvantage as the whole explanation for high entrepreneurship. Discussing entrepreneurial Pakistanis and East Indians in Britain, Aldrich, Cater, Jones, and McEvoy (1983:8) declared that "because of natives whites' prejudice and hostility" Asians in Britain must "seek employment below their skill level or else create their own employment opportunity by forming a small business." Ladbury (1984:105) finds that Turkish Cypriots in London opened small businesses because "that was all they could get." Min (1984:343) found that 90% of Korean entrepreneurs mentioned disadvantage as a major reason for their self-employment, and he assigned first importance to this cause. In Min's (1984:335) opinion, "disadvantage in the American job market" was a principal cause of Korean entrepreneurship in Atlanta. Similarly, Lubin's (1985: Ch. 7) comparative study of Soviet immigrants in the United States and Israel also stressed disadvantage, not cultural repertoires. In her opinion (p. 157), the chief motivation for entrepreneurship among the immigrants arose from "lack of other employment options."

Phizacklea (1988: Ch. 2) declared entrepreneurship an "escape route" for minority men confined to "dead-end manual jobs by racism and racial discrimination." Except for racism, these men would have obtained better jobs for which they were objectively qualified. Therefore, Phizacklea (1988:21) viewed their entrepreneurship "as a form of disguised unemployment." Blaschke and Ersoz (1986b) also turned to disadvantage in their account of Turkish entrepreneurship in West Berlin, concluding that "unemployment or the threat of unemployment" was the principal source of Turkish entrepreneurship. "Other than hard-to-come-by dependent employment, Turkish nationals are only left with one option for economic survival—that is, starting self-employed businesses."

The business cycle also offers indirect support for disadvantage theory. The business cycle literature has commonly reported a countercyclical relationship between aggregate unemployment and self-employment such that self-employment rises in periods of increased unemployment and declines with the return of full employment (Bregger, 1963; Light, 1983:367). One can also count upon the press to make this point whenever unemployment increases (McMillan, 1982; Mitchell, 1990). True, Becker (1984) found the evidence mixed in his review of existing literature. However, his own time series statistical data, 1948–1982, did support the countercyclical hypothesis in the nonagricultural sector. Also utilizing time series data, Steinmetz and Wright (1989) found no relationship between unemployment and self-employment until the unemployment rate was interacted with a time variable. When interacted, both the unemployment rate and the interaction term became significant predictors of self-employment rates.

THEORIES OF DISADVANTAGE

Summarizing this one-dimensional, contemporary view, we dub it the simple disadvantage hypothesis. The *simple disadvantage hypothesis* expects disadvantage in the labor market to encourage self-employment independent of the resources of those disadvantaged (see Aurand, 1983). Jettisoning the classic formula for entrepreneurship (resources + affinities), simple disadvantage became the baseline from which modern research proceeded. However, as simple disadvantage arguments proliferated, those offering them began to propose variations on the simple disadvantage hypothesis, a sign of theoretical maturation that actually returned research to the classic formula.

Confronting the evidence, simple disadvantage theory encountered problems of uneven fit. Several researchers found that disadvantage did not have identical effects upon workers at all socioeconomic levels. Reviewing disadvantage research, Johnson (1981) found data sparse and support only partial. According to Johnson, "non-manual workers" were more likely to undertake self-employment in response to unemployment than were manual workers. Among manual workers, Johnson found that the unskilled were "less likely to set up than skilled workers." Thus, unemployment's effects upon self-employment depended upon the skills of the unemployed, a resource constraint.

Haber (1985) examined the relationship between unemployment and self-employment in the period 1979–1983, a recession. In this period, self-employment grew by 6.9%, whereas wage and salary employment increased only 1.3%. Haber also found that the greatest growth of self-employment occurred among employed workers who opened a side business. Haber (1985:12) supposed that, when their hours were reduced during the recession, some wage and salary workers opened a side business to supplement their earnings from paid employment. Therefore, the effects of unemployment on self-employment were much less than those of underemployment. Haber supposed that the underemployed had more resources than did the unemployed; hence, they could more easily set up on their own account.

Studying the resurgence of self-employment in Europe, Keeble and Wever (1986:10–19) found results similar to those of Haber. Originally, they endorsed the "recession push" explanation they found in the existing literature. According to this explanation, unemployment, fear of unemployment, and blocked promotion opportunities compelled European workers to open their own business firms. Therefore, self-employment rates increased in Europe as economic conditions deteriorated. However, Keeble and Wever (1986) found that the occupational structure of localities influenced the extent to which local unemployment promoted self-employment. Managerial workers and others possessing higher educational qualifications were much more likely than others to undertake self-employment in response to unemployment or underemployment. Therefore, in localities with many managerial workers, unemployment and underemployment occasioned greater increase in self-employment than in other localities.

In his study of Vietnamese and Soviet Jewish immigrants in San Francisco, Gold (1988b:418) found "little evidence to indicate that small business is a direct alternative to unemployment." In Gold's opinion, the unemployed had a motive for self-employment, but they typically lacked the resources to succeed in it. Unemployed immigrants who tried self-employment usually failed. More commonly, the foreign born undertook self-employment because of "the low quality" of the jobs they could obtain, a situation of underemployment, not unemployment. When starting up their own business, the underemployed had access to the slender resources afforded by the disagreeable jobs they still held. The unemployed had no resources. Hence, the underemployed more commonly succeeded in developing viable business firms than did the unemployed.

Implicit in this literature we find a sophisticated version of disadvantage theory that transcends the classical view while incorporating all of its explanatory power. We call this implicit theory the resource-constraint variant of the disadvantage theory. The *resource-constraint variant* supposes that even the disadvantaged require resources to undertake and/or survive in self-employment. The resource-constraint formula for entrepreneurship is disadvantage + resources. On this view, disadvantage alone is insufficient to create entrepreneurs. The resource constraint variant resembles the classical formula of disadvantage + affinities. The difference is the substitution of resources for affinities in the formula. Affinities must be ethnocultural in the hard sense,[1] that is, they must belong to historic systems of cultural meaning. Resources include ethnocultural affinities such as religion, but they also include class resources as well as ethnocultural resources (such as institutions and social capital) that are not reducible to historic systems of cultural meaning. Resources are broader than affinities, and represent, for this reason, a theoretical improvement that broadens the scope of classical theory.

Although they offer alternative versions of how disadvantage causes entrepreneurship, the resource-constraint and simple disadvantage theories need not exclude one another. Conceivably, each fits different situations. Confronting labor force disadvantage, those with no resources turn to self-employment in the informal economy. A typical firm in the informal economy requires few resources. For example, fruit vendors at freeway entrances are self-employed, but their informal enterprise did not require extensive resources of money, skill, and knowledge. Anyone could do it. On the other hand, when people with resources confront disadvantage, they mobilize those resources to produce a bona fide business firm. A grocery store or dry cleaners requires resources that those merely disadvantaged simply lack. Lacking resources, they could not have responded to disadvantage by starting this firm.

TYPES OF DISADVANTAGE

Taking account of the difference between the resource-constraint variant and simple disadvantage theory, we also find it essential to distinguish two types of disadvantage that the existing literature conflates. These types we call resource disadvantage and labor market disadvantage. Groups experience *resource disadvantage* when, as a result of some current or past historical experience, such as slavery, their members enter the labor market with fewer resources than other groups. Resources include all attributes that improve the productivity of employees, including human capital, a positive work ethic, good diets, reliable health, contact networks, self-confidence, etc. Thus, if their group was or is prevented from obtaining education, group members enter the labor market with less education on the average than non-group members, a disadvantage that reduces their productivity. Even if these disadvantaged persons then earn the expected market return on their human capital, their incomes will be low because their human capital and productivity are low. Since their human capital is low because of prior exclusion, a condition that existed when they entered the labor market, we appropriately term these workers resource disadvantaged.

In contrast, *labor market disadvantage* arises when groups receive below-expected returns on their human capital for reasons unrelated to productivity.[2] Their human capital may be extensive or minimal. Labor market disadvantage means that qualified workers get no job or they do not get a job commensurate with their experience and education. Discrimination is a classic cause of labor market disadvantage. For example, labor market disadvantage exists when equally educated and productive women workers earn less than male counterparts or when women workers cannot obtain promotions for which they are qualified. Hiring discrimination and a ceiling on promotions are prominent forms of labor market disadvantage affecting women. However, when unqualified and unproductive women workers earn low wages, they do not suffer from labor market disadvantage, except to the extent that their wages are lower than equally unqualified and unproductive male workers. Naturally, their unqualified and unproductive situation may be itself the product of resource disadvantage, such as historic gender roles in society, but it is essential to distinguish disadvantage that arises in the labor market from disadvantage that arises in society.

Labor market disadvantage and resource disadvantage are two different disadvantages. Any group can suffer from neither, from either, or from both. When both are present, resource disadvantage may precede or follow labor market disadvantage. When resource disadvantage is in place before a worker enters the labor market, it precedes labor market disadvantage. When a woman who was not offered algebra in high school seeks a job, the consequences of her inferior education will narrow her career horizon, increasing the likelihood of labor market disadvantage too. On the other hand, today's resource disadvantage can reflect yesterday's labor market disadvantage. For example, unfair treatment of women workers in the 1940s produced a generation of women who did not have the career role models they would otherwise have had. This lack was a resource disadvantage that continues to hold back women workers in the labor force, the daughters of those earlier women. In such cases, prior labor-force disadvantage caused current resource disadvantage.

That said, resource disadvantage is worse than labor market disadvantage in that the resource-deprived lack the resources to undertake self-employment in response to labor market disadvantage.[3] Because they provide at least some workers with the option of self-employment, entrepreneurial resources reduce the exposure of groups to abuse, discrimination, or exploitation in the labor market. For this reason, whatever else it also is, entrepreneurship is one economic self-defense of those subject for any reason to unfair treatment in the labor market. Labor unions are another such defense. Arguably labor unions provide a more comprehensive defense because they benefit and include everyone. Entrepreneurship's direct benefit affects a minority. Nonetheless, groups that have entrepreneurs and labor unions are better defended than groups that have only labor unions.

Naturally, those never subject to unfair treatment in the labor market need no defense. One might suppose that this advantaged class includes native whites, the majority group in American society. On a simple reckoning, native whites are not disadvantaged in the labor market. However, some native whites are women, who experience gender discrimination in the labor market. Moreover, all native whites, if they live past 40, face hiring and promotion discrimination against older workers. Without entrepreneurial resources, older native whites have no defense when this nasty contingency arises. Finally, in many bureaucratic settings, especially universities, white males are "invisible victims" of affirmative action quotas that offer them the choice of self-employment or resignation to reverse discrimination (Lynch, 1989). Granted, disadvantage of nonwhites is worse than that of native whites, other things being equal, but the notion that native whites never face discrimination is preposterous and simplistic.[4]

Stressing resource endowments, the positive status, the resources theory of entrepreneurship explains superior entrepreneurship by superior resources. But by implication resources theory also explains inferior entrepreneurship by inferior resources. Here, inferior resources means resource disadvantage, not labor market disadvantage. Indeed, our guiding hypothesis is that resource-disadvantaged groups are unable to mount an entrepreneurial response to labor market disadvantage. In our data, these groups are African Americans and Hispanics, the least educated ethnoracial categories. Conversely, we propose that non-resource-disadvantaged groups (Asians, native whites, foreign whites) more easily respond to labor force disadvantage by starting businesses of their own. This capacity renders them sensitive to labor force disadvantage that the resource-disadvantaged must tolerate.

DISADVANTAGE MUST BE MEASURED

We now wish to rectify several conceptual and methodological flaws in the existing disadvantage literature. First, several researchers failed to define or to measure labor market disadvantage, simply assuming its presence from conditions thought to cause it. Evans claimed that the main disadvantage facing immigrant workers was nonfluency in the language of the host country.[5] In a series of papers dealing with immigrants in Australia, Evans (1987, 1989) examined the occupational effects of weak English skills. She found that belonging to a non-English language community increased the likelihood of an immigrant's self-employment. The reason, Evans (1989:270) supposed, is that "people with weak skills" in English have an incentive to seek "employment from their compatriots because they can get better jobs inside the enclave than they could in the broader labour market." In turn, regardless of linguistic disadvantage, an entrepreneur benefits from the linguistic disability of coethnics because their linguistic disability creates a captive labor force of workers paid "below the market value of their skills." In this situation, coethnic entrepreneurs "spring up to hire them," thus causing high rates of entrepreneurship in linguistically disadvantaged groups.

Although plausible, Evans' view mistakes cause and effect. Conditions that cause labor market disadvantage are not the same as labor market disadvantage, their effect. Thus, inferior language skills, health disability, racial or gender discrimination, etc. cause labor market disadvantage. However, these situations are not labor market disadvantage so they cannot measure it. Labor market disadvantage is the consequence of these conditions: higher than expected underemployment or unemployment among those who do not speak the language, who are diseased, who experience discrimination, or whatever. If we declare lack of English fluency a labor force disadvantage, we should have to declare groups disadvantaged that earn more than their expected return on their human capital and who have less than their expected unemployment *despite* lack of fluency in English. Such a situation is not impossible. *Groups* are not disadvantaged unless they actually suffer adverse consequences of mistreatment in the labor market.[6] Therefore, the best measure of labor market disadvantage of groups is the penalty disadvantage inflicts, not the condition that draws a penalty. No penalty means no disadvantage. Big penalty means big disadvantage.

Infinite Causes

Second, the possible causes of labor market disadvantage are both transitory and infinite so it is useless to enumerate them. In China, it became a disadvantage during the Cultural Revolution to have had educated parents, but, after the Cultural Revolution, it became an advantage again (Deng, 1993). French employers discriminate against those whose knowledge of art and music does not meet a high class standard (Bourdieu, 1979), and American employers discriminate against anyone who knows about these subjects. According to Henry Higgins, British employers discriminate against cockney speakers. That is why Eliza Doolittle operated her florist business on the streets of London. Japanese employers discriminate against Burakumin who are not, as far as non-Japanese can tell, any different from the discriminating employers. Hollywood studios discriminate against actresses with small busts, but modeling agencies discriminate against big busts.

The literature of entrepreneurship reflects the bewildering etiologies of disadvantage. Explaining Korean entrepreneurship, Min (1988:35–36, 56–61) turned to status incongruence, a form of underemployment. That is, he measured underemployment among Korean immigrant men by the discrepancy between their work status in Korea and their work status in Atlanta on the one hand, and, on the other, by the discrepancy between their educational background and their current work status. More than 90% of Min's (1988:57) respondents had held white-collar or professional employment in Korea, but only 17% held white-collar or professional jobs on their first U.S. job. In that sense, most Koreans were underemployed. Similarly, 68% of Korean entrepreneurs in Atlanta had completed four years of college or more, but 83% of Korean entrepreneurs were in manual occupations on their first American job. More than half of the Korean entrepreneurs were "status inconsistent with a high pre-immigrant occupation and a low occupation in this country" (Min, 1988:59). Unsurprisingly, the Korean entrepreneurs also regarded their first American job as inferior in income and prestige to their entitlement. About half reported that this dissatisfaction drove them to undertake self-employment.

Light and Bonacich (1988: Table 35) offered an opportunity cost definition of labor force disadvantage. They reported that Korean wage and salary earners in Los Angeles earned only 70% of the return on their human capital that non-Korean workers earned. On the other hand, self-employed Koreans earned 92% of the return that non-Koreans obtained on their human capital. Either way, Koreans were disadvantaged. However, the Koreans' disadvantage was 22% greater in wage and salary employment than in self-employment. Arising from relative disadvantage, the obvious financial incentive explained the Koreans' overrepresentation in self-employment. This treatment of underemployment turned exclusively on below-expected wages rather than, as did Min's, on subjective dissatisfaction with low prestige jobs.

Kim, Hurh, and Fernandez (1989) defined disadvantage in terms of inferior returns upon college diplomas awarded by foreign universities. They distinguished college-educated Asians who had graduated from U.S. institutions from those who had graduated from foreign institutions, a distinction never drawn before. They found that among three

national-origin groups, graduates of foreign universities were more frequently self-employed than graduates of American universities. This
result suggests that foreign college graduates were underemployed in
the American labor force and so turned in despair to self-employment.

Because the causes of disadvantage are infinitely expandable, we cannot measure disadvantage by enumerating its causes. However long,
any list of possible labor force disadvantages can always be expanded
by one. Therefore, as a research strategy, we must measure labor force
disadvantage in terms of two penalties, underemployment and unemployment. Here, at least, closure is possible. Unemployment means long-
and short-term joblessness among job-seeking workers. Unemployment
provides workers a zero return upon their human capital, which,
indeed, they might as well not possess. Unemployment is worse than
underemployment. Underemployment means lower earnings than one's
human capital normally commands, a disadvantage, but one that affords
at least some return upon human capital. One cause of underemployment is short hours. People who work 10 hours weekly are likely to
earn lower than expected returns upon their human capital even if their
hourly wages are satisfactory. That kind of underemployment amounts
to partial unemployment. Another kind of underemployment is low pay
relative to qualifications. When immigrant doctors pump gasoline, they
earn a fair wage for gasoline service station attendants, but their wage
is a much lower than the expected return upon their human capital.

Another meaning of underemployment is purely subjective. People
may reject jobs because the task is not one they deem appropriate for
someone like them, because they dislike the boss, because they are not
morning people, or any fancied reason. Unsuitability occurs when workers earn an expected return on their human capital, but reject their task.
This is the usual situation of immigrant professionals who run garment
factories or service stations: the money is satisfactory but the work is
infra dignitatem. We suppose that it is worse to be underpaid and dis-
satisfied with the job than merely to be underpaid, or merely dissatis-
fied. In any case, underemployment must become a state of conscious
dissatisfaction before it has consequences. When objectively underemployed people are happy in their wretched jobs, ignorance is bliss, and
underemployment produces no consequences in the labor market.

Disadvantage is Continuous

Third, simple disadvantage literature has failed to acknowledge
degrees of disadvantage. Some disadvantaged workers are more disadvantaged than others. In general, the merely resource disadvantaged are

more disadvantaged than the merely labor market disadvantaged, the long-term unemployed are more disadvantaged than the short-term unemployed, and the unemployed are more disadvantaged than the underemployed. The unemployed are more disadvantaged because the underemployed earn a return on their education, skill, and work experience whereas the unemployed earn none. Among the unemployed, the long-term unemployed are more disadvantaged than the short-term unemployed if only because the long-term unemployed have depleted their resources in the course of protracted unemployment (Podgursky and Swaim, 1987:224–225).

Both the underemployed and the unemployed have objective grounds for dissatisfaction with their labor force status and, hence, for attention to self-employment. But the underemployed have more choice about timing their entry into business than do the unemployed. They can wait until conditions are ripe rather than having to rush in desperation into overcrowded or unsuitable markets. Similarly, the underemployed can accrue financial resources and training for subsequent self-employment while working at their unsatisfactory jobs. Indeed, training underemployed coethnics for self-employment is a principal resource of small ethnic businesses (Cobas, Aickin, and Jardine, 1993; Bailey and Waldinger, 1991). In sum, the underemployed have more financial and skill resources for legitimate self-employment than do the permanently unemployed. In particular, when the underemployed have higher educational credentials and job skills unused in their occupation, they possess important resources for self-employment. Because the permanently unemployed typically lack much human capital, they have a reduced capacity for self-employment even if their need is higher. Worse, the longer they are unemployed, the more their human capital falls behind what their age cohort's employed members command.

True, those more disadvantaged have more incentive to undertake self-employment than do those less disadvantaged. Increasing the subjective intensity of unemployment (temporary, protracted, and permanent) increases the economic attractiveness of self-employment. For the permanently unemployed underclass of great cities, philanthropy, public welfare, and self-employment offer the only legal alternatives to starvation.[7] Public welfare and self-employment are incompatible in law because welfare recipients are not permitted to receive benefits while obtaining income from a business. Even though welfare and self-employment are not incompatible in practice, some welfare recipients still unlawfully operate business enterprises on the side. Instead of expressing indignation about this freeloading minority, the usual political response, one might ask why *all* welfare recipients do not also operate a clandestine small business on the side? Fear of detection is probably not the only reason. Some welfare recipients operate no business because, as a result of public welfare, they need not. Welfare supplies their modest needs. In addition, however, many welfare recipients do not operate a side business because, despite the incentive, they lack the resources. Only the "truly disadvantaged" lack all resources.

EVEN THE DISADVANTAGED REQUIRE RESOURCES

Simple disadvantage is enough to explain self-employment in the informal economy. The informal economy requires next to no resources. But even those sorely disadvantaged in the labor market need resources to undertake self-employment in the mainstream. Therefore, disadvantaged workers with more resources are the most likely to try or to succeed in self-employment. No matter how skilled or how educated, an unemployed person earns nothing. However, if highly skilled, the worker's economic loss is greater than if unskilled, because an unskilled person earns a lower return on his or her human capital when fully employed. In this sense, unemployment represents a greater absolute economic loss for the trained and experienced than for the unskilled beginner. This idea explains Johnson's (1981) findings above that more skilled workers were more likely to become self-employed than were less skilled workers. Additionally, disadvantaged workers with skills and education have more resources at their disposal with which they can undertake their own business firm in response to labor market disadvantage. It therefore follows that disadvantage should promote more entrepreneurship among those with resources than among those lacking them.

REVIEW

Based on this review and critique of the disadvantage literature, Table 5.1 summarizes our theoretical discussion.[8] Among groups suffering resource disadvantage, additional labor market disadvantage has no effect in stimulating compensatory entrepreneurship.[9] In this case, labor market disadvantage increases the need for self-employment without, however, providing the necessary resources. As W. S. Gilbert (1932:179) put it, "they would if they could, but they are not able." Only among groups not resource disadvantaged does labor market disadvantage encourage entrepreneurship. Those not disadvantaged have the

Table 5.1. Disadvantage and Entrepreneurship

Group Resource Disadvantage	Group Labor Market Disadvantage	
	Yes	No
Yes	Low entrepreneurship	Low entrepreneurship
No	High entrepreneurship	Average entrepreneurship

resources, but they lack the motive to undertake defensive entrepreneurship. Therefore, their self-employment rate is average.

High entrepreneurship groups suffer labor force disadvantage without resource disadvantage. Their labor force disadvantage provides a motive for defensive self-employment, and their extensive resources provide the means. Abused in the labor market, they have the means to start businesses of their own. Middleman minorities fit this model. Outsiders, and subject to discrimination on this account, middleman minorities have elaborated a cultural preparation for entrepreneurship that facilitates their defensive self-employment (Bonacich, 1973; Turner and Bonacich, 1980). Indeed, in some cases, middleman minorities make a virtue of necessity, turning defensive entrepreneurship into a source of gigantic capitalist profit. But labor force disadvantage does not have the same energizing effect upon nonmiddleman groups that lack a cultural heritage of entrepreneurship. Lacking cultural and class resources of entrepreneurial self-defense, underdogs must endure whatever abuse employers dish out, escaping only into crime or the informal economy. Similarly, women are more disadvantaged in the labor force than are men, but men's self-employment rate is three times that of women because, until quite recently, women have lacked the cultural and class resources that facilitate entrepreneurship in the mainstream. Now that they increasingly control those resources, women increasingly respond to employer discrimination by entrepreneurship.

MEASUREMENT ISSUES

To proceed to analysis, we must first define and explain the independent variables. Table 5.2 lists and defines these. These variables are current resources, labor market disadvantage, and resource disadvantage. To measure resource disadvantage we use ethnic self-identification. From Tables 4.2 and 4.3 we learned that, net of control variables, ethnic self-identification's effect on self-employment is powerful and unequal.

Table 5.2.   Variables Used in the Analyses[1]

Variables	Name and Operational Description of Variables
Dependent variables	
BRODMSER	Income-defined mean self-employment rate[2]
NAROMSER	Work-defined mean self-employment rate[3]
Independent variables	
Labor market disadvantage	
Unemployment	
UNEMP	Category mean percentage unemployed[4]
CWKSUNEMP	Category mean number of weeks unemployed — 13.13411[5]
Underemployment	
CWIFORED	Category mean weekly wage and salary income per category mean years of education — $21.11547[6]
Specific labor market disadvantage interaction variables	
4 specific supply intercept variables × 3 labor market disadvantage variables[7]	
Supply[8]	
Specific invariant supply (intercept variables)	
FBW	Dummy variable (foreign-born whites = 1; else = 0)
BLACK	Dummy variable (blacks = 1; else = 0)
ASIAN	Dummy variable (Asians = 1; else = 0)
HISPANIC	Dummy variable (Hispanics = 1; else = 0)
General variant supply or resources	
CCATPCTM	Category mean percentage male — .54
CCATED	Category mean years of education — 12.56
CCATAGE	Mean years of age — 36.67
CYRSINUS	Weighted category mean percentage of their lives in U.S. — .76832[9]
Specific supply interaction variables	
4 specific supply intercept variables × 3 general variant supply variables[7]	
Demand independent variables	
Regional economy[10]	
NYNJPA	Dummy variable (SMSA in NY, NJ, or PA = 1; else = 0)
ECENTRAL	Dummy variable (SMSA in East Central = 1; else = 0)
WCENTRAL	Dummy variable (SMSA in West Central = 1; else = 0)
SATLANTIC	Dummy variable (SMSA in South Atlantic = 1; else = 0)
MIDSOUTH	Dummy variable (SMSA in Mid-South = 1; else = 0)
CENTRLSO	Dummy variable (SMSA in Central South = 1; else = 0)
WESTMTNS	Dummy variable (SMSA in Western Mountains = 1; else = 0)
PACIFIC	Dummy variable (SMSA in Pacific = 1; else = 0)

[1] See Chapter 2, Appendix 2A, for detailed descriptions.

[2] This measure is identical to BRODMSER used in Chapter 2 and to CATMSER used in Chapters 3 and 4. Respondents were defined as self-employed (= 1) if they had reported any income gains or losses from self-employment (INCOME2). We calculated the self-employment rate by dividing the number of persons who reported self-employment income (NINCOME2) by the total number of persons in the civilian labor force for each category.

[3] This measure is identical to NAROMSER used in Chapter 2. Respondents were defined as self-employed (=1) if they had reported self-employment work in a business that was not incorporated or as an employee of their own corporation (SETOT).

[4] Values for UNEMP range from 0 to 31.25%. Because UNEMP has a meaningful zero

Table 5.2. (continued)

value, it does not need to be centered.

[5] Values for WKSUNEMP range from 1.5 to 35.0 weeks, therefore this variable is centered using the mean from the pooled sample as indicated in Table 5.2.

[6] For each of the five categories, CWIFORED = [(Category 1979 wage and salary income/Category mean number of weeks worked by wage and salary workers)/ Category mean years of education] – mean WIFORED for the pooled sample. Values for CWIFORED range from $9.83 to $33.90, therefore this variable is centered using the mean from the pooled sample as indicated in Table 5.2.

[7] There are no native-born white interaction variables, because native-born white is the omitted reference group. The labor market disadvantage variables, CWKSUNEMP and CWIFORED, were first centered, but not UNEMP or the dummy invariant supply vairables.

[8] See Table 4.1 for detailed descriptions of the operationalizations of the supply variables.

[9] Assuming that all native-born whites have lived all of their lives in the United States, we assigned them the value 1 for 100%. We also assigned this value for the native-born blacks, native-born Asians, and native-born Hispanics in the following equation:

For FB whites, YRSINUS = $\dfrac{\text{FB white mean number of years in the United States}}{\text{FB white mean age}}$

For blacks, Asians, and Hispanics, respectively, a weighted mean percentage years lived in the United States was calculated as follows:

$\dfrac{(N \text{ of NB group} \times 1) + [N \text{ of FB group} \times (\text{mean years in the U.S.}/\text{mean age})]}{N \text{ of NB group} + N \text{ of FB group}}$

If there were no foreign-born of a group in an SMSA, and/or a missing value for the foreign-born of a group, YRSINUS was assigned the value of 1 (i.e., 100%) for the native-born of that group in that SMSA. In one case, there was an error, in which the mean number of years in the United States for a foreign-born blacks was greater than their mean age. This error was ``corrected'' by assigning them the value for living in the United States of 100%. Values for this variable ranged from 13.67 to 100%, therefore this variable is centered using the mean from the pooled sample as indicated in Table 5.2. No interaction variables were tested for CYRSINUS, because there was no variation in the values of this variable for native-born whites.

[10] The omitted reference group is New England.

For African Americans and Hispanics, ethnic self-identification is strongly negative; for native whites, foreign whites, and Asians, it is positive. When ethnic identity has a negative effect on self-employment rate, we interpret the coefficient as resource disadvantage. That is, a negative identity coefficient stands for disadvantaging baggage that people lugged into the current situation from their historic past. The historical sources of this disadvantage are not clear in the census data, but the effects certainly are. Judging from Tables 4.2 and 4.3, we infer that African Americans and Hispanics lugged a resource disadvantage into the labor markets of great American cities whereas native whites, foreign whites, and Asians had no such disadvantaging burden to bear. This resource disadvantage is not reducible to current labor market disadvantage.

Following our discussion above, we measure the effects rather than the causes of labor market disadvantage. Only those experience labor market disadvantage who suffer its penalties. The penalties of disadvantage are unemployment and objective underemployment. Objective underemployment means money returns lower than one's human capital normally commands. We cannot measure subjective underemployment utilizing census data. We utilize two measures of unemployment: an ethnoracial category's rate of unemployment and its mean weeks of unemployment. We have one measure of underemployment: a category's mean weekly wage and salary income relative to its mean years of education. This measure shows whether the people of this category earn less than expected returns on their human capital, a sign of unfair treatment. Underemployment exists when ethnoracial minorities earn lower returns on human capital than do native whites. As before, measures of current resources are percentage of the labor force male, mean years of education, and mean age. In addition, we test the effects of American acculturation. We do this by measuring the mean percentage of years that each group has lived in the United States in each metropolitan area.

Since work-defined and income-defined self-employment yield two slightly different groups, with the income-defined lower status than the work-defined, we utilize both measures of self-employment. This comparison has never been made before because published literature routinely uses only the work-defined measure of self-employment. However, this comparison of two measures permits us to explore the possibility that disadvantage has different effects at the bottom and at the top of the self-employment spectrum. In general, we expect that resource-disadvantaged groups will respond more easily to labor force disadvantage by entrepreneurship in the informal economy than by entrepreneurship in the mainstream. Because the income-defined self-employed are slightly lower status than the work-defined self-employed (see Chapter 2), we expect the resource-disadvantaged to display slightly higher income-defined entrepreneurship than work-defined entrepreneurship.

Empirical Results

Table 5.3 compares our measures of underemployment and unemployment of the five ethnoracial categories. Native whites provide the reference standard against which we measure labor market disadvantage. The mean unemployment rate of native whites was 5.3 and their mean weeks of unemployment was 12.2. Relative to native whites,

African Americans and Hispanics were disadvantaged with respect to both unemployment rate and duration of unemployment. Blacks had the highest mean unemployment rate (10.6%) and the longest mean number of weeks unemployed (16.0). This was the worst unemployment problem of any ethnoracial category. Following our prior reasoning, this unenviable situation should confer the highest motive for entrepreneurship, but African Americans also suffer resource disadvantage, a condition that frustrates their entrepreneurship in the mainstream.[10] Asians and foreign whites had slightly lower rates of unemployment than did native whites as well as slightly shorter durations of unemployment. Asians and foreign whites were not disadvantaged with respect to unemployment, but blacks and Hispanics were.

Turning to underemployment, we find that native whites earned a mean salary of $12,679, which amounted to $985 per year of education. Foreign whites earned more money than native whites ($13,085), and 5% more money per year of education ($1,037). Relative to native whites, foreign whites were *not* underemployed. Asians earned as much as native whites. However, although better educated than native whites, Asians earned $890 per year of education, only 91% of what native whites received. Therefore, relative to native whites, Asians were underemployed; foreign whites were not. Hispanics earned much less than native-born whites, and when this shortfall is standardized into returns to education, we see that Hispanics too earned only 91% of what native-born whites received. Relative to native whites, Hispanics were underemployed to the same extent as Asians. African Americans were the most underemployed. Blacks earned less than native whites, and only 82% of the return on education of the native whites.

Since annual earnings ignores variations in weeks worked, we refined it, using weekly income. Weekly income yields about the same differences as did annual returns. Our baseline group, native whites, earned almost $22 per week for every year of education. Blacks earned about three dollars less! A white person with 10 years of education earned $220 a week in 1979. A black person with 10 years of education earned about $190 a week in 1979. Foreign whites earned one dollar more than native whites, and Asians and Hispanics earned about one dollar less than native whites. Thus, Asians, Hispanics, and African Americans experienced labor market disadvantage, but African Americans were the most disadvantaged in the labor market, presumably because of racial discrimination.

Comparing these measures of unemployment and underemployment disadvantage to the mean self-employment rates for the five ethnoracial categories, we find a negative relationship between disadvantage and self-employment. The two minorities with the lowest underemployment

Table 5.3. Means and Standard Deviations of Income-Defined and Work-Defined Self-Employment Rates and Labor Market Disadvantage Variables,[1] for Five Separate Categories

Variables	NB Whites		FB Whites		Blacks		Asians		Hispanics	
	Means	*SD*	*Means*	*SD*	*Means*	*SD*	*Means*	*SD*	*Means*	*SD*
Dependent variables										
Mean income-defined										
Self-employment rate	7.5	1.9	9.7	3.8	2.6	1.3	7.7	4.8	4.2	2.8
Mean work-defined										
Self-employment rate	7.9	2.1	11.0	4.7	2.5	1.3	8.2	4.7	4.2	2.9
Independent variables										
Labor market disadvantage										
Unemployment										
Mean unemployment rate (%)	5.3	2.0	4.9	3.0	10.6	4.5	5.1	3.5	8.8	5.0
Mean no. weeks unemployed	12.2	1.8	12.1	4.2	16.0	2.8	12.0	4.1	13.1	3.3

Underemployment									
Mean W & S income ($)	12,679	1,530	13,085	2,514	9,603	1,643	12,689	3,499	10,229	1,661
Yearly returns for W & S income per mean years of ed ($)	985	108	1,037	203	808	126	890	201	895	145
Ratio of yearly W & S income returns for category compared to returns for NB whites	—		1.1		.82		.90		.91	
Weekly returns for W & S income per mean years of ed ($)	21.92	2.28	23.10	4.08	18.81	2.88	20.53	4.15	20.97	3.28
Ratio of weekly W & S income returns for category compared to returns for NB whites	—		1.1		.86		.94		.96	
Supply									
Mean % of years in U.S.	100.0	0.0	48.0	4.2	98.3	2.7	41.6	11.9	84.9	10.4
N (No. of SMSAs)	272		245		245		180		230	

[1] See Table 5.2 for detailed descriptions of the operationalizations of these variables.

and unemployment (Asians, foreign whites) had the highest self-employment. The most disadvantaged minorities (blacks, Hispanics) had the lowest self-employment. If simple disadvantage caused self-employment, then African Americans and Hispanics ought to have had the highest rates of self-employment, not the lowest. Conversely, Asians and foreign whites ought to have had the least self-employment, but they had, in fact, the most. Therefore, we find no evidence for the simple disadvantage hypothesis in this elementary analysis of the census data.

However, these results do roughly fit the resource-constraint model (Table 5.1). African Americans and Hispanics are both resource-disadvantaged and disadvantaged in the labor market. Because of the resource disadvantage, these minorities cannot augment self-employment in response to labor market disadvantage. Therefore, their self-employment rates are low despite discrimination. In contrast, Asians are not resource disadvantaged, but they do suffer underemployment in the labor market. The Asians' labor market disadvantage is actually milder than that of blacks and Hispanics, but the Asians are able to mount more self-employment because they suffer no resource disadvantage. The Asians have high self-employment compatible with the supposition, widely supported in the literature, that they undertake self-employment in order to escape labor market disadvantage.

Foreign whites are neither resource disadvantaged nor, according to our data, disadvantaged in the labor market. They are not disadvantaged, and neither the simple nor the resource-constraint version of disadvantage theory predicts foreign white self-employment higher than native white self-employment. Yet, the foreign whites have the highest mean self-employment rate. The oldest of the four ethnoracial categories, the foreign whites may owe their high entrepreneurship to their age and human capital. At any rate, labor force disadvantage does not explain foreign white entrepreneurship unless we invoke real disadvantages that the census data do not measure.

POOLED GROUPS ANALYSIS

Turning to regression methods for a finer analysis, we want to distinguish any effects of resource disadvantage from those of labor market disadvantage. As before, we include the invariant supply variables that measure the effects of group identity.[11] Negative coefficients of ethnic identity are evidence of resource disadvantage.

We test the ability of the labor market disadvantage to explain variation in income-defined and work-defined self-employment rates net of resource disadvantage (variant supply), and demand.[12] Work-defined mean self-employment rates suggest exclusive engagement in self-employment work, whereas the income-defined rates also encompass those engaged in self-employment activities on a part-time basis or per-haps to supplement wage and salary work. Our income-defined definition of self-employment encompasses a much more heterogeneous group of entrepreneurs than does the work-defined definition. The former include a broad spectrum ranging from those engaging in supplementary, part-time self-employment, to those working exclusively in their own enterprises. Therefore, we expect differences in how these models predict the two types of self-employment.

We include the main effects of the three labor market disadvantage variables: mean percentage unemployed, mean number of weeks unemployed, and mean weekly wage and salary income returns per mean year of education. The response of the four minority groups to these labor market disadvantage variables sometimes differs from that of the native whites. Following Gujarati (1970:50–51), to determine whether the main effects of the labor market disadvantage variables are the same for all five groups, we include the invariant supply by labor market disadvantage interactions. These interactions indicate whether the effects of these labor market disadvantages on each of the four minority categories differ from the effects on native whites.[13] If the interaction variables are *not* significant as a "set,"[14] they will be deleted from the model. The modified model will be retested, but findings for the original model[15] will not be reported. If the interaction variables as a set *are* significant, we will retain them in the modified model.

We also test whether the four general variant supply variables (mean percentage males, mean years of education, mean years of age, and mean percentage years lived in the United States) have additive effects net of the labor market disadvantage factors. We check whether the effects of the general variant supply variables of the four minority groups differ significantly from the effects of the same variables for native-born whites, by testing these interaction variables. Finally, we control for regional economic differences.

EMPIRICAL RESULTS

Table 5.4 presents the modified models to predict income- and work-defined mean self-employment rates for the pooled sample. These models include the four minority categories, the main effects of labor market disadvantage, variant supply, and regional demand variables. They also include interactions of labor market disadvantage and supply variables

Table 5.4. Regression of Mean Income-Defined and Work-Defined Self-Employment Rates on Labor Market Disadvantage and Supply Variables,[1] Five Categories Pooled, in 272 Metropolitan Areas, N = 172 (Standardized Coefficients)

	Dependent Variables	
Independent variables	Income-Defined MSER[2]	Work-Defined MSER[2]
Invariant supply		
Foreign-born whites	.135	.048
Black	−.250	−.426***
Asian	.127	.047
Hispanic	−.119**	−.121**
Labor market disadvantage		
Unemployment		
Mean percent unemployed	−.005	.012
Weeks number of weeks unemployed	−.006	.026
Underemployment		
Weekly wage and salary income		
Per mean years of education	−.531***	−.348*
Specific labor market disadvantage[3]		
W & S income per yr ed × FBW	.149***	.185****
W & S income per yr ed × Black	.427*	.434*
W & S income per yr ed × Asian	.130***	.178****
W & S income per yr ed × Hispanic	.040	.067*
Variant supply		
Mean percentage male	.090***	.029
Mean years of education	.523****	.412****
Mean years of age	.346****	.367****
Mean percentage years lived in U.S.	.081	−.026
Specific supply interactions[4]		
Mean years of education × FBW	−.134*	−.088
Mean years of education × Black	−.080	.045
Mean years of education × Asian	−.222**	−.158*
Mean years of education × Hispanic	−.179**	−.100
Demand		
Regional economy		
NY, NJ and PA	.007	.006
East Central	.068	.021
West Central	.022	.036
South Atlantic	.133***	.196****
Mid-South	.088**	.090***
Central South	.179****	.222****
Western Mountains	.087**	.106****
Pacific	.251****	.203****
Adjusted R^2	.5294	.5797

[1] See Table 5.2 for detailed descriptions of the operationalizations of the variables used in these models.

Table 5.4.   (continued)

[2] Modified version in which only significant interaction coefficients are included in the model, and the others are deleted.
[3] The four mean percent unemployed × invariant supply, and the four mean weeks unemployed × invariant supply, interaction variables were not significant for either model. Therefore, they were deleted from the modified models for both dependent variables.
[4] The four mean percentage male × invariant supply, and the four mean age invariant supply, interaction variables were not significant for either model. Therefore, they were deleted from the modified models for both dependent variables.
"""" LE .0001.
""" LE .001.
"" LE .01.
" LE .05.

with the four minority groups. Because we analyzed them previously, in Chapter 4, we ignore the effects of variant supply and regional economy, which figure as control variables only.

Identical models do not produce identical effects on the work and income self-employment! First, the model explains work-defined mean self-employment rates slightly better than income-defined self-employment rates (adjusted R^2 = 58% for the latter versus 53% for the former). But this difference is not important. Second, the two models generate patterned differences in which variables reach significance. These patterned differences bear on substantive issues.

Our measures of labor market disadvantage do not eliminate the effects of resource disadvantage. Resource disadvantage is indicated by a negative coefficient of ethnic self-identification net of control variables and labor market disadvantage. A negative coefficient means that factors not in the model tend to inhibit group entrepreneurship, and, taken together, we call those factors resource disadvantage. As in earlier chapters, African-American and Hispanic self-identification continue to reduce self-employment net of control variables. The robust resource effects are quite significant. However, the resource disadvantage effect is not the same for income and work self-employment. Black self-identification reduces work-defined self-employment, the usual measure, but it has no effect on income self-employment. Since, as previously explained, income self-employment reaches farther down the business hierarchy into the informal economy than does work-defined self-employment, the result implies that resource disadvantages of African Americans mainly exist in the mainstream economy. They do not exist or are much attenuated in the informal economy. This result is compatible with the resource-constraint version of disadvantage theory.

True, we might expect similar results for Hispanics, another disadvantaged group, but we do not find them in Table 5.4. The negative effect of Hispanic self-identification is not much greater on work-defined than on income-defined self-employment. This comparability suggests an Hispanic resource deficit that is not more serious in the mainstream economy than in the informal economy. Possibly the discrepancy arises because the Hispanic resource deficit is less than the black deficit in work-defined self-employment. If intermediate deficits permit equal access to work-defined (class of worker) self-employment and income self-employment, whereas large deficits do not, we can understand why Hispanics have better access to work-defined self-employment than African Americans.

We turn to the effects of labor market disadvantage. Net of control variables, neither unemployment variable (rate or length) affects self-employment. In the simple disadvantage theory, we would expect a positive effect of unemployment on self-employment, and in the resource-constraint version a negative relationship. But we find no relationship. However, *under*employment is highly significant for both work and income self-employment. The less rewarding the weekly wage and salary returns to education, the more likely groups are to undertake self-employment. This result confirms our expectations of a negative relationship between underemployment and self-employment. Moreover, as expected, underemployment has a more powerful effect on income self-employment than on work-defined self-employment. We can explain that difference in terms of the reduced resources required to undertake income self-employment. Underemployment provides a motive for self-employment, and income self-employment requires fewer resources and less risk than does work-defined self-employment. On balance, these results support the resource-constraint version since those underemployed have more resources than those unemployed. After all, the underemployed have at least the resource of their unsatisfactory job. Therefore, underemployment should encourage more self-employment than unemployment.

Interaction effects speak to the question of whether the effects of specific labor market disadvantage are the same for the four minority categories and for native whites. If the minorities are not more disadvantaged in the labor market than native whites, then they should not differ from native whites in their response to under- and unemployment. However, the interaction terms show that minorities uniformly differ from native whites, suggesting more disadvantage. All four minority groups show positive interactions with human-capital adjusted wage and salary income. That is, underemployment augments self-employment less among minorities than among native whites. This effect means reduced sensitivity to underemployment. Minorities translate underemployment into entrepreneurship less promptly than native whites. Although the main effect of underemployment generally increases self-employment, minorities turn to self-employment at more disadvantaged income levels than do native whites. That is, when wages start to fall relative to human capital, minorities bail out of wage employment *after* native whites, who quit sooner. It is as if minorities pop out of wage employment into self-employment at higher levels of underemployment pressure than do whites.

Why should minorities, especially African Americans, be more tolerant of wage and salary underemployment than native whites? Explaining this white/minority difference, we propose that minority wage earners have a tendency to accommodate to wage and salary underemployment more severe than what comparably educated native whites will tolerate. Thus, underemployment of 10% looks hugely negative to native whites, but, expecting underemployment of 20%, blacks view that same 10% underemployment as relatively attractive. Therefore, blacks stay in underemployed wage and salary jobs in greater proportion than would comparably underemployed native whites. The same observation applies to all minorities, but blacks are the most underemployed of any, so the effect is most extreme for blacks.

The effects of underemployment on minorities are also slightly stronger in work-defined self-employment than in income self-employment. We attribute this sensitivity to the greater resources required to undertake work self-employment than income self-employment. Because the resources required are greater, the pressure of underemployment has to be greater to produce work-defined self-employment. Slight underemployment pops a minority wage earner into the informal economy; but massive underemployment is required to pop that same worker into mainstream entrepreneurship. The more difficult the option of self-employment, the more underemployment minorities tolerate before attempting it.

Turning now to education, we hypothesize that if minority workers experience no more labor force disadvantage than native white workers, we expect no difference between minorities and native whites in the effects of education on self-employment rates. However, the interaction effects of education and ethnic identity do show systematic white/minority differences. Although education generally raises self-employment rates, the main effect, three of four minority groups convert education into self-employment less efficiently than do native whites (Table 5.4). That is, net of other variables, increments in years of education induce smaller increases in self-employment rate among foreign-born whites, Asians, and Hispanics than among native-born whites and blacks. As a result, at the same level of education, Hispanic, Asian, and foreign-born white groups display lower self-employment rates than native whites and blacks. It is as if, relative to more venturesome native whites and blacks, Asians, Hispanics, and foreign whites cling to their wage and salary jobs rather than exploit their human capital for entrepreneurship. Clinging to a wage is the opposite of what one might expect from people disadvantaged in the mainstream labor market and compelled for this reason to undertake self-employment.

However, on closer examination, this result is by no means incompatible with disadvantage theory, and actually confirms it in a sense. After all, clinging to a wage occurs in our table net of underemployment, a strong predictor of entrepreneurship. In that context, clinging to a wage implies that unless compelled by actual disadvantage, Asian, Hispanic, and foreign-white employees prefer to stay in bureaucratic jobs rather than take a chance on self-employment. These are reluctant entrepreneurs after all, just as disadvantage theory predicts.

Two considerations support this interpretation. The first is the known preference of immigrant employees for wage jobs in the formal sector. Nee and Sernau (1994:856) found that immigrant Asian employees "expressed a desire to move toward the open and formal domains" of the labor market. "Many such workers avoid jobs in the informal and ethnic domains; they would rather work in well-established, formally organized and regulated firms, often in the public sector." Presumably the ethnic economy's harsh working conditions and long hours of labor explain this preference. Second, our data show that foreign whites, Hispanics, and Asians clung more tenaciously to their wage jobs relative to income-defined self-employment than to work-defined self-employment. As we have seen, income-defined self-employment is appreciably less desirable than work-defined self-employment. Therefore, in clinging to wage jobs, Hispanic, foreign white, and Asian employees were really expressing reluctance to enter the least desirable sector of self-employment. Relative to native whites, they clung much less to wage jobs against an option of *desirable* self-employment.

Among the African Americans, we find a similar pattern of clinging to wage jobs, especially relative to income-defined self-employment, the less attractive type. However, the African American results are too feeble to reach significance. Even if they clung a little to wage jobs, the African Americans apparently clung less than the other minorities (Table 5.4). That is, increments in education caused about the same increment in self-employment rate among African Americans that they caused among whites. African Americans exploited their human capital for entrepreneurship as aggressively as did native whites. Explaining this result, we propose that nativity connects African Americans with native whites whose preference pattern they, therefore, approximate. As native-born Americans, both African Americans and whites are advantaged relative to foreign-born minorities. If nativity improves access to mainstream entrepreneurship, eliminating the disagreeable option of poorly remunerated self-employment in a linguistic ghetto, then blacks as well as whites confront a self-employment horizon whose prospects do not include the worst characteristics of the immigrant economy. In this situation, bolder exploitation of human capital makes sense.

In summary, Table 5.4 provides evidence of both resource and labor market disadvantage among minorities. Some minorities are not resource disadvantaged, and foreign whites are not objectively disadvantaged in the labor market, but all minorities behave as if disadvantaged in the labor market. That is, minorities translate underemployment into entrepreneurship in different proportions than do native whites. Resource disadvantage robustly persists net of labor market disadvantage, suggesting that the two forms of disadvantage are quite distinct. Given our data and measurement, we hesitate to declare whether resource disadvantage is, on balance, more important than labor market disadvantage to the entrepreneurship of African Americans and Hispanics. That is a valid question that Weber and Sombart would have answered affirmatively. We are satisfied to point out that both disadvantages appear in our data, and they represent distinct and independent disadvantages.

Turning to disadvantage theory, Table 5.4 shows many results that require us to invoke resource-constraint ideas in order to explain them. In general, resource-constraints are more apparent in work-defined self-employment than in income self-employment, a discrepancy compatible with the lower level of self-employment earlier diagnosed among the income self-employed. Because work-defined self-employment requires more resources to undertake, minorities tolerate more underemployment before undertaking it. Requiring less resources, recourse to income self-employment is prompter.

According to the simple disadvantage theory, the main effect of mean percentage unemployed and mean weeks of unemployment should be positive. However, their effects are nil in our data. Possibly our cross-sectional analysis cannot obtain the effects on entrepreneurship that Steinmetz and Wright (1989) found for unemployment interacted with a time variable. Our data are strictly cross-sectional, a limitation in this analysis. However, even our cross-sectional data show that underemployment powerfully increases entrepreneurship. That is, the lower their wage and salary income returns to education, the more pressure groups feel to engage in self-employment on either a full-time or part-time basis. The strong effect of underemployment underscores the importance of resources to entrepreneurship since the underemployed have more resources than the unemployed.

DISCUSSION

A long, large, and even historical literature has developed around the disadvantage theory. Weber and Sombart thought that entrepreneurship was a product of religiously inspired affinities and disadvantage, but they stressed the affinities. In recent years, this classic formula was pared down to disadvantage alone. This recent literature has yielded widespread agreement that those disadvantaged in wage labor turn to entrepreneurship in self-protection. However, contemporary literature has also encountered many problems that suggest the desirability of retrieving the affinities argument. The concept of entrepreneurial resources includes the older affinities variable, expanding it to include wider material and cultural sources of entrepreneurship, not just religion.

We distinguish simple disadvantage theory, the model so popular in the 1980s, from a resource-constraint variant. Simple disadvantage theory predicts augmented self-employment in proportion to a group's disadvantage: the more disadvantaged, the more self-employment. Simple disadvantage theory does not invoke resource issues. The resource-constraint version maintains, in contrast, that those most disadvantaged in the labor market often lack the resources to undertake self-employment. Therefore, it predicts the most self-employment among persons slightly disadvantaged who are not resource-disadvantaged. Here the resources provide the means and the labor force disadvantage the motive. Entrepreneurship requires means as well as motive. In the simple disadvantage theory, the disadvantaged have ample motive for self-employment, but they often lack the means, material and cultural.

Reviewing the census data, we have found consistent support for the resource-constraint version and little for the simple disadvantage theory. The simple disadvantage theory runs into problems that the resource-constraint theory avoids. True, our evidence is often circumstantial, and we have had to infer motivations and preferences that we did not measure directly. These limitations are serious. Nonetheless, from these census data, we find support for the superior predictive ability of the resource-constraint version of disadvantage theory. Underemployment augments entrepreneurship more than unemployment, a discrepancy easily explained by the superior resources of the underemployed. Entry into the income self-employed requires fewer resources than entry into the work-defined self-employed, and is, for this reason, subject to less delay.

Of course, these census data assume firms of a sufficient size and permanence that census enumerators could find and measure them. The informal economy lies outside this range. The resources required to operate in the informal economy are appreciably fewer than those required in the mainstream economy. Naturally, one has to take resources into account when explaining participation in mainstream entrepreneurship. It is, however, highly likely that the simple disadvantage theory offers a satisfactory explanation for entrepreneurship in the informal economy. Indeed, those with resources normally avoid the informal economy since their resources permit entry into the mainstream. Comparing work-defined and income self-employed, our analysis finds some support for this conclusion in the data. As a group, the income-defined self-employed are lower class than the work-defined self-employed, and we find that the discrepancy affects the ease of access of minorities to the two forms of entrepreneurship.

Although impressed by the superiority of the resource constraint version, we do not believe that the simple disadvantage theory should be jettisoned. Rather, we recognize that simple disadvantage theory explains participation in the informal economy. Its resource-constraint variant better explains entrepreneurial participation in the economic mainstream. Although our results pertain to American immigrant and ethnic minorities, we find a direct line of intellectual continuity with classical theories of capitalism that confirms and supports this individual analysis.

NOTES

1. The distinction between hard and soft cultural theory is discussed in Light (1980).

2. Economists call this outcome market failure. See Sowell (1975: Ch. 6).

3. A starving pauper lacks the money and knowledge to farm, but starvation affords him the motive.

4. Who is more disadvantaged in the labor market: an 18-year-old black man who has completed high school or a 62-year-old white man who has the same educational credential? What if the older white man is also disabled, alcoholic, an ex-convict, and a homosexual? If we keep piling on the disabilities, the white man's disadvantage finally exceeds the black man's.

5. Sengstock (1967:187) explained the entrepreneurship of Roman Catholic Chaldeans in Detroit who were "forced into the grocery business" because they lacked marketable skills, and knew little English.

6. Individuals may be disadvantaged even when they receive better than expected treatment in the labor market. Such a person may have succeeded despite discrimination. But we cannot make the same claim of groups.

7. Crime offers an illegal alternative. The relationship of labor force disadvantage and self-employment parallels what Thornberry and Christenson (1984:400) find between unemployment and crime.

8.   Resemblances to Merton's (1957:140) anomie paradigm are inescapable. Entrepreneurship is a kind of innovation. Merton thought that innovation arose from the combination of blocked access to institutionalized means and introjection of cultural goals. Translated into the entrepreneurship lexicon, Merton's view becomes the simple disadvantage theory: subject to discrimination in the labor market, ambitious people turn to entrepreneurship. The trouble is, we hasten to point out, people who have introjected the cultural goals may lack the requisite resources, in which case innovation becomes retreatism.

9.   Entrepreneurship means legal activities accessible to measurement. Those engaged in the informal or illegal economy are likely to claim unemployment rather than to reveal their participation in the informal economy. Those without resources, therefore, lack access to the "legal" economic structure, and when they have the added burden of labor market disadvantage, they may have access only to the informal or illegal economic structure. In fact, resource disadvantage and labor market disadvantage may provide the motivation for their engagement in such activities.

10.   See Table 2.8, which presents the means and standard deviations for three of the supply resources: category mean years of education, mean years of age, and mean percentage male.

11.   These effects measure differences between the intercept coefficients of each ethnoracial category as dummy variables, compared to the intercept coefficient of native whites. Such differences show whether an ethnoracial category's intercept was significantly higher or lower than that of native whites.

12.   The two metropolitan demand variables, which were tested in Chapter 4, are not included in these labor market disadvantage models. Category mean wage and salary income is deleted because underemployment would be highly correlated with it, i.e., underemployment is measured by the category wage and salary returns per years of education. Metropolitan industrial structure is also omitted from these models.

13.   The differential slope dummy variables are interaction or multiplicative terms of the four intercept dummy variables (omitting native whites) times each of the disadvantage (and supply) variables. These differential slope coefficients test if "the response to change in a continuous independent variable differs between classified groups" (Schroeder, Sjoquist, and Stephan, 1986:58). That is, we ascertain whether the slopes of these independent variables for the four categories are the same or significantly differ from the slope obtained from native whites. In summary, the slope dummy variables tell us whether the differences in the effects for the same variables *within* each category differ significantly for the native-born whites who serve as the reference definition of a nondisadvantaged group.

14.   If any one interaction variable, such as "foreign white × mean percent unemployed," is significant, the other interactions for blacks, Asians, and Hispanics by mean percent unemployed will also be retained, irrespective of whether they are also significant. The four interaction variables are regarded as a "set."

15.   Original Pooled Sample Model 5.1, the regression of income-defined and work-defined MSER on 4 invariant supply dummy variables, 3 labor market

disadvantage variables, 12 specific labor market disadvantage interaction variables, 4 variant supply, 12 specific supply interaction variables, and 8 regional demand variables, is

$$
\begin{aligned}
Y = {} & b_1\text{FBW} + b_2\text{BLACK} + b_3\text{ASIAN} + b_4\text{HISPANIC} \\
& + b_5\text{UNEMP} + b_6\text{CWKSUNEMP} + b_7\text{CWIFORED} \\
& + b_8\text{UNEMP} \times \text{FBW} + b_9\text{UNEMP} \times \text{BLACK} \\
& + b_{10}\text{UNEMP} \times \text{ASIAN} + b_{11}\text{UNEMP} \times \text{HISPANIC} \\
& + b_{12}\text{CWKSUNEMP} \times \text{FBW} + b_{13}\text{CWKSUNEMP} \times \text{BLACK} \\
& + b_{14}\text{CWKSUNEMP} \times \text{ASIAN} + b_{15}\text{CWKSUNEMP} \times \text{HISPANIC} \\
& + b_{16}\text{CWIFORED} \times \text{FBW} + b_{17}\text{CWIFORED} \times \text{BLACK} \\
& + b_{18}\text{CWIFORED} \times \text{ASIAN} + b_{19}\text{CWIFORED} \times \text{HISPANIC} \\
& + b_{20}\text{CCATPCTM} + b_{21}\text{CCATED} + b_{22}\text{CCATAGE} + b_{23}\text{CYRSINUS} \\
& + b_{24}\text{CCATPCTM} \times \text{FBW} + b_{25}\text{CCATPCTM} \times \text{BLACK} \\
& + b_{26}\text{CCATPCTM} \times \text{ASIAN} + b_{27}\text{CCATPCTM} \times \text{HISPANIC} \\
& + b_{28}\text{CCATED} \times \text{FBW} + b_{29}\text{CCATED} \times \text{BLACK} \\
& + b_{30}\text{CCATED} \times \text{ASIAN} + b_{31}\text{CCATED} \times \text{HISPANIC} \\
& + b_{32}\text{CCATAGE} \times \text{FBW} + b_{33}\text{CCATAGE} \times \text{BLACK} \\
& + b_{34}\text{CCATAGE ASIAN} + b_{35}\text{CCATAGE HISPANIC} \\
& + b_{36}\text{NYNJPA} + b_{37}\text{ECENTRAL} + b_{38}\text{WCENTRAL} \\
& + b_{39}\text{SOATLANTIC} + b_{40}\text{MIDSOUTH} + b_{41}\text{CENTRALSO} \\
& + b_{42}\text{WESTMTNS} + b_{43}\text{PACIFIC} + b_0
\end{aligned}
$$

(Original Pooled 5.1)

6

Immigrant Entrepreneurs

Textbooks aside, with all their theoretical possibilities, the theory of capitalist concentration actually proposed the most parsimonious explanation of the entrepreneur population of the United States (Steinmetz and Wright, 1989). Derived from Marx (1965: Ch. 32) and supported by Mills (1951; also Bechofer and Elliott, 1985), the concentration theory explained the entrepreneur population by reference to an economic system that needs fewer entrepreneurs as it matures. A strictly demand-side explanation, concentration theory ignored supply-side issues in advanced capitalism, and minimized their importance in pre- or early capitalist societies. Although flawed in theory by exclusive attention to the demand side, the concentration theory agreed well with historical statistics. Between 1870 and 1972, the self-employed in the United States persistently declined as a proportion of the nonfarm labor force, a trend that was also observed in Europe. Although this decline was briefly interrupted during the Great Depression, the trend was sufficiently unidirectional to lend impressive confirmation to the concentration theory. Therefore, dissenters were few, and most sociologists viewed concentration as a master trend, like urbanization or population growth.

IMMIGRANTS AS ENTREPRENEURS

Traced strictly on the demand side, the concentration theory could not notice the unusual status of immigrant entrepreneurs on the supply side. This blindness posed a problem because in every decennial census between 1880 and 1980, the foreign born evidenced persistently higher rates of self-employment than did the native born (Light, 1972: Ch. 1; Light, 1984, Higgs, 1976:163; Conk, 1981:711–712; Borjas, 1985:17; Stark, 1991:372). This pattern suggested that immigrants were more inclined to entrepreneurship than were native-born Americans, presumably a supply-side effect in that the same opportunity conditions elicited higher rates of entrepreneurship from immigrants than from natives. Second, some immigrant and ethnic minorities displayed higher rates of self-employment than others. For example, whatever the general rate of self-employment in the nonfarm labor force, Jews were reliably above it and blacks, reliably below it (Light, 1972: Ch. 1; Higgs, 1976:162; Model, 1985). True, Goldscheider and Kobrin (1980:262–275) also found that successive generations of Jews in Providence, Rhode Island displayed successively lower rates of self-employment, a result compatible with the concentration theory. But the successive decline of self-employment did not affect the rank order of ethnic and immigrant minorities in entrepreneurship, thus suggesting that sociocultural characteristics of ethnic and immigrant communities, supply issues, affected entrepreneurship too.

When urban self-employment rates increased and then stabilized after 1972, concentration theory turned first to countercyclical effects of unemployment for an explanation (Bechofer and Elliott, 1985:201). Steinmetz and Wright (1989:975) found that the countercyclical effects of unemployment were actually weaker in the 1970s than they had earlier been. They then tried postindustrialism, reasoning that an expanded services sector characteristic of postindustrialism would offer expanded opportunities for small and medium business. Their evidence showed that growth of the service sector had supported the resurgence of self-employment, but the effects were not large enough to explain the whole increase in self-employment. Having exhausted demand-side explanations, the only explanations their data could examine, Steinmetz and Wright (1989:1007) speculated on the possible contribution of supply-side explanations such as changed tax laws, an older labor force, and women's increased participation in self-employment.

Their list is good, and bears further witness to the tendency of contemporary theory to seek balanced explanations that invoke both supply and demand. Alas, their list ignored immigration and ethnicity, variables known to influence self-employment. Resurgent immigration offers a plausible, supply variable that could explain all or some of the increased self-employment in the United States even if concentration continued to reduce the real money returns of entrepreneurship after 1972, the nadir of urban self-employment. As Brozen (1954:360) long ago observed, societies unable to generate sufficient entrepreneurs often utilize entrepreneurial immigrants. Thus, if immigrants accept the money rewards of entrepreneurship in greater proportion than natives, whether because of differences in work culture or superior organizing capacity, then the American labor force consists of a high (immigrant) and a low (native) entrepreneurship sector. In this circumstance, increased immigration would increase the high entrepreneurship sector relative to the low entrepreneurship sector, thus increasing the number of entrepreneurs in the economy, the money returns of entrepreneurship remaining the same or even declining. Admittedly, this supply-driven increase could prove transitory as acculturation homogenized work culture among immigrants and natives. Nonetheless, until homogenization was accomplished, a period of generations, immigration could in principle enhance aggregate self-employment in economies still undergoing concentration. Under this circumstance, capitalist concentration might emerge as the most important long-term factor governing self-employment, but a complete explanation of the entrepreneur population would require attention to immigration and acculturation, supply-side factors of secondary but nontrivial importance.

This scenario is plausible. Some evidence suggests that immigration did increase aggregate nonfarm self-employment in the period 1972–1984 by increasing the entrepreneur supply. The basic case is simple. Between at least 1880 and 1980, the foreign born regularly demonstrated a higher rate of nonfarm self-employment than the native born. Utilizing census data, we found that in the 272 metropolitan areas of the United States,[1] the rate of self-employment[2] among the foreign born exceeded the rate among the native born. Table 2.7 shows that, in 1980, the unweighted work-defined mean[3] self-employment rate among all foreign-born persons was 9.1% of the employed in 272 metropolitan areas, whereas, in the same year, the same unweighted mean self-employment among the native born was only 7.2%.[4] Moreover, the foreign born in the United States demonstrated a higher rate of self-employment than the native born among blacks, Asians, Hispanics, and whites alike, irrespective of whether 272 or 167 potential metropolitan areas are examined.

From approximately 1910 until 1972, the foreign born were a declining proportion of the U.S. population and labor force (Light and Sanchez, 1987:380). However, following the Immigration and Nationality Act of 1965, the resumption of international migration increased the proportion of the foreign born in the U.S. labor force. In 1970, the foreign born were 5.8% of the nonagricultural civilian labor force, whereas, in 1980, the foreign born were 7.2%. Since the foreign born were more frequently self-employed than the native born, renewed immigration might have increased nonfarm self-employment by increasing the representation of a high entrepreneurship component in the nonfarm labor force. If so, some of the resurgent entrepreneurship is explained by immigration, a supply-side variable.

Census evidence permits a preliminary evaluation of how much of the increase in the rate of nonfarm self-employment may be attributed to immigration. In the decade 1970–1980, the civilian labor force added 2,777,428 foreign-born workers, an increase of 66%. In the same decade, the increased rate of self-employment added 379,000 entrepreneurs to the nonfarm labor force net of employment growth. Assuming that 9.1% of immigrants became self-employed, the unweighted 1980 mean among the foreign born, then this foreign influx in the 1970s produced 252,746 new entrepreneurs. However, again assuming the 1980 mean, an "influx" of 2,777,428 native-born persons would have generated only 199,975 new entrepreneurs.[5] In this sense, the higher rate of self-employment among the foreign born added 54,771 self-employed to what would have been produced by an equivalent influx of native workers. Representing 2.2% of the aggregate increase in self-employment during the 1970s, these 54,771 foreign-born self-employed would constitute 14.1% of the self-employment resulting from the increased rate of self-employment during the decade.[6] This figure excludes increased self-employment resulting from increased size of the labor force.

GROWTH OF THE SERVICE SECTOR

Growth of employment in service industries provides a competing explanation for resurgent self-employment in that service industries have had a higher rate of self-employment than other industries. Even though the rate of self-employment in service industries declined from 8.7 to 7.7% of the industry's employed during the 1970s, the rate of service industry self-employment in 1980 was still slightly higher than that prevailing in the rest of the nonfarm labor force. In 1980, the rate of self-employment in service industries was 7.7% of the industry's employed, whereas the rate of self-employment in the entire nonfarm economy was 7.2%. Hence, the labor force's well-known shift to service employment might have produced a parallel increase in the proportion of the labor force self-employed (U.S. President, 1984:127–129). This demand-side explanation would not rescue the concentration theory from difficulty because the concentration theory ignores any effect of postindustrial transition upon the scale of enterprise. Nonetheless, if completely successful, a service sector explanation would exclude any supply-side variables, notably immigration.

However, like Steinmetz and Wright (1989), we find a service sector explanation only partially successful. Between 1970 and 1980, employment in service industries increased from 17.7 to 21.1% of the nonfarm employed.[7] If the service industry's share of nonfarm employment in 1980 had been the same as in 1970, then service industries would have employed only 17,695,000 instead of the observed

21,097,000 workers. Therefore, the difference between these two numbers (3,402,000) represents the gain in service industry employment caused by an increased share of total employment, and net of the increased size of the labor force. Had these 3,402,000 new service workers been employed in the general nonagricultural economy, then we would expect them to have produced self-employed workers at the rate of 7.2% rather than the higher service industry rate of 7.7%. Therefore, the shift of workers into service industries actually produced a gain of 17,010 self-employed workers in the nonfarm economy. These workers represent people whose self-employment was 379,000 higher in 1980 than it would have been had the self-employment rate stayed at the 1970 level. Therefore, the increase of service industry self-employment explains 4.5% of the aggregate increase in self-employment during the decade of the 1970s and net of increased employment in the nonagricultural civilian labor force. This demand-side chunk is less than one-third of the increased self-employment attributable to immigration, but it does not exclude an additional contribution from immigration.

CENSUS EVIDENCE

To develop a stricter test of the immigration hypothesis, we ascertained the relationship between the number of immigrants in the civilian labor force of the 272 largest American metropolitan areas and the total number who were self-employed in each metropolitan area. If immigration increased self-employment, then the growth of the foreign-born labor force should increase the aggregate number who were self-employed in metropolitan areas net of control variables.[8] Such a result would not only contribute to an explanation of the increasing trend in nonfarm self-employment, but also demonstrate a current supply-side effect upon the entrepreneur population.

Our first concern is whether an increased number of foreign-born workers in the civilian labor force increased the total number of self-employed in metropolitan areas, while controlling other supply, as well as demand factors. Table 6.2 identifies two variables bearing on this issue. Regressing the total number of work-defined self-employed in each of 272 metropolitan areas on the size of the two nativity groups in the metropolitan areas' labor force, models 1 and 2 find that for every additional 1,000 native-born workers in an area's labor force, 83 workers are self-employed. On the other hand, for every 1,000 foreign-born workers in an area, an additional 341 are self-employed! Therefore, an

Table 6.1. Variables Used in the Analyses[1]

Variables	Name and Operational Description of Variables
Dependent variables	
TSE	Total number of work-defined self-employed in each area[2]
NAROMSER	Work definition of mean self-employment rate of native-born whites, native-born blacks, or Koreans[3]
BRODMSER	Income definition of mean self-employment rate of native-born whites, native-born blacks, or Koreans[4]
INCOME2	Mean self-employment income of native-born whites, native-born blacks, or Koreans[1]
Independent variables[7]	
Demographic	
NUMNAT	Number of native-born labor force of area, in 1,000s[5]
NUMFOR	Number of foreign-born labor force of area, in 1,000s[5]
AREASIZE	Number in the labor force of SMSA, in 1,000s[5]
%FORBORN	Percentage foreign-born in area
FBMSER	Work-defined self-employment rate of foreign-born population in metropolitan area[3]
FBSE2TSE	Foreign-born self-employed as percentage of total self-employed[6]
KMSER	Work-defined self-employment rate of Koreans in area[3]
KSE2TSE	Korean self-employed as percentage of total self-employed[6]
NUMNBB	Number of native-born blacks in labor force of a metropolitan area[5]
NBB2FREQ	Native-born black labor force as percentage of total metropolitan area labor force
General supply[7]	
PCTMALE	Area mean percentage males
YRSED	Area mean years of education
AGE	Area mean years of age
Demand	
SMSAI1	Area mean wage and salary income, in 10,000s[7]
%SERVIND	Mean percentage of area labor force in aggregated service industries[7,8]
%RETIND	Mean percentage of area labor force in the retail industry[7]
8 Regions	8 dummy variables representing 8 regions of the United States[9]

[1] See Chapter 2, Appendix 2A, for detailed descriptions.
[2] The number self-employed of a category was calculated by multiplying the percentage who were self-employed in the category by the number who had valid responses for the class of worker question for each respective ethnoracial category in each respective metropolitan area.
[3] This measure is identical to NAROMSER used in Chapters 2 and 5.
[4] This measure is identical to BRODMSER used in Chapters 2 and 5 and to CATMSER used in Chapters 3 and 4.
[5] See Chapter 2, "Aggregate Characteristics," for a detailed description.
[6] FBSE2TSE = number of self-employed foreign born/total number of self-employed in each metropolitan area. For KSE2TSE, substitute "Korean" for "foreign born."
[7] Unlike earlier chapters, these variables are *not* centered in the analyses in Chapter 6.
[8] Aggregated service industries = finance, business and repair, personal, and entertainment.
[9] New England is the omitted region. (See Chapter 2, Appendix 2A, for the definition of the nine regions.)

Table 6.2. Regression of the Total Number of Self-Employed[1] in a Metropolitan Area, on Numbers of Native Born and Foreign Born, Supply and Demand Control Variables,[2] in 272 Metropolitan Areas[3] (Unstandardized Coefficients)

Independent Variables	Models		
	1	*2*	*3*
Demographic			
Number of native born	83.45****	—	59.87****
Number of foreign born	—	341.44****	133.51****
General supply			
SMSA mean percent male	1761.09	−2950.86	1025.34
SMSA mean years of education	69.13	182.56	100.74*
SMSA mean years of age	63.47	23.21	34.71
Demand			
Mean wage and salary income	−949.16**	2028.37****	−173.34
%Service industries	2006.60*	1327.70	689.91
%Retail industry	−1388.29	954.77	643.31
NY, NJ, and PA	15.13	385.27	25.56
East Central	18.04	190.72	−10.02
West Central	39.64	363.11	78.78
South Atlantic	40.46	406.12	107.27
Mid-South	33.33	394.29	95.03
Central South	171.13	551.58*	204.48*
Western Mountains	128.53	375.28	171.49
Pacific	538.51***	208.22	314.69***
Intercept	−3271.31	−4071.55	−3164.05**
Adjusted R^2	.9436	.8314	.9814

[1] The work definition of self-employment is used.
[2] See Table 6.1 for detailed descriptions of the operationalizations of the variables in Table 6.2.
[3] There are 272 areas irrespective of how many native-born whites, foreign-born whites, blacks, Asians, and Hispanics live in each.
**** LE .0001.
*** LE .001.
** LE .01.
* LE .05.

influx of foreigners would increase aggregate self-employment more than a comparable influx of native-born persons.

Finally, in model 3, when we enter both the number of native born and the number of foreign born to the equation, the foreign born contribute over twice the number of self-employed than the native born. That is, for every 1,000 native born in an area, 60 are self-employed, but for every 1,000 foreign born in an area, 134 are self-employed. These results are compatible with the hypothesis that an increase of immigrants in an area's civilian labor force resulted in a more than proportional increase in self-employment in that area, and might, therefore, have contributed to an increased rate of self-employment in the entire nonfarm labor force. We note that the strong collinear effect between the number of native born or foreign born and the number in an area who are self-employed is not surprising.

We find that area percentage in service industries in the second and third models is not significant, nor is percent retail industry significant in any of the models. When both the number of native born and the number of foreign born are entered into the same equation (model 3), only education and two regional variables are significant, but none of the other control variables. Thus, working in the Central Southern or the Pacific region significantly increases the number of self-employed compared to New England, over and above the numbers associated with increases in the sizes of either nativity group.

ESTIMATING THE SELF-EMPLOYED, 1980

If we regress our first two demographic variables on the number of work-defined self-employed in 272 metropolitan areas, we obtain the following metric coefficients,[9] where Y = estimated number of self-employed in an area, x_1 = the number of native born in an area, and x_2 = the number of foreign born in an area:

$$Y = 62.64 + .0597_{nb} \text{ (number of native born)} + .1382_{fb} \text{ (number of foreign born)} \tag{6.1}$$

Equation (6.2) offers a satisfactory method for estimating immigration's effect upon the nonfarm self-employed population in the decade 1970–1980. To accomplish this estimate, we first inserted the known size of the native and foreign segments of the 1980 civilian labor force into Eq. (6.1). The estimated total number of self-employed (Y') in all metropolitan areas, based on the metric coefficients for Eq. (6.1), where 97,449,100 = the true total number of native-born workers in the civilian labor force and 7,000,600 = the true total number of foreign-born workers in the civilian labor force is

$$Y' = 62.64 + .0597_{nb} (97,449,100) + .1382_{fb} (7,000,600)$$
$$= 6,785,257 \tag{6.2}$$

This procedure yielded an estimate of 6,785,257 nonagricultural self-employed in 1980. The 1980 U.S. Census (1984, Table 255) reported 6,677,891 nonagricultural self-employed in the civilian labor force.

Therefore, our estimate exceeded the report by 1.6%, a margin of error small enough for the purpose of this estimate.

We next rearranged the labor force components, adding to the native-born term the entire 2,764,861 persons by which the 1980 foreign-born civilian labor force exceeded the 1970 foreign-born labor force to create Eq. (6.3), an alternative estimated total number of self-employed (Y'').[10] Naturally, we subtracted the same 2,764,861 from the 1980 foreign-born civilian labor force so that the aggregate size of the civilian labor force in the second equation remained the same as in the first. In effect, we projected an estimate of the self-employed population based on an assumption of no growth in the 1970s and an "influx" of 2,746,861 native workers in that decade. The alternative estimated total number of self-employed is

$$Y'' = 62.64 + .0597_{nb} \, (100,213,961) + .1382_{fb} \, (4,235,739)$$
$$= 6,568,215 \tag{6.3}$$

Equation (6.2) shows the 1980 self-employed population we projected when the native and foreign components of the nonagricultural civilian labor force were entered in correspondence to their actual size. Equation (6.3) increases the native labor force by an influx equivalent to the net increase of the foreign labor force in the decade 1970–1980 while decreasing the foreign term by the same amount. This second equation [Eq.(6.3)] estimates the self-employed population that would have resulted had the same civilian labor force experienced an influx of native rather than of foreign workers. The estimate from Eq. (6.3) is 217,042 lower than from Eq. (6.2). This amount, therefore, represents our estimate of how much the immigration of the 1970s increased the nonfarm self-employed.

This increased self-employment (217,042) represented 3.3% of the actual self-employed population in 1980. Therefore, we estimate, immigration actually caused 1980s population of nonfarm self-employed to exceed by 3.3%, the number that a comparable influx of native workers would have generated. However, these 217,042 additional self-employed immigrants also represented 57.3% of the decade's 379,000 *increase* in nonfarm self-employment net of employment growth. This 57.3% share compares with the 14.1% share of the net increase that we explained with the cruder method above utilizing the unweighted mean self-employment of the native and foreign labor force segments. In view of their close fit and linear character, the regression equations offer, in our opinion, a better estimate of the actual increase in self-employment caused by immigration net of labor force growth. Either way, it is now doubly apparent that immigration, a supply-side factor, contributed importantly to the perplexing termination and reversal of the decline in the rate of nonfarm self-employment.

AREA LABOR FORCE SIZE AND NATIVITY

Table 6.3 continues our inquiry, considering two demographic measures: size of the area's labor force and the percentage of an area's labor force that is foreign born. Naturally, the aggregated labor force size produces a nearly linear explanation of self-employment in metropolitan areas. In itself this result is uninteresting as it merely demonstrates that the larger a labor force, the larger its self-employed sector. However, the

Table 6.3. Regression of the Total Number of Self-Employed[1] in a Metropolitan Area, on Area Labor Force Size and Percentage Foreign Born, General Supply and Demand Control Variables,[2] in 272 Metropolitan Areas[3] (Standardized Coefficients)

Independent Variables	Models			
	1	2	3	4
Demographic				
Area labor force size	.962****	.966****	—	—
%Foreign born	.055****	.044**	.429****	.431****
General supply				
SMSA mean percent male	—	.025	—	−.017
SMSA mean years of education	—	.040*	—	.186*
SMSA mean years of age	—	.033*	—	.118
Demand				
Mean wage and salary income	—	−.049**	—	.169
%Service industries	—	.015	—	.116
%Retail industry	—	−.001	—	−.123
NY, NJ, and PA	—	.011	—	.299***
East Central	—	.019	—	.386***
West Central	—	.023	—	.257**
South Atlantic	—	.039	—	.383***
Mid-South	—	.024	—	.249**
Central South	—	.045*	—	.323**
Western Mountains	—	.028	—	.168*
Pacific	—	.080****	—	.272**
Adjusted R^2	.9696	.9743	.1807	.3101

[1] The work definition of self-employment is used.
[2] See Table 6.1 for detailed descriptions of the operationalizations of these variables.
[3] See Table 6.2, note 3.
**** LE .0001.
*** LE .001.
** LE .01.
* LE .05.

addition of the percent of the area labor force who were foreign born and supply and demand control variables permit us to ascertain whether we can modify our accurate, but trivial, model if we know more about a metropolitan area than just its labor force size. In effect, our test asks whether nativity affects aggregate self-employment net of the number of workers in the metropolitan area and control variables.

Nativity does have an independent effect. Numerical size of a metropolitan area and percentage of the labor force foreign born alone account for about 97% of the explained variation in the number of self-employed workers in an area (model 1). When the control variables are added in model 2, little is added to the explanation of the total numbers of self-employed in metropolitan areas, but percent foreign born remains significant.

In models 3 and 4, we test the effects of just percent foreign born, deleting the expected powerful effect of area size. The effects of the control variables in model 4 are as follows: First, the more educated an area's labor force is, the more workers choose self-employment. Second, all eight regions produce more self-employed workers than New England. However, the percentage of an area's labor force that is working in service industries has no significant effect upon the number who become self-employed, nor do the other two demand variables.

Our results thus far have indicated that immigrants forced the aggregate self-employed population of metropolitan areas above the level that would have been expected from a comparable influx of native workers. Apparently, the number of self-employed in metropolitan areas expands and contracts in response to the entrepreneurial versatility of the labor force. That conclusion is theoretically important. If true, it means that the level of self-employment in a metropolitan area is not a simple function of metropolitan population size, but is also affected by nativity, a quality of the population. This quality reflects the entrepreneurial potential of the population, not its size.

This qualitative finding contradicts Lieberson (1980:294), who proposed that "the occupational composition of a community is essentially independent of the ethnic-racial composition of the population." Possibly true with respect to wage and salary occupations, Lieberson's proposal cannot be true of entrepreneurship unless we suppose that every metropolitan area has a quantum of market opportunities, strictly proportional to size, and that metropolitan areas always saturate all opportunities immanent in demand. That view reduces entrepreneurship to filling niches, overlooking the problem of missed opportunities. When entrepreneurs miss market opportunities, they fail to saturate the economic potential immanent in local markets. That failure results in suboptimal entrepreneurial performance. If entrepreneurship is the capacity to squeeze real business firms out of immanent demand potential, a locality's entrepreneurship can easily fall short of optimal performance. We may not assume that metropolitan economies always operate at optimal levels of self-employment.

EFFECT ON NATIVE ENTREPRENEURS

A related theoretical difficulty surfaces in regard to relationships between foreign and native entrepreneurs. If entrepreneurial opportunities are always saturated, and every locality always operates at optimal entrepreneurship, then foreign entrepreneurs can obtain a share of demand only at the expense of native entrepreneurs. The pie is not only fixed, it always reaches its maximum potential, so when foreigners take a bigger slice, they leave less for natives. However, if the self-employment rate of localities depends partially upon local entrepreneurship, and not just upon labor force size, then immigrants might expand the local economy's entrepreneur population, benefiting themselves, without reducing either the number or the income of native entrepreneurs.

The possible impact of foreign entrepreneurs upon native entrepreneurs offers another way to ascertain whether local economies can expand self-employment when the local population is especially entrepreneurial. On the one hand, immigrant entrepreneurship might have occurred at the expense of native-born entrepreneurs with immigrants appropriating all or some of the opportunities that natives would otherwise have enjoyed. True, on the basis of our own evidence, discussed above, we dismiss the view that the entrepreneur population of each metropolitan area has some upper limit, a simple function of population size, and that the upper limit is always reached in every metropolitan area. If that were so, then the higher rate of entrepreneurship among immigrants would require transfers of business opportunities from the native to the immigrant population, a zero-sum condition. However, even if immigrant entrepreneurs increase the aggregate population of entrepreneurs in a metropolitan area, as they apparently do, they may appropriate business opportunities that native entrepreneurs would otherwise have enjoyed, provided only that the immigrant-caused increase in aggregate entrepreneur population is less than the immigrant's self-employment. Suppose, for example, that immigrant entrepreneurs operated 200 firms, but added only 100 to the area's aggregate of firms. Under that circumstance, the rate of immigrant self-employment reduced the number of native-owned firms by 100 while increasing the rate of self-employment in the metropolitan area.

On the other hand, immigrant entrepreneurship might wholly augment and supplement native entrepreneurship. Foreign entrepreneurs might find and exploit economic opportunities natives missed, shunned, or underexploited. Under this circumstance, immigrant self-employment should have no effect upon the self-employment of native-born workers because foreigners exploit opportunities that natives would not have exploited on their own. That is, the rate of self-employment among the native born should be the same whatever the rate of self-employment among the foreign born because foreign born entrepreneurs increased aggregate self-employment by an amount equal to their own self-employment.

Two measures of immigrant self-employment are the mean self-employment rate of the foreign born and the percentage of all self-employed in a metropolitan area who were foreign born. Since native whites are the most advantaged category, they test the possibly deleterious effects of competition with immigrant entrepreneurs. If the foreign entrepreneurs compete with the native white entrepreneurs, then the more foreign entrepreneurs a metropolitan area contains, the fewer native white entrepreneurs there should be. Table 6.4A shows the results of regressing these two measures of immigrant entrepreneurship on native self-employment rates, both work and income. The effects (models 1 and 3) are negligible or slightly positive. There is no sign here that foreigners reduce native-white entrepreneurship.

When native-white supply characteristics and demand control variables are added, in models 2 and 4, the mean self-employment rate of the foreign born still has no effect upon the self-employment rate of native whites for either the work or the income definitions of self-employment. High rates of immigrant self-employment neither increase nor reduce self-employment of native whites. However, the higher the percentage of all self-employed in a metropolitan area who were foreign-born, the *lower* the percentage of native whites who were income-defined self-employed, a category heavy on part-time workers.[11] This last result is not substantively important. The negative relationship is a built-in feature of the mathematical relationship.

As the foreign born become a larger percentage of the labor force of an area, the native-born white self-employment rate decreases, but this decrease has no effect upon native whites' self-employment income (Table 6.4B). We believe that the adverse impact of foreign self-employment upon native-white self-employment is a statistical artifact of no real consequence. But we cannot ignore the independence of native white self-employment income and immigrant self-employment. No matter how numerous they were, absolutely or relatively, immigrants did not reduce the self-employment income of native white

Table 6.4. The Effects of Immigrant Self-Employment on Native-Born White Self-Employment Rates and Self-Employment Income,[1] in 272 Metropolitan Areas[2] (Standardized Coefficients)

A. Dependent Variables: Work-Defined and Income-Defined Self-Employment Rates

	Native-Born White Work-Defined SE Rates		Native-Born White Income Defined SE Rates	
Independent Variables	1	2	3	4
Demographic				
Foreign-born MSER[3]	.122*	.044	.046	.053
Foreign-born SE/total SE[3]	.174**	−.045	.083	−.128**
General supply[4]				
NB white mean percent male	—	−.043	—	−.088
NB white mean years of education	—	.307****	—	.378****
NB white mean years of age	—	.394****	—	.299****
Demand				
Mean wage and salary income	—	−.154**	—	−.198***
%Service industries	—	.020	—	.028
%Retail industry	—	.379****	—	.270****
NY, NJ, and PA	—	−.003	—	.072
East Central	—	−.000	—	.152*
West Central	—	.084	—	.148**
South Atlantic	—	.195**	—	.165**
Mid-South	—	.144**	—	.149**
Central South	—	.367****	—	.455****
Western Mountains	—	.203****	—	.292****
Pacific	—	.420****	—	.616****
Adjusted R^2	.0401	.7199	.0020	.7182

B. Dependent Variable: Mean Self-Employment Income

	Native White Mean SE Income	
Independent Variables	1	2
Demographic		
Foreign-born MSER[3]	.119*	.088
Foreign-born SE/total SE[3]	.317****	.048
General supply[4]		
NB white mean percent male	—	.000
NB white mean years of education	—	.177*
NB white mean years of age	—	.353****
Demand		
Mean wage and salary income	—	.236**
%Service industries	—	.184**
%Retail industry	—	.007
NY, NJ, and PA	—	−.073
East Central	—	−.068
West Central	—	.023

Table 6.4. *(continued)*

South Atlantic	—	.039
Mid-South	—	.176*
Central South	—	.324****
Western Mountains	—	−.076
Pacific	—	.036
Adjusted R^2	.1117	.4334

[1] See Table 6.1 for detailed descriptions of the operationalizations of these variables.
[2] See Table 6.2, note 3.
[3] The work definition of self-employment is used.
[4] General supply characteristics of native-born whites are used, instead of the area characteristics, which were used in Tables 6.2 and 6.3.
**** LE .0001.
*** LE .001.
** LE .01.
* LE .05.

entrepreneurs. There is no warrant in these data for the supposition that immigrants' self-employment rate reduced the number or the income of native white entrepreneurs.

AFRICAN-AMERICAN VERSUS IMMIGRANT ENTREPRENEURS

If immigrant entrepreneurs reduced the self-employment rates or earnings of any native-born counterparts, African Americans would probably feel the effect most. First, of all native-born groups, blacks have the lowest rate of self-employment, a possible sign of vulnerability to external competition. Second, overt conflicts between blacks and immigrant entrepreneurs have developed in many big cities (Light and Bonacich, 1988, Ch. 12; Light, Har-Chvi, and Kan, 1994a). Third, immigrant entrepreneurs cluster in central cities where blacks also work and reside, thus placing black entrepreneurs at special risk from immigrant business competition. Among the foreigners, Koreans have been the special subjects of African-American complaints in New York, Los Angeles, Washington, Chicago, Philadelphia, and other big cities (Chang, 1990). Therefore, to hone the analysis, we also assess the effect of Korean entrepreneurship upon black entrepreneurship and self-employment earnings. Inasmuch as nationalistic blacks have vociferously complained about Korean entrepreneurs in black neighborhoods (Light and Bonacich, 1988, Ch. 12; Johnson and Oliver, 1989; Min, 1992), identifying them as obstacles to African-American economic progress, the separate analysis of Koreans and blacks isolates the single most likely case in which to expect negative impact of foreign entrepreneurs upon the mean self-employment income and percentage self-employed of native entrepreneurs.

To assess this issue, Table 6.5A first shows the effect of the mean self-employment rate of the foreign born and the percentage of all self-employed in an area who were foreign born upon the rate of self-employment among native blacks and upon the mean self-employment income of native blacks (Table 6.5B). Table 6.6A and B then displays the statistical effect upon the self-employment rates and incomes of native blacks, of the mean self-employment rates of Koreans and the percentage of all self-employed in an area who were Korean, holding constant the same native-black resource and general economic variables in both conditions.

Table 6.5. The Effects of Immigrant Self-Employment on Native-Born Black Self-Employment Rates and Self-Employment Income,[1] in 245 Metropolitan Areas[2] (Standardized Coefficients)

A. Dependent Variables: Work-Defined and Income-Defined Self-Employment Rates

	Native-Born Black Work-Defined Self-Employment Rates		Native-Born Black Income-Defined Self-Employment Rates	
Independent Variables	*Model 1a*	*Model 1b*	*Model 2a*	*Model 2b*
Demographic				
Foreign-born MSER[3]	.052	.024	−.052	−.021
Foreign-born SE/total SE[3]	.037	−.035	.036	−.070
General supply[4]				
NB black mean percent male	—	.013	—	.138*
NB black mean years of education	—	.255**	—	.358****
NB black mean years of age	—	.292****	—	.190**
Demand				
Mean wage and salary income	—	.098	—	.063
%Service industries	—	−.001	—	.183*
%Retail industry	—	.283***	—	.179*
NY, NJ, and PA	—	−.219*	—	−.174
East Central	—	−.280*	—	−.120
West Central	—	−.113	—	−.025
South Atlantic	—	−.125	—	−.038
Mid-South	—	−.089	—	−.046
Central South	—	−.004	—	.050
Western Mountains	—	.004	—	−.195*
Pacific	—	−.001	—	.057
Adjusted R^2	−.0040	.1986	−.0043	.2742

Table 6.5. *(continued)*

	B. Dependent Variables: Mean Self-Employment Income	
	Native-Born Black Self-Employment Income	
Independent Variables	Model 3a[5]	Model 3b[5]
Demographic		
Foreign-born MSER[3]	.054	.064
Foreign-born SE/total SE[3]	.098	.067
General supply[4]		
NB black mean percent male	—	−.063
NB black mean years of education	—	.009
NB black mean years of age	—	.049
Demand		
Mean wage and salary income	—	.104
%Service industries	—	−.094
%Retail industry	—	−.103
NY, NJ, and PA	—	−.211
East Central	—	−.304*
West Central	—	−.012
South Atlantic	—	−.158
Mid-South	—	−.129
Central South	—	−.212
Western Mountains	—	−.038
Pacific	—	−.138
Adjusted R^2	.0043	.0245

[1] See Table 6.1 for detailed descriptions of the operationalization of these variables.
[2] The 245 areas in which there are a minimum threshold of 20 native-born blacks, in the 5% PUMS sample.
[3] The work definition of self-employment is used.
[4] General supply characteristics of native-born blacks are used, instead of the area means, which were used in Tables 6.2 and 6.3.
[5] Due to missing cases, the Ns are reduced to 233 areas.
**** LE .0001.
*** LE .001.
** LE .01.
* LE .05.

Neither immigrant entrepreneurship in general (Table 6.5) nor specifically Korean entrepreneurship (Table 6.6) reduces either the self-employment of the native blacks or their money returns from self-employment.[12] For the latter, this was even true in the 46 metropolitan areas in which more than a threshold number of both native-born blacks and Koreans resided. Agreeing with Boyd (1990), who reached the same conclusion, our data show no evidence that Korean entrepreneurs displaced African-American entrepreneurs. Obviously, this result does not prove that immigrant firms did not cluster in black

Table 6.6. The Effects of Korean Self-Employment on Native-Born Black Self-Employment Rates and Self-Employment Income,[1] in Metropolitan Areas (Standardized Coefficients)

	A. Dependent Variables: Work-Defined and Income-Defined Self-Employment Rates							
	Native-Born Black Work-Defined Self-Employment Rates				Native-Born Black Income-Defined Self-Employment Rates			
	Model 1a		Model 1b		Model 2a		Model 2b	
Independent Variables	208 Areas[2]	46 Areas[3]	208 Areas[2]	46 Areas[3]	208 Areas[2]	46 Areas[3]	208 Areas[2]	46 Areas[3]
Demographic								
Korean MSER[4]	-.001	-.003	.050	.182	-.074	-.138	-.013	.126
Korean SE/total SE[4]	.074	.207	-.055	-.052	.192**	.458**	.021	.233
General supply[5]								
NBB mean percent male	—	—	.060	.222	—	—	.158*	.196
NBB mean years education	—	—	.218*	.196	—	—	.305***	.136
NBB mean years age	—	—	.290**	.540**	—	—	.165*	.024
Demand								
Mean wage and salary income	—	—	.072	.074	—	—	.056	.217
%Service industries	—	—	.014	.019	—	—	.161*	-.103
%Retail industry	—	—	.358***	.480*	—	—	.237**	.401
NY, NJ, and PA	—	—	-.224*	-.282	—	—	-.142	-.257
East Central	—	—	-.334*	-.239	—	—	-.118	-.259
West Central	—	—	-.101	.034	—	—	.004	-.081
South Atlantic	—	—	-.192	.113	—	—	-.026	-.076
Mid-South[6]	—	—	-.116	—	—	—	-.023	—
Central South	—	—	-.027	.245	—	—	.123	-.001
Western Mountains	—	—	-.025	.223	—	—	-.189*	.102
Pacific	—	—	-.026	.339	—	—	.072	.008
Adjusted R^2	-.0043	-.0019	.2448	.4751	.0235	.1605	.2930	.4345

A. Dependent Variable: Mean Self-Employment Income

| | Native-Born Black Self-Employment Income | | | |
| | Model 3a | | Model 3b | |
Independent Variables	198 Areas[2]	46 Areas[3]	198 Areas[2]	46 Areas[3]
Demographic				
Korean MSER[4]	-.004	.317*	-.036	.170
Korean SE/total SE[4]	-.028	-.171	.017	.059
General supply[5]				
NB black mean percent male	—	—	.086	-.028
NB black mean years of education	—	—	-.075	-.310
NB black mean years of age	—	—	.076	.328
Demand				
Mean wage and salary income	—	—	.095	.666*
%Service industries	—	—	-.013	.008
%Retail industry	—	—	-.061	.044
NY, NJ, and PA	—	—	-.288*	-.520
East Central	—	—	-.453**	-.431
West Central	—	—	-.082	-.086
South Atlantic	—	—	-.301*	-.311
Mid-South[6]	—	—	-.256*	—
Central South	—	—	-.356**	-.206
Western Mountains	—	—	-.169	-.076
Pacific	—	—	-.301*	-.167
Adjusted R^2	-.0094	.0616	.0361	.2525

[1] See Table 6.1 for detailed descriptions of the operationalizations of these variables.
[2] Maximum number of areas that do not have any missing values for any of the variables.
[3] The number of areas in which there are a minimum threshold number of 20 Koreans and 20 native-born blacks, in the 5% PUMS sample.
[4] The work definition of self-employment is used.
[5] General supply characteristics of native-born blacks are used, instead of area means, which were used in Tables 6.2 and 6.3.
[6] Due to few cases in the Mid-South, this region had to be omitted in addition to New England, as the reference category.
**** LE .0001. *** LE .001. ** LE .01. * LE .05.

neighborhoods. They did. However, any clustering had no effect upon African-American entrepreneurship by 1980, presumably because immigrant firms filled economic niches that went unfilled when no foreign or Korean entrepreneurs were present to fill them.

KOREAN SETTLEMENTS

Although Korean entrepreneurs did not affect the income or the number of African-American entrepreneurs, Korean entrepreneurs possibly gravitated to cities in which blacks were numerous. Razin (1988:7) proposed that groups with low self-employment rates "increase opportunities for other groups" who occupy entrepreneurial niches that would otherwise remain empty. In this case, Koreans should gravitate to cities in which blacks are numerous, taking advantage of the economic slack created by low-resource neighbors. This slack would exist inside and outside the black neighborhoods precisely because blacks themselves did not produce the expected number of entrepreneurs, thus permitting Koreans to exploit their untapped opportunities. In effect, Razin proposes that Koreans settled in areas containing large African-American populations because such areas contained untapped entrepreneurial opportunities Koreans could exploit.

To examine this possibility, Table 6.7 regresses Korean work and income self-employment rates on number and characteristics of metropolitan   populations in 224 metropolitan areas[13] that contained blacks above threshold levels. In actuality, African Americans and Koreans coexisted in only 46 of these 224 areas. But a strict test of the settlement hypothesis requires us to include all metropolitan areas in which blacks lived, predicting that Koreans will overselect for entrepreneurship those areas in which blacks are most numerous.

In these 46 metropolitan areas, native blacks range from 3,140 in Honolulu to 54,700 in New York City.[14] Koreans, on the other hand, range from a low of 400[15] in Cincinnati, Indianapolis, and Vallejo, CA, to a high of 12,400, also in New York City. Thus, native blacks always outnumber Koreans in these metropolitan areas. However, increasing the number of native-born blacks in an area was positively significant only in the first model[16] for the work-defined self-employment rates of Koreans. When control variables are added, this effect is no longer significant. In these 46 areas, the self-employment success of Koreans cannot be attributed to the demographic characteristics of native blacks as competitors or as consumers.

The number of native blacks in an area and their percentage of an area's labor force are irrelevant to explaining the work-defined self-

Table 6.7. The Effects of Native-Born Black Self-Employment on Korean Self-Employment Rates,[1] in 224 Metropolitan Areas[2] (Standardized Coefficients)

Independent Variables	Korean Work-Defined MSER	Korean Income-Defined MSER
Demographic		
Number of NB blacks	.014	.036
NB blacks as % of area labor force	.207	.250*
General supply[3]		
NB black mean percent male	−.018	−.010
NB black mean years of education	−.054	−.095
NB black mean years of age	−.018	−.042
Demand		
Mean wage and salary income	.121	.036
%Service industries	.008	.031
%Retail industry	.125	.061
NY, NJ, and PA	−.046	−.117
East Central	−.097	−.105
West Central	−.119	−.137
South Atlantic	−.105	−.208
Mid-South	−.071	−.050
Central South	−.107	−.153
Western Mountains	−.099	−.101
Pacific	−.080	−.018
Adjusted R^2	−.0061	.0139

[1] See Table 6.1 for detailed descriptions of the operationalizations of these variables.
[2] Maximum number of areas that do not have any missing values for any of the variables.
[3] General supply characteristics of native-born blacks are used, instead of area means, which were used in Tables 6.2 and 6.3.
* LE .05.

employment rates of Koreans in America's largest metropolitan areas. However, increasing the percentage of an area's labor force that is native black *does* significantly increase the engagement of Koreans income-only self-employment, a type heavily affected by part-timers. However, explained variation is minuscule, and the supply characteristics of the native black population have no impact on either type of self-employment. None of the demand factors is significant for either model, including the percentage working in service industries. Needless to say, these models are not significant as a whole. They explain next to no variation in Korean self-employment rates, and lead us to conclude that Korean settlement and black population were largely independent. Koreans did not overselect for settlement metropolitan areas in which large African-American populations existed.

CONCLUSION

Textbook treatments of entrepreneurship have long claimed that supply as well as demand affect its level. However, this claim was hard to vindicate because changes in entrepreneurship's rate could not be attributed to specific demand-side or supply-side causes. Additionally, the success of the concentration theory discouraged research on entrepreneurship's supply-side in advanced economies.

This chapter has identified immigration as a supply-side factor that affects aggregate entrepreneurship. We measured its effect upon the entrepreneur population of 272 American metropolitan areas between 1970 and 1980. Because immigrants have a higher rate of self-employment than do native workers, they increase the aggregate level of self-employment in the nonfarm economy. The resumption of immigration in 1965 increased the proportion of immigrants in the labor force of American metropolitan areas, thus contributing between 14 and 57% of the surprising increase in rate of nonfarm self-employment between 1970 and 1980. The choice of estimates depends upon which method of estimation one employs, but we believe that the higher estimate is more accurate.

Immigrant entrepreneurs increased the aggregate self-employment in the nonfarm economy without reducing either the rate of, or mean money returns to, self-employment among the native-born whites. We also found no evidence that the rate of or money returns earned by immigrant entrepreneurs had any effect upon native blacks, presumably the most vulnerable to foreign competition of any population segment. This result implies that foreign entrepreneurs in African-American communities filled niches that went unfilled when no foreigners were available to fill them. They did not obstruct the entrepreneurial possibilities of either blacks or native whites. However, we found some evidence that native blacks, as consumers, slightly increased the income-defined self-employment rates of Koreans.

In a world of dog-eat-dog competition these results are refreshing. At least with respect to entrepreneurship, a process that increases the size of total material welfare, one group's success does not occur at the expense of another. That lugubrious situation would arise if metropolitan areas imposed maximum self-employment rates that were always reached. In such a case, new entrepreneurs could only have high self-employment rates if the rate of self-employment among existing entrepreneurs were reduced. Dog would indeed eat dog. However, our data show some upward flexibility in the number of entrepreneurs that metropolitan areas can support just as if the immigrant entrepreneurs were creating new economic opportunities such that their success did not jeopardize the material welfare of others. Entrepreneurship is the point at which metropolitan areas experience the ability to create new opportunities that simply increase material welfare. In the language of sociology, entrepreneurship is a point at which agency overcomes structure (Sewell, 1992:27).

NOTES

* This chapter is an expanded version of an earlier article by Ivan Light and Angel Sanchez, "Immigrant Entrepreneurs in 272 SMSA's," *Sociological Perspectives* 30(1987):373–399

1. The maximum number of metropolitan areas selected for analysis is 272. However, a category or group may have representation in less than 272 areas if it did not have the minimum of 400 persons in the civilian nonagricultural labor force in all 272 areas.

2. Utilizing the work (narrow) definition of self-employment. (See Chapter 2, "Who Are the Self-Employed?")

3. See Chapter 2, "Self-Employment Rates; Weighted and Unweighted Rates."

4. The mean self-employment rates for all foreign-born persons in 167 metropolitan areas were slightly less (8.8%) than for the 272 areas. The 167 areas have a minimum threshold number of native whites, foreign whites, blacks, Asians, and Hispanics.

5. Based on the unweighted mean work definition of the self-employment rate of the native born of 7.2%.

6. Statistical sources for these calculations are U.S. Bureau of the Census (1984, 1973).

7. See note 6.

8. That is, general supply and demand variables, see Table 6.1 for a description of variables used in this analysis.

9. These coefficients are not shown in Table 6.2.

10. Where 100,213,961 = the true total number of native-born workers in the civilian labor force, 97,449,100 + 2,746,861, the increased number of foreign born in the civilian labor force between 1970 and 1980, and 4,235,739 = the true total number of foreign-born workers in the civilian labor force, 7,000,600 - 2,746,861, the increased number of foreign born in the civilian labor force between 1970 and 1980.

11. That is, the income definition of self-employment.

12. In the augmented models, 1b, 2b, and 3b, in Tables 6.5 and 6.6.

13. Maximum number of areas that do not have any missing values for any of the variables.

14. These are weighted numbers, i.e., each frequency × 20 to estimate a 100% sample.

15. That is, our threshold number.

16. This model is not shown in Table 6.7.

Rethinking Entrepreneurship

In Horatio Alger's nineteenth-century childrens' novels, initially disadvantaged young men overcome obstacles "by luck and pluck." Although Alger (1869) never claimed that hard work and determination alone could overcome any obstacles and achieve eventual success, his name is popularly linked to just that claim.[1] Whatever Alger may have meant, in contemporary American culture, the "Horatio Alger tradition" stands for a philosophy of rugged individualism less radical than Ayn Rand's (1943, 1957), but sharing with that writer a profound faith in the ability of determined individuals to succeed by dint of supreme efforts (Murray, 1984:186).

Horatio Alger did not invent the Horatio Alger tradition. Self-help and individualism were already prominent values in Benjamin Franklin's writings, a century earlier. Because these values have long been core features of American culture, self-help and individualism naturally find ready constituencies when advanced as solutions to social problems (Smith and Stone, 1989). Of these nostrums, the grandfather is probably the recommendation that the poor lift themselves "by their bootstraps." This recommendation simultaneously affirms cherished values of self-help and individualism and rejects government interference in the economy. Entrepreneurship offers an example of self-help values scarcely less central than the bootstrap recommendation, and has, indeed, often been identified as the bootstrap (Gilder, 1981:65).[2]

John Benson (1983:4–6) noted that a century ago most working-class families extended their wage income with various forms of petty self-employment. The entrepreneurship solution to poverty is self-employment (Green and Pryde, 1990). If people suffer poverty because of discrimination, those people should open business firms, thus positioning themselves for progression from dependent employees, to self-employed owners, to employers. This progression Abraham Lincoln dubbed "the true condition of the laborer" (Mayer, 1953:160). As the marketplace allows all entrants to compete for success, prejudice excludes no one from opening his or her own business firm. Once open, firms depend for success upon hard work and ingenuity, resources available in principle to anyone. Therefore, when individual members of disadvantaged groups initiate and manage their own business firms, so runs the Alger theory, they position themselves for self-advancement, and in so doing advance the interests of the whole disadvantaged class to which they belong. In this manner, entrepreneurship eliminates the poverty of the entrepreneur, and reduces the poverty of her or his coethnic employees.

Because entrepreneurship is a cultural cliché, Americans unthinkingly fit this complex subject into outmoded ideological frameworks, thus frustrating innovation, research, and even dialogue. The rigidity and intolerance that surround this subject are profound. On the left, ideologues denounce entrepreneurship's "key symbolic role" in justifying capitalism (Clegg, Boreham, and Dow, 1986:82).[3] We agree that entrepreneurship props up capitalism by improving the performance of market economies, a result that, when projected into the ideological arena, promotes the perpetuation of capitalism. However, even if so, the ultraleftist argument to that effect also implicitly perpetuates capitalism too since it concedes that this part of the capitalist system still works. People retain economic systems that work.[4] Fearing that entrepreneurship still works, ultraleftists seek to discourage poor and working class individuals from becoming entrepreneurs lest they lose enthusiasm for revolution. Such a misguided policy requires poor people to await for the revolution rather than to feed themselves and their families by means currently in hand. Worse, this self-contradicting policy sacrifices the material interest of poor and working individuals in order to salvage a theory that proclaims the supremacy of material interests.

On the right, ideologues glibly assume that entrepreneurship expresses and belongs to a conservative political ideology, an assumption that ironically mirrors what the ultraleftists also believe (Gilder, 1981:31, 65). In actuality, this assumption misinterprets the political implications of entrepreneurship. In fact, entrepreneurship is not a touchstone that divides liberals and conservatives. The political difference that long has separated liberals and conservatives is the role of government in the economy, especially its activist role in redressing economic inequalities, managing health care, parity price supports, rent controls, minimum wage requirements, regulation of airwaves, public housing, national parks, and the like (Friedman, 1962:35–36; Thatcher, 1989:86).[5]

Unlike any of these divisive issues, entrepreneurship fits within both liberal and conservative economic agendas. Under conservative administration, government scales back interventionist economic policies, leaving only the labor market and self-employment as vehicles for redressing poverty and encouraging economic growth (Murray, 1984). Thus, expressing a conservative's optimistic faith in markets, Patrick

Buchanan (1988:14) predicts prosperity for all "if only we provide enough incentives for entrepreneurs to bring full employment." In his opinion, government needs no economic policy other than getting out of the way of entrepreneurs.

Lambasting his opponents with the same message, candidate Ronald Reagan (1968:138) declared that Democrats believe "only in centralized government and an all-powerful state." But Reagan's partisan claim misrepresents what Democrats believe. In actuality, liberals like George McGovern endorse government interventions in the economy when the private sector does not provide full employment. But even in McGovern's liberal view, entrepreneurship offers a private sector vehicle for redressing social inequalities as well as the preferred agency for economic action.[6] McGovern is not alone. Writing for the Democratic Policy Commission, Kirk and Matheson (1986:55) declare that economic opportunity means "a supportive environment for entrepreneurs." Democrats propose to shore up this environment by means of increasing the federal role in research and development, sponsoring entrepreneur/university partnerships, developing state-funded "incubator projects," and federal strategic block grants for entrepreneurs. This is activist, liberal government, but its goal is the support of entrepreneurship, not its suppression (Mokry, 1988:25–26).

In sum, entrepreneurship enjoys political support from liberals as well as from conservatives, who differ principally about what to do in case entrepreneurship falls short of providing full employment. That philosophical difference pertains to the larger political/economic context within which conservatives and liberals locate entrepreneurship. Conservatives treat entrepreneurship as the only vehicle for rectifying economic inequalities and promoting economic growth. They are comfortable when persistent poverty defies market solutions because they believe no other solutions exist. Liberals have more faith in government's interventionist role in supporting the market. Confronting shortfalls in economic growth or persistent poverty, liberal administrations offer supplementary social programs and interventions without disconnecting entrepreneurship in the market economy.

We do not cry peace where there is no peace, and concede that liberals and conservatives have important philosophical differences. But, contrary to the ranting ideologues, entrepreneurship is not that difference. On the contrary, entrepreneurship is common to both. Because it persists under either liberal or conservative administrations, enjoying the support of both, encouragement of entrepreneurship is actually a bipartisan element of government economic policy. Supporting and encouraging entrepreneurship simply makes common sense whether one defines oneself as a liberal or as a conservative.

Entrepreneurship is part of a liberal economic policy, not the whole
of it. From a liberal perspective, entrepreneurship alone represents an
inadequate economic policy, not a pernicious policy. Therefore, liberals
like Michael Dukakis supplement entrepreneurship with government
intervention, even government intervention in the supply of entrepreneurs (Dukakis and Kanter, 1988: Ch. 2). This supplementation takes
the form of government loan programs targeted to minority-owned
businesses and government procurement policies that favor minority-
owned suppliers. Whether these interventions are effective or well-
advised is an important but technical issue. The point is simply that
entrepreneurship's encouragement is neither a partisan issue nor a
uniquely conservative faith. Currently, both major American political
parties believe that entrepreneurship promotes economic development
and reduces poverty—and even Russian ex-Communists like Boris
Yeltsin have come around to this way of thinking (Szelenyi, 1988;
Schillinger and Jenswold, 1988). The partisan issue concerns the social
programs that administrations do or do not offer to encourage entrepreneurship in the private economy.

In our opinion, to stress entrepreneurship alone does not constitute a
sufficient political response to this country's economic challenges, and
we advocate in addition paring wasteful defense spending, development
of a national, industrial policy, job-creating programs of tax-supported
public works, single-payer health care reform, and temporary, self-
destructing tariff protection for basic industries. If these are characteristically liberal views, we accept the political label. Nonetheless, we
maintain that alongside these interventionist economic programs, just
encouraging entrepreneurship can have a significant, cost-effective
impact upon the reduction of poverty, the promotion of economic
growth, job creation, and even the reduction of intergroup conflicts in
society. We wish to contribute here to a nonpartisan, technical discussion
of how best to encourage entrepreneurship. That discussion should interest liberals and conservatives alike. This is a core subject that requires
some ideological rethinking in order to contribute to human welfare.

ENTREPRENEURSHIP POLICY

Although they agree on encouraging entrepreneurship, liberals and
conservatives disagree on how best to accomplish that goal. This dis-
agreement concerns means, not ends. Until social science began to study
the subject, policies to promote entrepreneurship descended from apri-

oristic, deductive reasoning derived from classical liberalism, a political philosophy developed in the nineteenth century. Liberalism proposes that entrepreneurs are profit-seeking individualists whose optimization requires minimum government. Minimum government means low taxes so that entrepreneurs keep the money they earn, thus maximizing their monetary incentive to work. More incentive means more and better entrepreneurs. Additionally, low taxes make low profit ventures feasible, thus squeezing the maximum of economic development from demand conditions. Minimum government also means small and efficient governments that stay out of the marketplace. Government rules, paperwork, oversight, and penalties encumber entrepreneurs in activities that redirect their attention from running their business. Time spent filling out forms for the government is time one cannot spend on improving one's business. Therefore, entrepreneurs who spend little time coping with the government have an economic advantage over entrepreneurs who spend much time. If entrepreneurs hire employees to deal with the government, directing their own attention to their business, their business has to carry a burden of unproductive employees. For all these reasons, Jack Kemp (1994) declares that "the key to job creation" is "unleashing the creative power of America's entrepreneurs and small business owners through lower taxes."

Without rejecting this liberal wisdom, persuasive as far as it goes, we note that it concentrates wholly upon demand conditions, ignoring entrepreneurial resources. That is not surprising because resources lie on the supply side, which classic liberalism did not consider (Bradford and Osborne, 1976:316). One easily sees, when the observation is made, that even optimal demand-side conditions cannot create entrepreneurs when people have inadequate resources, nor can demand conditions guarantee optimal entrepreneur populations when resources are lacking or maldistributed (Kasarda, 1989:44). The resources of entrepreneurship require attention in a comprehensive entrepreneurship policy that wishes to exploit existing social science knowledge. Although entrepreneurial supply was not studied in the last century, when liberal philosophers were spinning their theories, we now know that entrepreneurs emerge from groups that stockpile and transmit essential resources (Taylor and Singleton, 1993; Putnam, 1993). These resources include but are not limited to money. Chen (1986:101) even declares that "the principal reason" for low entrepreneurship is lack of information, not lack of money.

As a result of several decades of research on entrepreneur supply, social science can now improve an entrepreneurship policy that ignores resources. This policy approach is novel in the United States.[7] We do not know where that search will end, but education for entrepreneurship is an obvious starting point. In addition to social networks, entrepreneurs need complex skills, knowledge, motivations, and values. Without these resources, they cannot respond to opportunities however favorable the tax climate. After all, the entrepreneurs of the informal economy pay no taxes right now. They evade all government regulation. For them enterprise zones already exist. Yet Jones (1988:167) found them "largely incapable of transforming their skills into those necessary for the successful operation of a sedentary retail site." It should be public policy to increase entrepreneurial skills in the population in order to improve the market's exploitation of latent demand conditions. To lend money to unqualified entrepreneurs is a proven recipe for disaster.[8]

As matters now stand, and have long stood, entrepreneurs acquire entrepreneurial resources from family, neighborhood, ethnic group, and class in the course of lifelong socialization. This system adequately serves affluent people who are related by friendship, blood, and marriage to existing entrepreneurs. These people acquire by inheritance the class and ethnic resources their entrepreneurship requires. We may appropriately inquire whether this mode of training entrepreneurs is optimal or whether any cost-effective room for improvement exists. Optimal training would provide all the entrepreneurs the market requires to extract maximum economic development from demand conditions. If societies do not produce enough entrepreneurs, or the ones they produce have the wrong skills, then the current system is not producing an optimal entrepreneur supply.

American society is producing plenty of young people who know how to peddle dope in the alley, to sell their bodies on the streetcorner, and to use a gun to rob (Sullivan, 1989). These are entrepreneurial resources in ample supply in inner cities whose people do not inherit class and ethnic resources of entrepreneurship (Padilla, 1992). Hagan (1994:77) declares their criminality "deviant formations of social and cultural capital that diverge from and oppose convention." Alas, one cannot look over the dilapidated inner cities of the United States, filled with unemployed people, and come away satisfied that the existing system is also optimizing the supply of entrepreneurs who know how to run laundromats, plumbing supply warehouses, or discount clothing stores.

Government enhancement of entrepreneurship supply is not the same as government set-aside programs. Reserving some government contracts exclusively for minority or women entrepreneurs, set-aside programs operate strictly on the demand side, expecting supply to materialize when demand strengthens through the usual market signals. The acknowledged failure of set-aside programs, riddled with corruption, is more evidence that governments need to expand the supply of entrepreneurial resources in populations whose entrepreneur production is low (Waldinger et al., 1990:190–192; Baltimore City, 1992). Just increasing demand for minority or women entrepreneurs raises the price of the underrepresented entrepreneurs, enabling those already endowed with entrepreneurial resources to earn rent on them. In a low-resources environment, the supply of entrepreneurs is unresponsive to their price.

Nor is it as if government has no history of improving entrepreneurial supply. Through public education governments already support entrepreneurship in the form of academic skills. Additionally, Marilyn Kourilsky's "mini-society" program has created a widely utilized vehicle for entrepreneurship education in public elementary schools (Hartman, 1989). Public universities train students in the technical skills that high-tech entrepreneurs require. That is why regions rich in higher education, like route 128 in Boston or the Silicon Valley in San Jose, develop dense populations of high tech firms whose entrepreneurs exploit their connections to the university as well as the technical expertise they acquired in them (Whitley, 1991:178). In effect, public higher education is already training students in upper-level entrepreneurship skills (Locke, 1993:58).

But what is public education doing to improve entrepreneurial resources among truly disadvantaged populations whose young people leave school? Balkin (1989: Ch. 7) has surveyed programs for entrepreneurship education of low-income people. These programs are new, but several different types already exist. Balkin distinguishes industry-linked programs, general self-employment training programs, unemployment insurance demonstration projects, and self-employment investment demonstrations. Industry-linked programs train people for entrepreneurship in a specific industry such as horticulture, arts and crafts, and daycare centers. General self-employment training programs offer preparation intended to equip students with generalized business competence that will assist them in many industries. An example is the Womens' Economic Development Corporation (WEDCO), founded in 1982. Eighty-seven percent of program participants are female heads of household on welfare. Trainees' average time on welfare exceeds 4 years.

Unemployment insurance demonstration projects imitate British and French legislation that encourages the unemployed to become self-employed. Instead of successive weekly unemployment payments, program participants receive a lump sum payment of their unemployment benefit, but they are required to invest this lump sum in a business of their own. Finally, self-employment investment demonstrations remove the legal obstacles that inhibit self-employment among welfare recipients.

Because these programs are new, one cannot reach conclusions about their cost-effectiveness (Balkin, 1989:136). Nonetheless, the process is not hit or miss. Programs that do not work can be jettisoned, and programs that work badly can be improved.

Balkin (1993) has also discovered and investigated programs that train prison inmates for entrepreneurship after their release. Prisoners keenly want access to entrepreneurship education (Dosti, 1994). Actual prison programs fall short of demand. Utilizing a survey method, Balkin discovered entrepreneurship training programs in the prison systems of Virginia, Texas, South Dakota, Delaware, Florida, and New Jersey. Operating through informants, Balkin found additional programs in prisons located in Alberta, Rhode Island, Washington, Illinois, Wisconsin, and Vermont. "How to Make an Honest Buck for a Change" is the title of an entrepreneurship education program at the Calgary Correctional Centre in Alberta. Taught between 1988 and 1992, the course met for 180 hours of instruction. The instructor, Harry Cotton, taught six classes a year to classes of 8 to 12 students. Cotton estimates that three-quarters of the inmates in the Calgary Correctional Centre aspire to become business owners upon release. However, inmates are not easy to redirect into entrepreneurship. Prisoners have low literacy and low numeracy. They have lifestyle commitments to the cool world, fervent faith in get-rich-quick schemes, weak family supports, crimino-genic social networks, and practical knowledge of how to steal.

All these demonstration projects target the aged, the unemployed, welfare mothers, prisoners, and other exceptionally disadvantaged adults. Although such people have immense interest in entrepreneur-ship, a product of their disadvantage in the labor market, they are also those least likely to succeed in it. Therefore, the most cost-effective entre-preneurship education redirects youth into entrepreneurship before they become addicts, inmates, or welfare mothers. Conceivably, expansion and improvement of entrepreneurship education in the schools would cost money, but, if successful, the public investment could amply repay society in the form of enhanced economic growth and reduced crime and welfare dependency in the long-term future. Equally conceivably, however, entrepreneurship education would cost little and yield a quick pay-back. Curricular changes are inexpensive. For starters, American trade schools might imitate Danish and Italian trade schools, which suc-cessfully generate young entrepreneurs (Whitley, 1991:177). We also pro-pose that social science develop entrepreneurship into an applied subject suitable for junior high schools. Applied entrepreneurship education should include values clarification, which means linking values to con-sequences for self and society. The most successful entrepreneurs find values in their work, not just money.

TYPES OF ENTREPRENEURS

Most entrepreneurs are not affluent, and many are downright marginal, a reality concealed for decades by elitist theories of entrepreneurship. *Survivalist* entrepreneurs selected entrepreneurship in preference to low-wage employment or underemployment, their realistic alternatives (Jones, 1988). Because their reasons for this selection vary, we divide survivalist entrepreneurs into two types: value entrepreneurs and disadvantaged entrepreneurs. *Value entrepreneurs* choose low return self-employment in preference to low-wage jobs. Bates (1987:547) finds that *nonminority* females are the largest group in this category. Many women want self-employment because it permits them to juggle home and work more flexibly than do wage jobs. Their preferences represent social values, a strictly supply-side issue (Mead, 1986:73, 80). Others prefer the entrepreneur's independence, social status, life-style, or self-concept to what a low wage job offers them. For example, Gold (1992:265; see also Ma Mung, 1994) found that many Vietnamese chose self-employment "because of its ability to provide them with a level of independence, prestige, and flexibility unavailable under other conditions of employment." Again, in their study of entrepreneurial aspirations among young Americans 18–25 years of age, Day and Willette (1987:IV-34) found that "being an important person in the community" significantly increased the probability of selecting entrepreneurship among blacks. Relative to whites, Asians, and Hispanic youth, young African Americans perceived the business owner as an important person, an autonomous social value that promoted their aspiration for entrepreneurship.

Whatever their reasons, value entrepreneurs select self-employment for reasons that include nonmonetary considerations (Aronson, 1991:xi–xii). This value-induced selection produces a strictly supply-side variable influencing the rate of entrepreneurship in a group, a class, or a society. Value entrepreneurs need not earn more in self-employment than in wage and salary employment, and they often earn less. After all, those who have accepted financial disadvantage just to become entrepreneurs have demonstrated that social values (not money) prompted their occupational choice. Pure cases of value entrepreneurship exist, but in most cases, entrepreneurship's perceived value coexists with financial motives among those who become entrepreneurs.

Despite their reputation for wealth, a manifestation of the cultural clichés that dog this subject, the self-employed are not wealthy. Average earnings from self-employment in 272 metropolitan areas in 1980 was about 5% less than the average wage and salary income for native whites and foreign whites, and 14% less for blacks. Mean self-employment income was only higher than mean wage and salary income for Asians and Hispanics. In all five ethnoracial categories many and often most entrepreneurs earned no more than wage earners of their own group. Among this large class, value entrepreneurs must have been numerous in that a very large number of self-employed persons presumably earned no more from self-employment than they would have from wage or salary employment. For such persons, value considerations presumably played a deciding role in their occupational choice.

We distinguish value entrepreneurs from *disadvantaged entrepreneurs*. Disadvantaged entrepreneurs undertake self-employment because, as a result of labor market disadvantage, they earn higher returns on their human capital in self-employment than in wage and salary employment (Light, 1979; Min, 1988: Ch. 5). Therefore, by definition, disadvantaged entrepreneurs earn more from self-employment than they could in wage and salary employment. Labor force disadvantage may arise from physical disability, ethnoracial discrimination, unrecognized educational credentials, exclusion from referral networks, or any other cause. Higher returns in self-employment need not mean returns equal to those of native whites with the same education and experience. It is necessary only that workers disadvantaged in the general labor market experience less disadvantage in entrepreneurship than in wage labor.

Both disadvantaged and value entrepreneurship often represent second choices of public policy just as lifeboats were a second choice of passengers on the *Titanic*. That is, the passengers would have preferred to ride the *Titanic* in style and comfort, but when that great ship went down, they were glad to ride in a lifeboat. In the same sense, high wage jobs and lucrative self-employment are laudatory objectives of public policy; however, where high wage jobs and profitable business do not exist, and cannot be brought into existence, value entrepreneurship at least offers low wage workers a choice of low-income life-styles. Similarly, discriminatory employment practices produce below average returns on human capital, a condition of labor force disadvantage. Although disadvantaged entrepreneurship offers a semisolution to an individual's labor market disadvantage, from the point of view of public policy, discrimination in employment and labor force disadvantage are undesirable conditions. Happily, entrepreneurship education is inexpensive. It need not prevent or inhibit the most aggressive programs of public works job creation that liberals might advocate.

We do not advocate low-wage jobs or disadvantages. Realistically speaking, however, neither low wage jobs nor labor force disadvantage is about to disappear, so it is well that entrepreneurship exists to relieve both conditions. In the extreme case of labor force disadvantage, permanent unemployment, destitution looms and Balkin (1992) even finds entrepreneurs among the homeless. Entrepreneurship is superior to destitution for both economic and social reasons. First, even marginal entrepreneurs produce goods and services that enhance the community's wealth, whereas the destitute unemployed consume without producing.[9] Second, as producers, even marginal entrepreneurs participate in the polity and the culture, helping in the process to tame the crime, apathy, hopelessness, and substance abuse that accompany destitution and racism. Here we are addressing noneconomic benefits of entrepreneurship. We do not know what or how big they are, but think that cost-effective programs of entrepreneurship enhancement will have noneconomic benefits as well as economic benefits.

ENTREPRENEURSHIP AND CRIME

Restricting entrepreneurship to legal trades excludes illegal entrepreneurship from consideration. Illegal entrepreneurs sell proscribed goods and services like drugs, prostitution, usurious loans, stolen property, and gambling plays (Light, 1977a, 1977b; Myers, 1978:49). At least at the retail level, illegal entrepreneurs are the common products of deprived socioeconomic environments. First, illegal entrepreneurs satisfy a consumer demand that is itself in many cases a product of deprived socioeconomic conditions. For example, numbers banks provide informal financial services (saving and investment) in neighborhoods underserved by mainstream financial institutions (Light, 1977a). Again, insofar as some hopeless people turn to addictive drugs for solace, and their hopelessness is a product of protracted poverty and discrimination from which they see no escape, illegal drug vendors tap a consumer market that is itself the whole or partial product of long-term poverty and discrimination. Second, many illegal entrepreneurs earn no more in crime than in legal employment. As such, their personal alternative to illegal entrepreneurship was unemployment or low wage work.

These value entrepreneurs preferred criminal self-employment to wage labor because of the attractiveness of the criminal life style, not just its higher incomes. Many criminals enjoy their occupation, and have elaborated an occupational subculture to celebrate its pleasures. What Katz (1988:313–317) labeled "seductions of crime" are the life-style attractions crime offers criminals, whether in the ecstatic enjoyment of brazen misdeeds or in the social recognition successful criminality affords both in the barrio and in the UCLA Graduate School of Management.[10] However, for most blue-collar criminals, style is crime's main attraction. Katz has shown that crime is a value entrepreneurship. Money rewards matter, but they need not exceed those of lawful alternatives, and usually fall short without discouraging criminal careers whose principal motive is the flamboyant personal style illegal life-styles afford. Naturally, a capable few move up to the criminal big time (Myers, 1978:50). For these disadvantaged entrepreneurs, criminal self-employment improves the rewards alternately available in straight employments as Merton (1957: Ch. 6) long ago explained. These success stories are, however, rare. In crime, as in business, most entrepreneurs earn modest rewards.

Whatever one's opinion of these illegal entrepreneurs—drug dealers, fences, prostitutes, loan sharks, etc.—one cannot deny that they help themselves rather than awaiting a government hand-out. As Karl Marx (1956:159) also noted, criminals reduce unemployment by opening their own illegal firms. Except for these illegal firms, the criminals would be unemployed. Of course, in helping themselves, many illegal entrepreneurs vend goods and services that further impoverish their already impoverished neighborhoods. In the case of vendors of addictive drugs, the point requires no elaboration. However, numbers banks provide credit services at usurious rates, thus causing the poor to pay more for financial services than do the nonpoor. The same observation arguably belongs to prostitutes and fences both of whom employ themselves in a traffic that indirectly undermines community welfare if only by undermining community morale, security, and family integrity, and by attracting rowdies.

In this respect, illegal entrepreneurs differ in an important way from legal ones. Most legal entrepreneurs contribute goods and services that enrich and enhance the community in which they work.[11] As prosaic as it is, a dry cleaning establishment solves social problems (La Guire, 1988). The owner justly obtains income for removing stains, and so improving the community. In contrast, a glamorous career in street corner cocaine vending impoverishes the community in which the vendor operates. Like a tobacco company or a polluting factory, both legitimate enterprises, cocaine vendors damage their customers and their community. Because most legal and most illegal entrepreneurs have these quite different social consequences, the former productive, the latter parasitic, social policy needs to slow the flow of youthful labor into wealth-destroying entrepreneurship and to enhance its flow into wealth-creating entrepreneurship, even survivalist entrepreneurship. If they can do the one, they can do the other. This is a policy of *entrepreneurial redirection* rather than a policy of entrepreneurial stimulation. Redirection policy is ideally successful when a young person who would have later become a fence, drug dealer, or a prostitute opens a dry cleaning establishment, a body shop, or a plumbing supply warehouse instead.

ENCOURAGING ENTREPRENEURIAL REDIRECTION

Discouraging as it is, America's massive and shameful crime problem proves that her young people do not lack initiative, a spirit of self-help, or independence. In this regard, criminal and legitimate entrepreneurs converge in their values. Indeed, entrepreneurship itself epitomizes social values for which criminals express respect. Criminals and convicts frequently express disdain for low wage labor, but identify self-employment in legitimate business as a respectable alternative to crime (Akerstrom, 1983). This coincidence of appraisal offers some ground for believing that some criminals or criminally inclined young persons might be attracted into legitimate entrepreneurship instead if they had or could obtain access to the requisite resources.

These resources include more than money. Of course, money is a key entrepreneurial resource. Entrepreneurs need money for initial capitalization. Equalization of borrowing opportunities is, therefore, one appropriate way to increase the opportunity for legal entrepreneurship among low-income persons. However, it is not sufficient because money is by no means the only necessary resource. This situation is fortunate because capital loans are not a free resource, and their corrective record to date is unimpressive.

Entrepreneurs also need social networks, skills, knowledge, values, and attitudes (Taylor and Singleton, 1993; Birley, 1985). Some of these skills are directly vocational. Accounting is that kind of skill, and a social investment in public education produces its social dividend when a student, having acquired that useful skill, becomes an accountant rather than a shoplifter. However, directly vocational skills like accounting are products of a prior desire for self-employment; and that desire is what needs to be channeled into constructive ventures. In their careful study, Day and Willette (1987:xii) found that among youths of all ethnoracial backgrounds, personal knowledge of a self-employed person, usually a relative or parent, was the best predictor of plans for one's own legal self-employment. Of course, this knowledge was highly unequal as young people of ethnoracial categories with high rates of legal self-employment (whites, Asians) knew more entrepreneurs than did young people from ethnoracial categories with low rates of legal entrepreneurship (blacks, Hispanics). The predictable result was reproduction of existing and unequal rates of entrepreneurship in the next generation (Fratoe, 1988:35–37). In contrast, of course, slum youths knew many illegal entrepreneurs and learned from them the appropriate skills, knowledge, beliefs, and attitudes for survivalist entrepreneurship in crime. Unless disturbed, this knowledge gap guarantees that the next generation of slum youths will contain more than its share of illegal entrepreneurs and less than its share of legal ones. In this way, the failures of the past reproduce themselves in the future.

Breaking these vicious cycles requires external interventions. The appropriate task of social policy is to direct the intervention such that the highest volume of entrepreneurial redirection results from each intervention. A neglected resource, junior high school education, is a cost-effective device for entrepreneurial redirection. But, education inside the classroom is just one form whose usefulness is limited by the tendency of the most troubled students to leave school early. Education outside the classroom takes the form of media exposure, films, call-in talk shows, advertising, art, celebrity endorsements, prestige association, social recognition, and whatever else works. Prisons can become entrepreneurship academies, a crime-fighting technique prisoners themselves request (Dosti, 1994). Whether inside or outside the classroom, what needs communication is the truth about entrepreneurship: some entrepreneurs impoverish their communities; others enrich them.

If education could shift youths' perceptions about entrepreneurship, some young adults who now select value entrepreneurship in crime, a cool occupation, would select instead value entrepreneurship in business, a productive occupation. In this case, entrepreneurial redirection would occur because of perceptual shifts affecting entrepreneurial supply rather than because of declines in the reward of crime, a demand-side issue. Demand-side approaches to criminal redirection have proven ineffective, and it is even unlikely that they can ever be effective because crime is lucrative (Myers, 1978:47–48). In this situation, cost-effective supply-side solutions merit a trial. Confronting a climate of public intolerance of impoverishing entrepreneurship in crime, at least some entrepreneurial youths would select enriching rather than impoverishing entrepreneurship, thus simultaneously reducing their community's crime problem and enhancing its wealth. Of course, if one thinks in terms of instant solutions, this modest proposal offers inadequate drama. The course we propose does not offer a means for eliminating social problems at one stroke. If, however, one thinks in terms of long-range, cost-effective interventions, educational intervention on the supply side offers a means for increasing entrepreneurship and reducing crime by making entrepreneurs out of people whose only other realistic option was criminality. Even with limited success, the potential savings to society are gigantic.

DEBUNKING AS EDUCATION

Fortunately, we need not wait for politicians to begin the process of entrepreneurial redirection. To start, social science can confront and debunk two potent myths that inhibit the entrepreneurship of disadvantaged youth. These are the myths of capital starvation and the myth of market saturation. The first myth concerns the availability of the financial means to finance wealth-producing small business enterprises. The poor are hopeless and fatalistic (Sudhir, 1994). Disadvantaged youths commonly believe that legitimate firms require initial capitalization that is beyond their capability to acquire now or ever in the future (Macleod, 1987:70). For example, in their comparative study of San Francisco and Washington D.C., Day and Willette (1987:v) found that black youths "showed the highest inclination toward business ownership" of any of the four ethnoracial groups they studied. On measure after measure, African-American youths appeared more interested in entrepreneurship as an occupation than did white, Asian, or Hispanic youths. Yet, when asked whether they knew someone who would lend them between $5,000 and $15,000 to start their own business, only 41% of young black men answered yes compared to 57% of all young men (1987: IV:34). Blacks also perceived nonavailability of start-up capital as a bigger problem than did nonblacks.

This combination of high aspirations and perceived nonaccess to the requisite means evokes Merton's (1957: Ch. 6) classic formula for criminality. Embracing the defeatist notion that wealth-producing entrepreneurship is impossible, disadvantaged but entrepreneurially inclined youth conclude that only entrepreneurship in crime is realistically available to people like them (Padilla, 1992). The belief has some merit. After all, vending drugs or turning tricks requires little capital. A prostitute needs only what nature provided. A hold-up man's equity consists of a pistol. The requisite motives, skills, and values are also available in the neighborhood through a process Edwin Sutherland (1949:234) called "differential association." In contrast, a yogurt store or a dry-cleaning establishment requires equity capital and the ability to borrow more. Barriers to entrepreneurial entry are plainly lower in crime than in wealth-producing enterprises.

Nonetheless, plausible as it appears, this worldly-wise objection is wrong. In a special report, the U.S. Census Bureau found that among entrepreneurs of every ethnoracial category, two-thirds either required no capital to start their business or started their business without borrowing any capital (Fratoe, 1988:40). Only 10% of black business owners had borrowed any money from commercial banks (Green and Pryde,

1990:380). Evidently, many households saved the wherewithal to start a small business. Immigrants show us how the feat is accomplished. In the last 15 years, the resumption of immigration to the United States has released millions of impoverished persons into our nation's largest metropolitan areas. Although these immigrants often speak little English, lack educational credentials accepted in this country, and lack access to hiring networks, they maintain rates of self-employment higher than those of native-born Americans. Admittedly, some new immigrants arrive with money, education, and experience that represent significant business resources. Nonetheless, immigrants in general are less endowed with class resources of money and education than are the native born in general, but the immigrants nonetheless manage higher rates of self-employment than do the native born.

Studies recurrently show that immigrant entrepreneurs raised most of their initial capitalization from their own savings (Fratoe, 1988:40; Min, 1984:34). Some of these savings were brought from abroad. Most were obtained from wage and salary income in this country. Contrary to the numerous myths, federal and state loan assistance was of modest or negligible importance as an entrepreneurial resource. In 1982, only 1.3% of black entrepreneurs indicated that they had borrowed capital from any government program, and the percentage was even lower among Asians, Hispanics, and nonminority males (Fratoe, 1988:40). Many Americans are skeptical about thrift, and relentless taxation of small savings balances does nothing to improve their opinion. Americans are among the most thriftless people in the world. As a nation, Americans saved only 3.9% of their disposable incomes (Shilling, 1988). This rate is not only lower than earlier in our history, it is also one of the lowest rates in the world (Thurow, 1992:160). In contrast, Japanese households routinely save 17% of their disposable incomes, and Korean households save 36%. With a Korean saving rate, an American household with $15,000 in yearly disposable income would set aside $5,400 a year, and $54,000 in a decade. However, with an American savings rate, the same American household would save $600 yearly or $6,000 in a decade. Yet one does not really need to be Korean to save money for one's own business. In point of fact, 70% of black entrepreneurs started their firms with less than $5,000 in capitalization, so even an American savings rate yields enough to start a business (Fratoe, 1988:39).

Of course, the United States must acknowledge and deal with the destructive lending and investment policies of mainstream financial institutions (Shiver, 1991; Delugach, 1988; Light, 1983:399–400, 408–409). Legislation is essential to control this abuse of financial power. At the same time, Asian immigrant entrepreneurs are acquiring capital despite these obstacles. Many Asian nationalities make effective use of indigenous rotating credit associations to assist them in saving and to link their community's savings to their community's financial needs (Light, Im, and Deng, 1990). This linkage is broken when banks and insurance companies refuse to lend money back to the communities that originally saved it.

Rotating credit associations are informal savings and lending associations in which members make regular contributions to a shared fund whose use is rotated among the membership until all have taken. The practice is widespread in Africa, Central America, and Asia (Light and Bonacich, 1988: Ch. 10; Velez-Ibanez, 1983). Although mostly oriented toward consumption and home ownership, rotating credit associations also contribute to entrepreneurship (Werbner, 1990:133–134). In a 1987 study of 110 Korean garment manufacturers in Los Angeles, two-thirds reported having utilized *kye*, the Korean rotating credit association, for saving, and one-third had utilized *kye* proceeds as part of their start-up capital (Light, Im, and Deng, 1990). As these Korean entrepreneurs employed 40 workers on the average, the Korean *kye* had supported the development of significant business firms. If more Americans understood that many Korean immigrants saved the money to start their own business firms, they would have more faith in saving.

Thriftlessness and ignorance permit Americans to waste millions of dollars in legal and illegal lotteries that drain resources from their communities (Light, 1977a). Unfortunately, that drainage is only part of the damage. These same public shortcomings have encouraged the spread of unsound rumors that purport to explain the remarkable entrepreneurial success of immigrants, especially Asian immigrants. According to these rumors, widely believed in the public, Asian immigrants have been the beneficiaries of government largesse denied native-born citizens (Johnson and Oliver, 1989:458). This alleged largesse has given them the wherewithal to open so many small business firms. Although the rumors lack substance, they offer pseudoexplanations to a public that is genuinely puzzled by the entrepreneurial success of Asian immigrants. These pseudoexplanations are, however, self-defeating since they reinforce the belief that only those with political influence can become self-employed. Because this erroneous belief is itself part of the cycle of misinformation that locks native youths out of small business, exploding the false rumors is an essential educational task, subsumable within the larger educational task discussed above. It is not only that in the absence of valid knowledge, the demonology stirs up unnecessary and misguided intergroup tensions, pitting indigenous have-nots against foreigners (Light and Bonacich, 1988:318–327). It is also that the misguided demonology reinforces the defeatism that locks native workers out of constructive entrepreneurship.

THE SATURATION THEORY

The second myth is more sophisticated than the financial objection, and it has defenders in the academy as well as on the street corner. The *saturation* theory maintains that the American economy has no room for additional entrepreneurs. Therefore, even if school drop-outs, unemployed workers, welfare mothers, or active criminals could be redirected into constructive, wealth-creating enterprises, they would find no niche because the economy already contains all the small firms it can absorb. Admittedly, there must exist some limit on the number of self-employed persons any economy can support. If everyone tried to become self-employed, almost everyone would fail. It makes no sense to redirect more workers into entrepreneurship if the market already has all the entrepreneurs it can absorb (Watts, 1987:145).

Plausible though it is, the saturation thesis hides two fallacies. First, the saturation thesis implies that ethnoracial groups and categories are in mutually exclusive competition for entrepreneurial opportunities. The more one group gets, the less others get (Bonacich, 1993:689–690). If new entrepreneurs invade these saturated opportunities, they succeed only by driving out those who already enjoy the coveted opportunities. Like a crowded elevator, the economy already has enough entrepreneurs; therefore, anyone new who wishes to get aboard must first expel an occupant. Force is one way to accomplish this task, and the Los Angeles riot and arson of 1992 illustrates the technique (Light, Har-Chvi, and Kan, 1993).

This zero sum corollary has much following in social science, in the American public at large, and in African-American communities where Korean entrepreneurs are a significant commercial presence. The saturation argument offers rational support for anti-immigrant commercial campaigns that seek to mobilize local buying power for indigenous merchants.[12] Boycotting alien merchants blasts them out of commercial niches they occupy, thus opening the coveted opportunity to indigenous entrepreneurs or would-be entrepreneurs (Kwong and Lum, 1988). Hitler's Nazis utilized similar arguments in boycotting Jewish businesses. From the Nazi point of view, Jewish firms soaked up entrepreneurial opportunities that would otherwise have been available to real Germans. If Nazi-organized boycotts could drive out the Jews, so the theory went, then their vacated stores would become available to Aryans.

Despite its superficial plausibility, the saturation theory is conceptually and empirically wrong. That the saturation theory is conceptually wrong is easy to demonstrate. To state that a limit on the population of entrepreneurs must exist, as does Lieberson (1980:376, 380, 381), is not to demonstrate that this limit is always reached in every metropolitan area. Such an unlikely claim requires separate empirical demonstration that no one has thus far offered. Possibly, all, most, or some of those 272 metropolitan areas might increase their entrepreneur population by 4% just by tapping the population of unemployed workers, a project that some European countries have begun to attempt. If not 4%, then possibly 2%, and so forth. In any event there is no warrant for the supposition that because the population of entrepreneurs must have an upward limit that limit has already been reached everywhere (Young, 1988:5).

Empirical evidence does not support the saturation theory either. Utilizing Census data from 272 metropolitan areas, Chapter 6 showed that, net of economic control variables, increases in the percentage foreign born of a metropolitan area tended to increase that area's entrepreneur population. As the foreign born were already known to have a larger proportion of self-employed than the native born, this statistical result implies that where the supply of entrepreneurs was larger, the entrepreneur population was also larger. That conclusion is incompatible with the saturation theory according to which a larger share of entrepreneurial opportunities for group A must come at the expense of group B. If the saturation theory were correct, the percentage of foreign born in the population of a metropolitan area could have no effect on the entrepreneur population of that area as the entrepreneur population was already at its maximum.

Chapter 6 also examined the statistical effect of foreign-born entrepreneurs upon the entrepreneurship of native blacks as well as upon the financial returns to entrepreneurship obtained by native black entrepreneurs. To amplify the effect, we added Korean entrepreneurs to the equation, seeking to ascertain whether the rate of Korean entrepreneurship had any adverse effect upon the rate of native African-American entrepreneurship or upon the money returns of native blacks in self-employment. If the saturation theory were correct, then metropolitan areas with a high rate of foreign entrepreneurship and Korean entrepreneurship ought to have shown a reduced rate of black entrepreneurship, and vice versa. In fact, foreign entrepreneurship and Korean entrepreneurship alike were statistically independent of black entrepreneurship. That is, African-American entrepreneurship and entrepreneurial income were unaffected by foreign and Korean entrepreneurship. As above, this result implies that even if a limit exists, American metropolitan areas have not, in fact, reached that saturated upper limit of entrepreneurial population. Hence, it would be possible to redirect at least some of the unemployed and the illegally self-employed into constructive forms of self-employment.

If the saturation objection is empirically and conceptually false, as we maintain, then the saturation theory itself emerges as an obstacle to entrepreneurial redirection and a conservative ideology propping up the status quo in American inner cities. Defeatism is an acceptable philosophy when facts warrant it, as in late-Hitlerian Germany, but the facts do not warrant the defeatism of the saturation theory. The popular and academic saturation theory directs energy into intergroup conflict and away from concrete steps to improve local economies by directing underemployed and unemployed workers into productive self-employment. When people believe a falsehood, they need education. An educational campaign to expand entrepreneurship requires a frank debunking of the saturation theory. Many people believe the saturation theory, and those who do are part of the problem whether they teach it in the academy or on the corner. We do not wish, however, to substitute a demonology of our own for the one we explode. In our opinion, one can demonstrate the fallacy of saturationism, and thus bring rational people to appreciation of the feasibility of entrepreneurial redirection as well as of its desirability. But if public education were not essential, in a climate intolerant of discourse on this sacred subject of entrepreneurship, everyone would already understand this issue.

CONCLUSION

Some economic problems we have, and some we give ourselves. Intolerance and rigidity inhibit a rational discourse about entrepreneurship, a symbol of Americanism so familiar that its discussion is unnecessary. Both on the left and on the right, people cling to outmoded ideologies that, by stopping thought, promote economic paralysis in the status quo. Some controversies are misguided and unnecessary; this is one. Whatever their political differences, conservatives and liberals agree on the desirability of enhancing entrepreneurship in the private economy. The method for doing that is a matter of technique that can take advantage of contemporary social science research, a resource unavailable to Liberal philosophers of the nineteenth century.

Entrepreneurship is patently suboptimal in the dilapidated inner cities of the United States. Moreover, the data provided in our book and elsewhere in the literature (Kasarda, 1989:44; Horton, 1988:199; Nee and Sanders, 1985:88–89) show that one cannot explain this shortfall on the basis of shortfalls of human or financial capital. People are not taking full advantage of opportunities they could in principal exploit (Fratoe,

1988:49). Therefore, entrepreneurship could be expanded now. Expanded entrepreneurship could make a serious contribution to economic growth, crime reduction, and poverty's alleviation in America's cities. We are making our problems worse than they have to be.

One issue is how to expand entrepreneurial supply. Classical liberalism stops with minimum government and low taxes. These prescriptions take no account of entrepreneurship education as a way to enhance entrepreneurship supply. We now know that low taxes and minimum government do not produce entrepreneurs among populations whose resources are low. Entrepreneurs require resources some of which are learned. Schools do not teach what young entrepreneurs need to know. Not a nostrum or cure-all, entrepreneurship education belongs on a list of practical, cost-effective measures intended to enhance wealth creation and to reduce inner city unemployment, welfare dependency, and crime. Although the subject is in its infancy, some cost-effective policy prescriptions are possible. First, the United States can copy the vocational education of Denmark and Italy, which graduate entrepreneurs from their secondary schools, not criminals. Second, we can study and expand existing programs in entrepreneurship education of the disadvantaged. Third, we can develop a technology of applied social science from the existing basic social science research in entrepreneurship. Introducing this applied science into the curriculum will improve entrepreneurship education.

By expanding entrepreneurship education from the classroom into media and prisons, American society reaches people who do not frequent classrooms. When every prison contains an entrepreneurship academy, open to selected volunteers, some promising inmates will learn entrepreneurship alternatives to recidivism. Coming out of prison, they will have the resources to promote economic development, creating jobs and reducing poverty in their communities. As is, the prisons teach inmates how to avoid getting caught next time. When committing crimes, they destroy existing wealth, interfere with economic growth, and compel the diversion of resources to social control. Even prisons can become part of the solution to inner city economic problems.

Fourth, social science must challenge patently false claims and beliefs, and not just report them. For entrepreneurship to increase its contribution to national well-being, it is essential to engage and explode mythology that masquerades as truth. This mythology is itself part of the frustrating cycle that locks disadvantaged people into poverty, crime, and unemployment. Lack of true knowledge about the economy is lack of a crucial resource that entrepreneurs require. People cannot become entrepreneurs if they know this option is impossible.

We have targeted two destructive mythologies that merit demolition. These are the myth of saturation and the myth of capital starvation. The myth of saturation tells people that all the opportunities are already occupied. By implication, the only way to make space for one's own business is to drive out the Koreans, the Jews, or whoever else is already running a business in your neighborhood. Then you can occupy their space. At best, the saturation theory encourages defeatism and resignation. At worst, it encourages intergroup hostility, looting, and arson. If the saturation theory were correct, our situation would be lamentable indeed. But, the saturation theory is not correct, its conclusions are false if plausible, and widespread acceptance of this view makes our urban situation worse than it need be. Debunking the false theory is an essential part of harnessing creative energy that is now wasted on hatred.

The myth of capital starvation tells people that entrepreneurship requires vast financial resources. Very well known and incontrovertible evidence shows that this proposition is wrong. Nonetheless, believing it, people conclude that they have no chance. Worse, the myth of capital starvation encourages invidious rumors that purport to explain how entrepreneurial immigrants started in business. Even when these rumors contain some truth, as in the federal government's loan assistance to Cuban refugees, they overlook the assisted immigrants (Vietnamese, Lao) who did not turn to entrepreneurship (Portes, 1987:359). But the rumors are usually without support. According to one persistent rumor, the United States government provided Koreans with privileged access to loan capital. That is why so many Koreans became entrepreneurs. These rumors have no basis in reality, but those who believe the myth of capital starvation must look for external explanations. When these patently false rumors exacerbate intergroup tensions, then what started as the myth of capital starvation turns into hatred and violence. Properly educated, the same energy could create new businesses in crime-wracked, dilapidated cities.

Rotating credit associations are a realistic vehicle for encouraging saving, home ownership, and entrepreneurship in inner cities. Alas, instead of supporting these informal thrift institutions, brought to our shores by new immigrants from Asia and Latin America, American courts have undertaken to force immigrant communities underserved by the banking system to rely exclusively on the banking system (Light, 1993). These policies are destructive and thoughtless as well as ethnocentric. Fortunately, government can change this destructive policy at no cost to the taxpayer, legalizing and domesticating rotating credit and savings associations so that native-born Americans can benefit from them too.

NOTES

1. "Early trial and struggle, as the history of the majority of our successful men abundantly attests, tends to strengthen and invigorate the character" (Alger, 1869:v). Scharnhorst (1985:91) declares this sentence the kernel of Alger's message.

2. Several of Horatio Alger's books depict entrepreneurship as a way out of poverty. In *Paul the Peddler*, an enterprising young man winds up as owner of a necktie stand. In *Slow And Sure*, Paul rises "from the humble position of a street merchant to be the proprietor of a shop" (quoted in Scharnhorst, 1985:93). But the careers of Alger heroes were often divided between self-employment and wage employment, and ultimate success was a product of marrying the boss's daughter as much as hard work. "Like other Alger heroes, Childs eventually saved enough money to open a shop, and began a confectionery business.... He sold his stand at a good profit, however, and took a position as a clerk.... Within a short time he became a trusted and valued employee, married Peterson's daughter, and...was made a partner in the business" (Gardner, 1964:269).

3. Edna Bonacich (1987:453) declares that "unless one has the well-being of humanity as one's goal, the capitalist ethic of self- or group-interest prevails." If capitalism is defined as adherence to self- or group interest in conduct, then capitalism has existed from the first appearance of humankind.

4. Social systems do not collapse until, having exhausted all their potential for growth, they become fetters on economic development. If entrepreneurship still works, even a little, capitalism has not exhausted all its potential for growth. An appropriate leftist argument would claim that entrepreneurship cannot improve conditions of life among the poor and working class, but this argument is empirically false.

5. George F. Will (1987:66, 71) claims that since President Nixon declared himself a Keynesian, conservatives have actually accepted the wisdom of economic management, questioning only the liberals' methods.

6. "The highest domestic priority of my administration will be to ensure that every American able to work has a job to do. This job guarantee will and must depend upon a reinvigorated private economy.... But it is our commitment that whatever employment the private sector does not provide, the federal government will either stimulate or provide itself" (George McGovern, 1972).

7. But O'Farrell (1986:165, 180–181) treats the same issue in Ireland.

8. "To lend money to entrepreneurs who lack managerial capacity is merely to throw it down the drain.... The main deficiency of local enterprise is not capital but knowledge and experience" (Lewis, 1954:11–12).

9. For expanded discussion, see Light, Sabagh, Bozorgmehr, and Der-Martirosian (1994).

10. The UCLA Graduate School of Management hired Mike Milken to teach a course on "creative finance." When the press complained that Milken was a

convicted embezzler, the Regents of the University attempted to back out of the contract. See *Los Angeles Times* (March 19, 1994:B7).

11.   Legalization is not the real issue. Many legal business firms impose negative externalities upon communities too. For example, polluting industries make communities pay the cost of their pollution. Tobacco firms impose health costs upon the users, the users' families, and the users' communities. Sport stadiums impose traffic congestion upon the neighborhood, and so forth. If public welfare were the only guideline of public policy, many currently legal industries and industrial practices would be banned, regulated, or taxed. Of course, public welfare is not the only influence upon public policy, but this lamentable reality renders it all the more urgent that we expose the disparities.

12.   These issues are discussed at greater length in Light, Har-Chvi, and Kan (1994b).

References

Abrams, I. J. 1978. "Determining Consumer Demand and Marketing Opportunities for Nutritional Products." *Food Technology* 32:79–85.

Acheson, James M. 1986. "Constraints on Entrepreneurship: Transaction Costs and Market Efficiency." Ch. 2 in *Entrepreneurship and Social Change*, edited by Sidney M. Greenfield and Arnold Strickon. Lanham, MD: University Press of America.

Acs, Zoltan J., and David Audretsch. 1990. *Innovation and Small Firms*. Cambridge: MIT Press.

Aiken, Leona S., and Stephen G. West. 1991. *Multiple Regression: Testing and Interpreting Interactions*. Newbury Park: Sage.

Akerstrom, Malin, 1983. "Crooks and Squares," Ph.D. dissertation, University of Lund, Sweden.

Akst, Daniel. 1990. *Wonder Boy: Barry Minkow, the Kid Who Swindled Wall Street*. New York: Scribners.

Aldrich, Howard, and Jane Weiss. 1981. "Differentiation Within the U.S. Capitalist Class." *American Sociological Review* 46:279–290.

Aldrich, Howard, John Cater, Trevor Jones, and David McEvoy. 1983. "From Periphery to Peripheral: The South Asian Petite Bourgeoisie in England." *Research in Sociology of Work* 2: 1–32.

Aldrich, Howard, Trevor P. Jones, and David McEvoy. 1984. "Ethnic Advantage and Minority Business Development." Ch. 11 in *Ethnic Communities in Business*, edited by Robin Ward and Richard Jenkins. New York: Cambridge University Press.

Alexander, Alec P. 1967. "The Supply of Industrial Entrepreneurship." *Explorations in Entrepreneurial History* 4:136–149.

Alger, Horatio. 1869. *Luck and Pluck*. Boston: Loring.

Archer, Melanie. 1991. "Self-Employment and Occupational Structure in an Industrializing City: Detroit, 1880." *Social Forces* 69:785–809.

Aronson, Robert L. 1991. *Self-Employment: A Labor Market Perspective*. Ithaca, New York: ILR Press.

Aurand, Harold W. 1983. "Self-Employment Last Resort of the Unemployed." *International Social Science Review* 58:7–11.

Auster, Ellen, and Howard Aldrich. 1984. "Small Business Vulnerability, Ethnic Enclaves, and Ethnic Enterprise." Ch. 3 in *Ethnic Communities in Business*, edited by Robin Ward. Cambridge: Cambridge University Press.

Bailey, Thomas R. 1987. *Immigrant and Native Workers*. Boulder: Westview Press.

Bailey, Thomas R., and Roger Waldinger. 1991. "Primary, Secondary, and Enclave Labor Markets: A Training Systems Approach." *American Sociological Review* 56:432–445.

Balkin, Steven. 1989. *Self-Employment for Low-Income People*. New York: Praeger.

_____. 1992. "Entrepreneurial Activities of Homeless Men." *Journal of Sociology and Social Welfare* 19:129–150.

_____. 1993. "A Survey of Entrepreneurial Training Programs for Prison Inmates." Chicago: The Prison Small Business Project of Roosevelt University.

Baltimore City Grand Jury. 1992. "Special Report Concerning the Maryland Minority Business Enterprise Program." Xeroxed document.

Basu, Ellen Oxfeld. 1991. "Profit, Loss and Fate." *Modern China* 17:227–259.

Bates, Timothy. 1985a. "Urban Economic Transformation and Minority Business Opportunities." *The Review of Black Political Economy* 13:24–36.

_____. 1985b. "Entrepreneur Human Capital Endowments and Minority Business Viability." *Journal of Human Resources* 20:540–554.

_____. 1987. "Self-Employed Minorities: Traits and Trends." *Social Science Quarterly* 68:539–551.

_____. 1994a. "An Analysis of Korean-Immigrant-Owned Small- Business Start-Ups with Comparisons to African-American and Non-Minority Firms." *Urban Affairs Review* 30:227–248.

_____. 1994b. "Social Resources Generated by Group Support Networks May Not Be Beneficial to Immigrant-Owned Small Businesses." *Social Forces* 72:671–689.

Bearse, Peter J. 1981. "A Study of Entrepreneurship by Region and SMSA Size." *Frontiers of Entrepreneurship Research.* Wellesley, MA: Babson College.

_____. 1985. "What We Know about Minority Entrepreneurship." *The Entrepreneurial Economy* 4:4–6.

_____. 1987. "The Ecology of Enterprise." Paper Prepared for the Northeast Meetings of the Regional Science Association, Binghamton, New York, May 29.

Bechofer, Frank, and Brian Elliott. 1985. "The Petite Bourgeoisie in Late Capitalism." *Annual Review of Sociology* 11:181–207.

Becker, Eugene H. 1984. "Self Employed Workers: An Update to 1983." *Monthly Labor Review* 107:14–18.

Bell, Daniel. 1973. *The Coming of Post-Industrial Society.* New York: Basic Books.

_____. 1976. *The Cultural Contradictions of Capitalism.* New York: Basic Books.

Bendix, Reinhard. 1956. *Work and Authority in Industry.* New York: John Wiley.

Benson, John. 1983. *The Penny Capitalists.* New Brunswick, NJ: Rutgers University.

Berg, Ivar. 1981. "Introduction." Ch. 1 in *Sociological Perspectives on Labor Markets,* edited by Ivar Berg. New York: Academic Press.

Birch, David L. 1981. "Who Creates Jobs?" *The Public Interest* 54:3–14.

_____. 1987. *Job Creation in America: How Our Smallest Companies Put the Most People to Work.* New York: Free Press.

Birley, Sue. 1985. "The Role of Networks in the Entrepreneurial Process." *Journal of Business Venturing* 1:107–117.

Blalock, Hubert M. 1960. *Social Statistics.* New York: McGraw- Hill.

Blaschke, Jochen, and Ahmet Ersoz. 1986a. "The Turkish Economy in West Berlin." *International Small Business Journal* 4:38–45.

_____. 1986b. "Life Histories: The Establishment of Turkish Small Businesses in West Berlin." Unpublished paper, City University of New York, April.

Boissevain, Jeremy, 1984. "Small Entrepreneurs in Contemporary Europe." Pp. 20–38 in *Ethnic Communities in Business*, edited by Robin Ward and Richard Jenkins. New York: Cambridge University Press.

Boissevain, Jeremy, and Hanneke Grotenbreg. 1987. "Culture, Structure, and Ethnic Enterprise: The Surinamese of Amsterdam." *Ethnic and Racial Studies* 9:1–23.

Boissevain, Jeremy, Jochen Blaschke, Hanneke Grotenbreg, Isaac Joseph, Ivan Light, Marlene Sway, Roger Waldinger, and Pnina Werbner. 1990. "Ethnic Entrepreneurs and Ethnic Strategies." Ch. 5 in *Ethnic Entrepreneurs*, edited by Roger Waldinger, Howard Aldrich, and Robin Ward. Newbury Park, CA: Sage.

Bonacich, Edna. 1973. "A Theory of Middleman Minorities." *American Sociological Review* 38:583–594.

_____. 1987. "Making It in America." *Sociological Perspectives* 30:446–466.

_____. 1993. "The Other Side of Ethnic Entrepreneurship: A Dialogue with Waldinger, Aldrich, Ward and Associates." *International Migration Review* 27(3):685–702.

Borjas, George J. 1985. "The Self-Employment of Immigrants." IRP Discussion Papers, University of Wisconsin, Madison.

_____. 1986. "The Self-Employment Experience of Immigrants." *The Journal of Human Resources* 21:485–506.

Borjas, George J., and Stephen G. Bronars. 1989. "Consumer Discrimination and Self-Employment." *Journal of Political Economy* 97:581–605.

Bourdieu, Pierre. 1979. *La Distinction*. Paris: Editions de Minuit.

Boyd, Robert L. 1990. "Black and Asian Self-Employment in Large Metropolitan Areas: A Comparative Analysis." *Social Problems* 37:258–273.

_____. 1991. "A Contextual Analysis of Black Self-Employment in Large Metropolitan Areas, 1970–1980." *Social Forces* 70(2):409–429.

Bradford, William D., and Alfred E. Osborne, Jr. 1976. "The Entrepreneurship Decision and Black Economic Development." *The American Economic Review* 66:316–319.

Bregger, John E. 1963. "Self-Employed in the United States, 1948–1962." *Monthly Labor Review* 86:37–43.

Brockhaus, Robert H. 1982. "The Psychology of the Entrepreneur." Ch. 3 in *Encyclopedia of Entrepreneurship*, edited by Calvin Kent, Donald Sexton, and Karl Vesper. Englewood Cliffs, NJ: Prentice-Hall.

Brown, Charles, James Hamilton, and James Medoff. 1990. *Employers Large and Small*. Cambridge: Harvard University.

Browning, Harley and Joachim Singelmann. 1978. "The Transformation of the U.S. Labor Force." *Politics and Society* 8:481–509.

Brozen, Yale. 1954. "Determinants of Entrepreneurial Ability." *Social Research* 21:339–364.

Brubaker, Rogers. 1985. "Rethinking Classical Theory: The Sociological Vision of Pierre Bourdieu." *Theory and Society* 14:745–776.

Bruck, Connie. 1988. *The Predator's Ball*. New York: Penguin.

Buchanan, Patrick. 1988. *Right From the Beginning*. Boston: Little, Brown.

Buckley, Jerry. 1991. "The Pizza Man Chooses God." *US News and World Report* July 29:43–44.

Burr, Angela. 1986. "A British View of Prescribing Pharmaceutical Heroin to Opiate Addicts: A Critique of the Heroin Solution with Special Reference to the Picadilly and Kensington Market Drug Scenes in London." *The International Journal of the Addictions* 21:83–96.

Butler, John, and Cedric Herring. 1991. "Ethnicity and Entrepreneurship in America." *Sociological Perspectives* 34:79–94.

Cain, Glen G. 1986. "The Economic Analysis of Labor Market Discrimination: A Survey." Pp. 693–776 in *Handbook of Labor Economics*, edited by Orley Ashenfelter and Richard Layard. Amsterdam: North Holland.

Calvo, Guillermo, and Stanislaw Wellisz. 1980. "Technology, Entrepreneurs, and Firm Size." Ch. 9 in *Entrepreneurship*, edited by Mark Casson. Brookfield, VT: Edward Elgar.

Carland, James W., Frank Hoy, William R. Boulton, and Jo Ann C. Carland. 1984. "Differentiating Entrepreneurs from Small Business Owners." *Academy of Management Review* 9:354–359.

Castles, Stephen, Jock Collins, Katherine Gibson, David Tait, and Caroline Alcorso. 1991. *The Global Milkbar and the Local Sweatshop: Ethnic Small Business and the Economic Restructuring of Sydney.* Sydney: Office of Multicultural Affairs of the Department of Prime Minister and Cabinet, and the Centre for Multicultural Studies of the University of Wollongong.

Cauthorn, Robert C. 1989. *Contributions to a Theory of Entrepreneurship.* New York: Garland.

Chan, Janet, and Yuet-Wah Cheung. 1985. "Ethnic Resources and Business Enterprise: A Study of Chinese Businesses in Toronto." *Human Organization* 44:142–154.

Chang, Edward Tea. 1990. "New Urban Crisis: Korean—Black Conflicts in Los Angeles." Ph.D. dissertation, University of California at Riverside.

Chell, Elizabeth, Jean Haworth, and Sally Brearley. 1991. *The Entrepreneurial Personality.* London: Routledge.

Chen, Gavin. 1986. "Minority Business Development: An International Comparison." *The Review of Black Political Economy* 15:93–111.

Clegg, Stewart, Paul Boreham, and Geoff Dow. 1986. *Class, Politics, and the Economy.* London: Routledge & Kegan Paul.

Cobas, Jose, and Ione DeOllos. 1989. "Family Ties, Co-Ethnic Bonds, and Ethnic Entrepreneurship." *Sociological Perspectives* 32:403–411.

Cobas, Jose, Mikel Aickin, and Douglas S. Jardine. 1993. "Industrial Segmentation, The Ethnic Economy, and Job Mobility: The Case of Cuban Exiles in Florida." *Quality and Quantity* 27:249–270.

Cochran, Thomas C. 1965. "Role and Sanction in American Entrepreneurial History." Pp. 93–114 in *Explorations in Enterprise*, edited by Hugh G. J. Aitken. Cambridge: Harvard University Press.

Cohen, Abner. 1969. *Custom and Politics in Urban Africa.* Berkeley: University of California.

_____. 1971. "Cultural Strategies in the Organization of Trading Diasporas." Pp. 266–284 in *The Development of Indigenous Trade and Markets in West Africa*, edited by Claude Meillassoux. London: Oxford University Press.

Coleman, James S. 1988. "Social Capital in the Creation of Human Capital." *American Journal of Sociology* 94:S95–S122.

Conk, Margo A. 1981. "Immigrant Workers in the City, 1870–1930: Agents of Growth or Threats to Democracy?" *Social Science Quarterly* 62:704–720.

Conti, Joseph G., and Brad Stetson. 1993. "The Coming Battle for Black Leadership." Ch. 1 in *Challenging the Civil Rights Establishment*, edited by Joseph G. Conti and Brad Stetson. Westport, CT: Praeger.

Corley, T. A. B. 1993. "The Entrepreneur: The Central Issue in Business History?" Ch. 2 in *Entrepreneurship, Networks, and Modern Business*, edited by Jonathan Brown and Mary B. Rose. Manchester: Manchester University.

Cowan, Ruth S. 1983. *More Work for Mother*. New York: Basic Books.

Cummings, S. 1980. *Self-Help in Urban America: Patterns of Minority Economic Development*. Port Washington, NY: Kennikart Press.

Curran, James, and Roger Burrows. 1987. "The Social Analysis of Small Business: Some Emerging Themes." Ch. 10 in *Entrepreneurship in Europe*, edited by Robert Goffee and Richard Scase. London: Croom Helm.

Dallalfar, Arlene. 1989. "Iranian Immigrant Women in Los Angeles: The Reconstruction of Work, Ethnicity, and Community." Ph.D. dissertation, University of California at Los Angeles.

Day, Harry, and JoAnne Willette. 1987. *Attitudes and Inclinations of Minority Youth Toward Business Ownership*. Arlington, VA: Development Associates, Inc.

Delugach, Al. 1988. "State Suit Alleges Mortgage Firm 'Redlined' Blacks." *Los Angeles Times* Aug. 11:IV,1.

Deng, Zhong. 1993. "Status Attainment in China." Ph.D. dissertation, University of California at Los Angeles.

De Soto, Hernando. 1989. *The Other Path*. Translated by June Abbott. London: I. B. Tauris.

Dogan, Mattei, and Robert Pahre. 1990. *Creative Marginality*. Boulder, CO: Westview.

Dosti, Ben. 1994. "Despair Drives Them to Crime." *Los Angeles Times* March 7:B5.

Drucker, Peter F. 1985. *Innovation and Entrepreneurship: Practices and Principles*. New York: Harper & Row.

DuBois, William Edward Burghardt. 1966. "Of Mr. Booker T. Washington and Others." Pp. 509–539 in *Negro Social and Political Thought, 1850–1920*, edited by Howard Brotz. New York: Basic Books.

Dukakis, Michael S., and Rosabeth Moss Kanter. 1988. *Creating the Future*. New York: Summit.

Espiritu, Yen Le. 1992. *Asian American Pan-Ethnicity*. Philadelphia: Temple University.

Evans, David S., and Linda S. Leighton. 1989. "Some Empirical Aspects of Entrepreneurship." *American Economic Review* 79:519–535.

Evans, M. D. R. 1987. "Language Skill, Language Usage, and Opportunity: Immigrants in the Australian Labour Market." *Sociology* 21:253–274.

_____. 1989. "Immigrant Entrepreneurship: Effects of Ethnic Market Size and Isolated Labor Pool." *American Sociological Review* 54:950–962.

Fain, Scott. 1980. "Self-Employed Americans: Their Number Has Increased." *Monthly Labor Review* 103:3–8.

Fairlie, Robert W., and Bruce D. Meyer. 1993. "The Ethnic and Racial Character of Self Employment." Paper presented at the Department of Economics, UCLA March 19, 1993.

Featherman, David L., and Robert M. Hauser. 1978. *Opportunity and Change.* New York: Academic Press.

Foner, Nancy. 1985. "Race and Color: Jamaican Migrants in London and New York City." *International Migration Review* 19:708–727.

Ford, Henry. 1922. *My Life and Work.* Garden City, NY: Doubleday Page.

_____. 1929. *My Philosophy of Industry.* New York: Coward-McCann.

Fratoe, Frank. 1986. "A Sociological Analysis of Minority Business." *Review of Black Political Economy* 15:5–29.

_____. 1988. "Social Capital of Black Business Owners." *Review of Black Political Economy* 16:33–50.

Fratoe, Frank, and R. L. Meeks. 1985. "Business Participation Rates of the 50 Largest U.S. Ancestry Groups: Preliminary Report." Research Division, Minority Business Development Agency, U.S. Department of Commerce.

Fredland, Eric J., and Roger D. Little. 1981. "Self-Employed Workers: Returns to Education and Training." *Economics of Educational Review* 1:316–319.

Friedman, Milton. 1962. *Capitalism and Freedom.* Chicago: University of Chicago.

_____. 1976. *Price Theory.* Chicago: Aldine.

Fuchs, Victor R. 1982. "Self-Employment and Labor Force Participation of Older Males." *The Journal of Human Resources* 17:339–357.

Gardner, Paul. 1964. *Horatio Alger.* Mendota, IL: Wayside Press.

Gershenkron, Alexander. 1953–54. "Social Attitudes, Entrepreneurship and Economic Development." *Explorations in Entrepreneurial History* 6:1–19.

Gilbert, W. S. 1932. *Plays and Poems of W. S. Gilbert.* New York: Random House.

Gilder, George. 1981. *Wealth and Poverty.* New York: Basic Books.

Gold, Steven J. 1988a. "Refugees and Small Business: The Case of Soviet Jews and Vietnamese." *Ethnic and Racial Studies* 11:411–438.

_____. 1988b. "The Employment Potential of Refugee Entrepreneurship: Soviet Jews and Vietnamese in California." Report to U.S. Department of Labor, International Division, Contract #41USC252C3.

_____. 1992. *Refugee Communities.* Newbury Park: Sage.

Goldscheider, Calvin, and Frances L. Kobrin. 1980. "Ethnic Continuity and the Process of Self-Employment." *Ethnicity* 7:256–278.

Gorz, Andre. 1982. *Farewell to the Working Class: An Essay on Post-Industrial Socialism.* London: Pluto Press.

Granovetter, Mark. 1981. "Toward a Sociological Theory of Income Differences." Ch. 2 in *Sociological Perspectives on Labor Markets,* edited by Ivar Berg. New York: Academic Press.

_____. 1984. "Small Is Bountiful: Labor Markets and Establishment Size." *American Sociological Review* 49:323–334.

_____. 1990. "The Old and the New Economic Sociology: A History and an Agenda." Ch. 3 in *Beyond the Marketplace*, edited by Roger Friedland and A. F. Robertson. Hawthorne, NY: Aldine de Gruyter.

Green, Shelley, and Paul Pryde. 1990. *Black Entrepreneurship in America*. New Brunswick, NJ: Transaction.

Greene, Richard. 1982. "Tracking Job Growth in Private Industry." *Monthly Labor Review* 105:3–9.

Gujarati, Damodar. 1970. "Use of Dummy Variables in Testing for Equality between Sets of Coefficients in Two Linear Regressions: A Note." *The American Statistician* 24:50–52.

Guttman, Peter M. 1977. "The Subterranean Economy." *The Financial Analyst's Journal* 33:26–27.

Haber, Sheldon E. 1985. "Phase II Final Report: A New Perspective on Business Ownership." Report prepared for the U.S. Small Business Administration, Office of Advocacy by Simon and Company, under Contract #SBA 8559-AER-84.

Haber, Sheldon, Enrique J. Lamas, and Jules H. Lichtenstein. 1987. "On Their Own: The Self-Employed and Others in Private Business." *Monthly Labor Review* 110:17–23.

Hage, Jerald, and Charles H. Powers. 1992. *Post-Industrial Lives*. Newbury Park CA: Sage.

Hagan, John. 1994. *Crime and Disrepute*. Thousand Oaks CA: Pine Forge.

Hagen, Everett. 1962. *On the Theory of Social Change*, Homewood, IL: Dorsey.

Hanushek, Eric A., and John E. Jackson. 1977. *Statistical Methods for Social Scientists*. New York: Academic Press.

Harding, Philip, and Richard Jenkins. 1989. *The Myth of the Hidden Economy*. Milton Keynes: Open University.

Harrell, Stevan. 1985. "Why Do the Chinese Work So Hard?" *Modern China* 11:203–226.

Hartley, Keith, and John Hutton. 1989. "Large Purchasers." Ch. 6 in *Barriers to Growth in Small Firms*, edited by J. Barber, J.S. Metcalfe, and M. Porteous. London: Routledge.

Hartman, Curtis. 1989. "Business School." *Inc.* 11:52–60.

Hechter, Michael. 1976. "Ethnicity and Industrialization: On Proliferation of the Cultural Division of Labor." *Ethnicity* 3:214–224.

Hess, Darrel. 1990. "Korean Garment Manufacturing in Los Angeles." Master's thesis, University of California at Los Angeles.

Higgs, Robert. 1976. "Participation of Blacks and Immigrants in the American Merchant Class, 1890–1910: Some Demographic Relations." *Explorations in Economic History* 13:153–164.

Hisrich, Robert D., and Candida Brush. 1986. "Characteristics of the Minority Entrepreneur." *Journal of Small Business Management* 24:1–8.

Hoffman, Constance A., and Martin N. Marger. 1991. "Patterns of Immigrant Enterprise in Six Metropolitan Areas." *Sociology and Social Research* 75:144–157.

Horton, Hayward Derrick. 1988. "Occupational Differentiation and Black Entrepreneurship." *National Journal of Sociology* 2:187–201.

Hughes, Jonathan. 1965. *The Vital Few*. Boston: Houghton Mifflin.

Hurley, Jayne, and Stephen Schmidt. 1993. "A Wok on the Wild Side." *Nutrition Action Healthletter* 20 (September):10–12.

Johannisson, Bengt. 1988. "Regional Variations in Emerging Entrepreneurial Networks." Paper presented at the 28th Congress of the Regional Science Association, Stockholm, August 23, 1988.

Johnson, James H., and Melvin L. Oliver. 1989. "Interethnic Minority Conflict in Urban America: The Effects of Economic and Social Dislocations." *Urban Geography* 10:449–463.

Johnson, Peter. 1981. "Unemployment and Self-Employment: A Survey." *Industrial Relations Journal* 12:5–15.

Jones, Trevor, David McEvoy, and Giles Barrett. 1994. "Labour Intensive Practices in the Ethnic Minority Firm." Ch. 5 in *Employment, the Small Firm, and the Labour Market*, edited by J. Atkinson and D. Storey. London: Routledge.

Jones, Yvonne V. 1988. "Street Peddlers as Entrepreneurs: Economic Adaptation to an Urban Area." *Urban Anthropology* 17:143–170.

Kallen, Evelyn, and Merrijoy Kelner. 1983. *Ethnicity, Opportunity and Successful Entrepreneurship in Canada*. Toronto: Institute for Behavioral Research of York University.

Kasarda, John D. 1989. "Urban Industrial Transition and the Underclass." *Annals of the American Academy of Political and Social Science* 501:26–47.

Katz, Jack. 1988. *Seductions of Crime*. New York: Basic Books.

Keeble, David, and Egbert Weaver. 1986. "Introduction." Pp. 1–34 in *New Films and Regional Development in Europe*, edited by David Keebel and Egbert Weaver. Beckenman UK: Croom Helm.

Kemp, Jack. 1994. "Forget Europe as a Model for Creating Jobs." *Los Angeles Times* March 20:M5.

Kenney, Martin. 1986. "Schumpeterian Innovation and Entrepreneurs in Capitalism: A Case Study of the U.S. Biotechnology Industry." *Research Policy* 15:21.

Kilby, Peter. 1971. "Hunting the Heffalump." Pp. 1–40 in *Entrepreneurship and Economic Development*, edited by Peter Kilby. New York: Free Press.

Kim, Kwang Chung, and Won Moo Hurh. 1985. "Ethnic Resources Utilization of Korean Immigrant Entrepreneurs in the Chicago Minority Area." *International Migration Review* 19:82–111.

Kim, Kwang Chung, Won Moo Hurh, and Marilyn Fernandez. 1989. "Intra-Group Differences in Business Participation: A Comparative Analysis of Three Asian Immigrant Groups." *International Migration Review* 23:73–95.

Kirk, Paul, and Scott Matheson. 1986. *Opportunity for Every American*. Report of the Industrial and Entrepreneurial Economy Committee of the Democratic Policy Commission. Washington, DC: The Commission.

Klein, Lawrence R. 1983. *The Economics of Supply and Demand*. Baltimore: Johns Hopkins.

Knight, Frank. 1921. *Risk, Uncertainty, and Profit*. Boston: Houghton Mifflin.

Kwong, Peter, and Joann Lum. 1988. "From Soul to Seoul: Koreans on 125th Street." *Village Voice* July 12:10–12.

Ladbury, Sarah. 1984. "Choice, Chance or No Alternative? Turkish Cypriots in Business in London." Pp. 105–124 in *Ethnic Communities in Business*, edited by Robin Ward and Richard Jenkins. Cambridge: Cambridge University.

La Guire, Lennie. 1988. "Meet the Lees: How One Korean Couple Have Cleaned Up as Entrepreneurs." *Los Angeles Herald- Examiner Asian Pacific Sketchbook Special Reprint* May 6–27:5.

Landa, Janet. 1991 "Culture and Entrepreneurship in Less-Developed Countries: Ethnic Trading Networks as Economic Organizations." Ch. 4 in *The Culture of Entrepreneurship*, edited by Brigitte Berger. San Francisco: ICS.

Langlois, Andre, and Eran Razin. 1989. "Self-Employment among Ethnic Minorities in Canadian Metropolitan Areas." *Canadian Journal of Regional Science* 12:335–354.

Lengyel, Gyoergy. 1989. "Entrepreneurial Inclinations," Pp. 79–93 in *Research Review: Hungary Under the Reform*, edited by Andreas Toth and Laszlo Gabor. Budapest: Coordinating Council of Program Ts-3.

Lewis, W. Arthur. 1954. "Aspects of Industrialization." *Nigerian Trade Journal* 2:11–12.

Lieberson, Stanley. 1980. *A Piece of the Pie.* Los Angeles: University of California.

———. 1985. *Making It Count.* Berkeley: University of California.

Light, Ivan. 1972. *Ethnic Enterprise in America.* Berkeley: University of California Press.

———. 1974a. "From Vice District to Tourist Attraction: The Moral Career of American Chinatowns, 1880–1940." *Pacific Historical Review* 43:367–394.

———. 1974b. "Reassessments of Sociological History: C. Wright Mills and the Power Elite." *Theory and Society* 1:361–374.

———. 1977a. "Numbers Gambling among Blacks: A Financial Institution." *American Sociological Review* 42:892–904.

———. 1977b. "The Ethnic Vice Industry, 1880–1944." *American Sociological Review* 42:464–479.

———. 1979. "Disadvantaged Minorities in Self-Employment." *International Journal of Comparative Sociology* 20:31–45.

———. 1980. "Asian Enterprise in America." Pp. 33–57 in *Self- Help in America*, edited by Scott Cummings. Pt. Washington, NY: Kennikat.

———. 1981. "Ethnic succession." Pp. 54–85 in *Ethnic Change*, edited by Charles Keyes. Seattle: University of Washington.

———. 1983. *Cities in World Perspective.* New York: Macmillan.

———. 1984. "Immigrant and Ethnic Enterprise in North America." *Ethnic and Racial Studies* 7:195–216.

———. 1993. "Lending Support to Kyes." *Los Angeles Times* Oct. 24, City Times Section, p. 22.

Light, Ivan, and Angel A. Sanchez. 1987. "Immigrant Entrepreneurs in 272 SMSAs." *Sociological Perspectives* 30:373–399.

Light, Ivan, and Edna Bonacich. 1988. *Immigrant Entrepreneurs; Koreans in Los Angeles; 1965–1982.* Berkeley: University of California.

Light, Ivan, and Stavros Karageorgis. 1994. "The Ethnic Economy." Pp. 647–671 in *Handbook of Economic Sociology*, edited by Neil Smelser and Richard Swedberg. New York: Russell Sage Foundation.

Light, Ivan, Hadas Har-Chvi, and Kenneth Kan. 1994a. "Black/Korean Conflicts in Los Angeles." Pp. 1–21 in *Managing Divided Cities*, edited by Seamus Dunn. Newbury Park: Sage.

_____. 1994b. "Resolving Status Dilemmas." Paper presented at the International Sociological Association Conference, Bielefeld, Germany, July 18.

Light, Ivan, Jung-Kwuon Im, and Zhong Deng. 1990. "Korean Rotating Credit Associations in Los Angeles." *Amerasia* 16:35–54.

Light, Ivan, Georges Sabagh, Mehdi Bozorgmehr, and Claudia Der- Martirosian. 1994. "Beyond the Ethnic Enclave Economy." *Social Problems* 41:65–80.

Lindner, Marc. 1992. *Farewell to the Self-Employed*. New York: Greenwood.

Locke, Robert R. 1993. "Education and Entrepreneurship: an Historian's View." Pp. 55–74 in *Entrepreneurship, Networks, and Modern Business*, edited by Jonathan Brown and Mary B. Rose. Manchester: Manchester University.

Lockwood, William W. 1954. *The Economic Development of Japan*. Princeton, NJ: Princeton University.

Loscocco, Karyn A., and Joyce Robinson. 1991. "Barriers to Women's Small-Business Success in the United States." *Gender and Society* 5(4):511–532.

Love, John F. 1986. *McDonald's*. Toronto: Bantam Books.

Lovell-Troy, Lawrence A. 1990. The Social Bases of Ethnic Enterprise. New York: Garland.

Lubin, Nancy, 1985. "Small Business Owners." Ch. 7 in *New Lives: The Adjustment of Soviet and Jewish Immigrants in the US and Israel*, edited by Rita J. Simon. Lexington, MA: Lexington Books.

Lynch, Frederick W. 1989. *Invisible Victims: White Males and the Crisis of Affirmative Action*. Westport, CT: Greenwood Press.

Macaulay, Stewart. 1963. "Non-Contractual Relations in Business." *American Sociological Review* 28:55–66.

MacDonald, Ronan. 1971. "Schumpeter and Max Weber: Central Visions and Social Theories." Ch. 3 in *Entrepreneurship and Economic Development*, edited by Peter Kilby. New York: Free Press.

Macleod, Jay. 1987. *Ain't No Makin' It*. Boulder, CO: Westview Press.

Ma Mung, Emmanuel. 1994. "L'Entreprenariat Ethnique en France." *Sociologie du Travail* 36:185–209.

Marceau, Jane. 1989a. *A Family Business? The Making of an International Business Elite*. Cambridge: Cambridge University Press.

_____. 1989b. "France." Ch. 3 in *The Capitalist Class*, edited by Tom Bottomore and Robert J. Brym. New York: Harvester Wheatsheaf.

Mars, Gerald, and Robin Ward. 1984. "Ethnic Business Development in Britain: Opportunities and Resources." Ch. 1 in *Ethnic Communities in Business*, edited by Robin Ward and Richard Jenkins. Cambridge: Cambridge University.

Marsh, Robert M., and Hiroshi Mannari. 1986. "Entrepreneurship in Medium and Large-Scale Japanese Firms." Ch. 1 in *Entrepreneurship and Social*

Change, edited by Sidney M. Greenfield and Arnold Strickon. Lanham, MD: University Press of America.

Martinelli, Alberto, and Antonio M. Chiesi. 1989. "Italy." Ch. 5 in *The Capitalist Class*, edited by Tom Bottomore and Robert J. Brym. New York: New York University.

Martinelli, Alberto, and Neil J. Smelser, eds. 1990. *Economy and Society*. Newbury Park, CA: Sage.

Marx, Karl. 1956. *Selected Writings in Sociology and Social Philosophy*, translated by T.B. Bottomore. New York: McGraw-Hill.

_____. 1965. *Capital*, Vol. I. Moscow: Progress Publishers.

Mayer, Kurt. 1953. "Business Enterprise: Traditional Symbol of Opportunity." *British Journal of Sociology* 4:160–180.

McClelland, David C., and David G. Winter. 1971. *Motivating Economic Achievement*. With Sara K. Winter and Others. New York: Free Press.

McGovern, George S. 1972. "Remarks Accepting the Democratic Nomination for the Presidency of the United States, July 13, 1972." Pp. 125–130 in *McGovern: The Man and His Beliefs*, edited by Shirley MacLaine. New York: Norton.

McLure, Marcia Lumadue. 1990. "Characteristics Associated with Entrepreneurial Success." Ph.D. dissertation, University of California at Los Angeles.

McMillan, Penelope. 1982. "New Entrepreneurs Try Marketplace." *Los Angeles Times* Dec. 13, (2):1.

Mead, Lawrence M. 1986. *Beyond Entitlement*. New York: Free Press.

Merton, Robert King. 1957. *Social Theory and Social Structure*. New York: Free Press.

Miller, Daniel R., and Guy E. Swanson. 1958. *The Changing American Parent*. New York: John Wiley.

Mills, C.W. 1951. *White Collar*. New York: Oxford University.

Min, Pyong Gap. 1984. "From White Collar Occupations to Small Business: Korean Immigrants' Occupational Adjustment." *The Sociological Quarterly* 25:333–352.

_____. 1988. *Ethnic Business Enterprise: Korean Small Business in Atlanta*. New York: Center for Migration Studies.

_____. 1989. *Some Positive Functions of Ethnic business for an Immigrant Community: Koreans in Los Angeles*. Final Report Submitted to the National Science Foundation, Sociology Division.

_____. 1992. "The Prevalence and Causes of Blacks' Rejection of Korean Merchants." Unpublished paper, Queens College of the City University of New York.

Min, Pyong Gap, and Charles Jaret. 1985. "Ethnic Business Success: The Case of Korean Small Business in Atlanta." *Sociology and Social Research* 69:412–435.

Minervini, Roberto. 1973. *Storia della Pizza*. Naples: Societa Editrice Napoletana.

Mitchell, Jacqueline. 1990. "Fear of Layoff Spurs Employees to Launch Part-Time Businesses." *Wall Street Journal* May 25, (1):1.

Model, Suzanne. 1985. "A Comparative Perspective on the Ethnic Enclave: Blacks, Italians, and Jews in New York City." *International Migration Review* 19:64–81.

Mokry, Benjamin W. *Entrepreneurship and Public Policy: Can Government Stimulate Business Startups?* New York: Quorum Books.

Morgan, Karen J., and Basile Goungetas. 1986. "Snacking and Eating Away From Home." Pp. 91–125 in *What Is America Eating?* Washington, DC: National Academy Press.

Murray, Charles. 1984. *Losing Ground: American Social Policy, 1950–1980.* New York: Basic Books.

Myers, Robert E. 1983. "Immigrant Occupational Achievement: A Comparative Case Study of Koreans, Soviet Jews, and Vietnamese in the Philadelphia Area." Ph.D. dissertation, University of Pennsylvania.

Myers, Samuel L., Jr. 1978. "The Economics of Crime in the Urban Ghetto." *The Review of Black Political Economy* 9:43–59.

Nafziger, E. Wayne. 1977. *African Capitalism: A Case Study of Nigerian Entrepreneurship.* Stanford, CA: Hoover Institution Press.

Nee, Victor, and Jimy Sanders. 1985. "The Road to Parity: Determinants of the Socioeconomic Achievements of Asian Americans". *Ethnic and Racial Studies* 8:75–93.

Nee, Victor, and Scott Sernau. 1994. "Job Transitions in an Immigrant Metropolis: Ethnic Boundaries and the Mixed Economy." *American Sociological Review* 59:849–872.

O'Brian, David J., and Stephen S. Fugita. 1984. "Mobilization of a Traditionally Petit Bourgeois Ethnic Group." *Social Forces* 63:522–536.

O'Farrell, Patrick N. 1986. "The Nature of New Firms in Ireland: Empirical Evidence and Policy Implications." Ch. 8 in *New Firms and Regional Development in Europe*, edited by David Keeble and Egbert Wever. London: Croom Helm.

O'Neill, Ken, Ranjit Bhambri, Terry Faulkner, and Tom Cannon. 1987. *Small Business Development: Some Current Issues.* Brookfield, VT: Avebury.

Ong, Paul. 1981. "Factors Influencing the Size of the Black Business Community." *The Review of Black Political Economy* 11:313–319.

Orru, Marco. 1991. "The Explanation of Economic Structures." *Theory and Society* 20:539–553.

Orum, Anthony. 1990. "Getting Down to Cases." *Newsletter of the Community and Urban Sociology Section of the American Sociological Association* 19:4–6.

Padilla, Felix M. 1992. *The Gang as an American Enterprise.* New Brunswick, NJ: Rutgers University Press.

Parsons, Talcott. 1928. "Capitalism in Recent German Literature: Sombart and Weber." *The Journal of Political Economy* 6:641–666.

Parsons, Talcott, and Neil J. Smelser. 1956. *Economy and Society.* Glencoe, IL: Free Press.

Patterson, Orlando. 1975. "Context and Choice in Ethnic Allegiance: A Theoretical Framework and a Caribbean Case Study. Ch. 10 in *Ethnicity*, edited by Nathan Glazer and Daniel P. Moynihan. Cambridge: Harvard University.

Paulin, William L., Robert E. Coffey, and Mark E. Spaulding. 1982. "Entrepreneurship Research: Methods and Directions." Ch. 18 in *Encyclopedia of Entrepreneurship*, edited by Calvin A. Kent, Donald L. Sexton, and Karl H. Vesper. Englewood Cliffs, NJ: Prentice-Hall.

Phizacklea, Annie. 1988. "Entrepreneurship, Ethnicity, and Gender." Ch. 2 in *Enterprising Women*, edited by Sallie Westwood and Parminder Bhachu. London: Routledge.

Piore, Michael J., and Charles F. Sabel. 1984. *The Second Industrial Divide*. New York: Basic Books.

Podgursky, Michael, and Paul Swaim. 1987. "Duration of Joblessness Following Displacement." *Industrial Relations* 26:213–226.

Polanyi, Karl. 1957. *The Great Transformation*. Boston: Beacon.

Portes, Alejandro. 1987. "The Social Origins of the Cuban Enclave Economy of Miami." *Sociological Perspectives* 30:340–372.

Portes, Alejandro, and Robert Bach. 1985. *Latin Journey*. Berkeley: University of California.

Portes, Alejandro, and Reuben Rumbaut. 1990. *Immigrant America*. Los Angeles: University of California.

Portes, Alejandro, and Julia Sensenbrenner. 1993. "Embeddedness and Immigration: Notes on the Social Determinants of Economic Action." *American Journal of Sociology* 98(6):1320–1350.

Portes, Alejandro, and Alex Stepick. 1985. "Unwelcome Immigrants: The Labor Market Experiences of 1980 (Mariel) Cuban and Haitian Refugees in South Florida." *American Sociological Review* 50:493–514.

Portes, Alejandro, and Min Zhou. 1992. "Divergent Destinies: Immigration, Poverty, and Entrepreneurship in the United States." Written for the Project on Poverty, Inequality, and the Crisis of Social Policy of the Joint Center for Political and Economic Studies, Washington, DC.

Portes, Alejandro, Juan M. Clark, and Manuel M. Lopez. 1981–82. "Six Years Later: The Process of Incorporation of Cuban Exiles in the United States: 1973–1979." *Cuban Studies* 11/12:1–24.

Putnam, Robert D. 1993. "The Prosperous Community: Social Capital and Public Life." *The American Prospect* Spring 1993:35–37.

Ragin, Charles C. 1987. *The Comparative Method*. Berkeley: University of California.

Rainnie, Al. 1985. "Small Firms, Big Problems: The Political Economy of Small Business." *Capital and Class* 25:140–168.

Rand, Ayn. 1943. *The Fountainhead*. New York: Bobbs Merrill.

_____. 1957. *Atlas Shrugged*. New York: Random House.

Ray, Robert N. 1975. "A Report on Self-Employed Americans in 1973." *Monthly Labor Review* 98:49–54.

Razin, Eran. 1988. "Entrepreneurship Among Foreign Immigrants in the Los Angeles and San Francisco Metropolitan Regions." *Urban Geography* 9:283–301.

_____. 1993. "Immigrant Entrepreneurs in Israel, Canada, and California." Ch. 5 in *Immigration and Entrepreneurship*, edited by Ivan Light and Parminder Bhachu. New Brunswick, NJ: Transaction.

Reagan, Ronald. 1968. *The Creative Society*. New York: Devin- Adair.

_____. 1984. *Economic Report of the President*. Washington, DC: U.S. Government Printing Office.

Redding, S. Gordon. 1991. "Culture and Entrepreneurial Behavior among the Overseas Chinese." Ch. 8 in *The Culture of Entrepreneurship*, edited by Brigitte Berger. San Francisco: ICS.

Rekers, A. M., M. J. Dijest, and R. Van Kempen. 1990. "The Influence of Urban Contexts on Ethnic Enterprises in the Netherlands." Paper presented at the Annual Meeting of the Association of American Geographers, April 19–22, Toronto, Canada.

Reynolds, Paul D. 1989. "New Firms and Economic Change: Recent Findings and Policy Implications." Paper presented at the Annual Meeting of the American Sociological Association, San Francisco Hilton Hotel, Aug. 13.

Riesman, David. 1950. *The Lonely Crowd*. New Haven: Yale University.

Sabagh, Georges, and Mehdi Bozorgmehr. 1987. "Are the Characteristics of Exiles Different Than the Immigrants? The Case of Iranians in Los Angeles." *Sociology and Social Research* 71:77–84.

SAS Institute. 1985a. *SAS User's Guide: Basics, Version 5 Edition*. Cary, NC: SAS Institute, Inc.

_____. 1985b. *SAS User's Guide: Statistics, Version 5 Edition*. Cary, NC: SAS Institute, Inc.

Scharnhorst, Gary. 1985. *The Lost Life of Horatio Alger, Jr.*. Bloomington, IN: Indiana University.

Schillinger, Elisabeth, and Joel Jenswold. 1988. "Cooperative Business Ventures in the Soviet Union: The Impact of Social Forces on Private Enterprise." *Sociology and Social Research* 73:22–30.

Schroeder, Larry D., David L. Sjoquist, and Paula E. Stephan. 1986. *Understanding Regression Analysis: An Introductory Guide*. QASS Series #57. Newbury Park, CA: Sage.

Schumpeter, Joseph. 1934. *The Theory of Economic Development*, translated by Redvers Opie. Cambridge, MA: Harvard University Press.

_____. 1943. *Capitalism, Socialism, and Democracy*. London: Allen & Unwin.

_____. 1988. *Essays on Entrepreneurs, Innovations, Business Cycles, and the Evolution of Capitalism*. New Brunswick, NJ: Transaction.

_____. 1991. "Comments on a Plan for the Study of Entrepreneurship." Ch. 10 in *Joseph A. Schumpeter: The Economics and Sociology of Capitalism*, edited by Richard Swedberg. Princeton: Princeton University.

Scott, Allen J. 1988. *Metropolis*. Berkeley: University of California.

Sengstock, Mary Catherine. 1967. "Maintenance of Social Interaction Patterns in an Ethnic Group." Ph.D. dissertation, Washington University.

Sewell, William H. 1992. "A Theory of Structure: Duality, Agency, and Transformation." *American Journal of Sociology* 98:1–29.

Shilling, A., Gary. 1988. "When Saving Drains the Economy." *Los Angeles Times* August 28:(IV)2.

Shiver, Jube, Jr. 1991. "South L.A. Patrons Pay a Hefty Price as Banks Leave." *Los Angeles Times*, November 26:A23.

Simon, Julian L. 1989. *The Economic Consequences of Immigration*. Oxford: Basil Blackwell and the Cato Institute.

Smelser, Neil J. 1976. *The Sociology of Economic Life*, 2nd ed. Englewood Cliffs, NJ: Prentice-Hall.

Smith, Dwight C., Jr. 1978. "Organized Crime and Entrepreneurship." *International Journal of Criminology and Penology* 6(S):161–177.

_____. 1980. "Paragons, Pariahs, and Pirates: A Spectrum-Based Theory of Enterprise." *Crime and Delinquency* 26:358–386.

Smith, Kevin B., and Lorene H. Stone. 1989. "Rags, Riches, and Bootstraps: Beliefs about the Causes of Wealth and Poverty." *The Sociological Quarterly* 30:93–107.

Sombart, Werner. 1951. *The Jews and Modern Capitalism*. Glencoe, IL: Free Press.

Sowell, Thomas. 1975. *Race and Economics*. New York: David McKay.

Stark, Oded. 1991. *The Migration of Labor*. Cambridge: Basil Blackwell.

Stein, Barry A. 1974. *Size, Efficiency and Community Enterprise*. Cambridge, MA: Center for Community Economic Development.

Steinmetz, George, and Erik Olin Wright. 1989. "The Fall and Rise of the Petty Bourgeoisie: Changing Patterns of Self- Employment in the Postwar United States." *American Journal of Sociology* 94:973–1018.

Stinchcombe, Arthur. 1983. *Economic Sociology*. New York: Academic Press.

Stites, Richard W. 1985. "Industrial Work as an Entrepreneurial Strategy." *Modern China* 11:227–246.

Sudhir, Venkateoh. 1994. "Getting Ahead: Social Mobility Among the Urban Poor." *Sociological Perspectives* 37:159–182.

Sullivan, Mercer L. 1989. *Getting Paid: Youth Crime and Work in the Inner City*. Ithaca: Cornell University.

Sullivan, Teresa A., and Stephen D. McCracken. 1988. "Black Entrepreneurs: Patterns and Rates of Return to Self-Employment." *National Journal of Sociology* 2:167–185.

Sutherland, Edwin. 1949. *White Collar Crime*. New York: Dryden.

Sway, Marlene. 1984. "Economic Adaptability: The Case of the Gypsies." *Urban Life* 13:83–98.

_____. 1988. *Familiar Strangers*. Urbana: University of Illinois.

Swedberg, Richard. 1987. "Economic Sociology: Past and Present." *Contemporary Sociology* 35:1–215.

Swinton, David H. and John Handy. 1983. *The Determinants of the Growth of Black Owned Businesses: A Preliminary Analysis*. Atlanta: Southern Center for Studies in Public Policy of Clark College. Under Contract with U.S. Department of Commerce, Minority Business Development Agency.

Szelenyi, Ivan. 1988. *Socialist Entrepreneurs*. Madison: University of Wisconsin.

Tannahill, Reay. 1973. *Food in History*. London: Eyre Methuen.

Taub, Richard, and Doris L. Taub. 1989. *Entrepreneurship in India's Small-Scale Industries*. New Delhi: Manohar.

Takahashi, Dean. 1990. "A Dogged Inventor Makes the Computer Industry Say Hello Mr. Chip." *Los Angeles Times* Oct. 21:D3.

Taylor, Michael, and Sara Singleton. 1993. "The Communal Resource: Transaction Cost and the Solution of Collective Action Problems." *Politics and Society* 21:195–214.

Teitz, Michael, Amy Glasmeier, and Douglas Svensson. 1981. *Small Business and Employment Growth in California*. Berkeley: Institute of Urban and Regional Development.

Thatcher, Margaret. 1989. *The Revival of Britain*. London: Aurum.

Thornberry, Terence P. and R. L. Christenson, 1984. "Unemployment and Criminal Involvement: An Investigation of Reciprocal Causal Structures." *American Sociological Review* 49:398–411.

Thurow, Lester C. 1992. *Head to Head*. New York: William Morrow.

Timms, D.W.G. 1975. "The Dissimilarity Between Overseas-Born and Australian Born in Queensland: Dimensions of Assimilation." Ch. 20 in *Urban Social Segregation*, edited by Ceri Peach. London: Longman.

Tuchman, Gaye, and Harry Gene Levine. 1993. "New York Jews and Chinese Food: The Social Construction of an Ethnic Pattern." *Journal of Contemporary Ethnography* 22:382–407.

Turner, Jonathan, and Edna Bonacich. 1980. "Toward a Composite Theory of Middleman Minorities." *Ethnicity* 7:144–158.

Trump, Donald. 1987. *The Art of the Deal*. New York: Random House.

U.S. Bureau of the Census. 1973. *Census of Population, 1970, Subject Reports, Final Report: National Origin and Language*. Washington, DC: Government Printing Office.

_____. 1983. *Census of the Population and Housing, 1980: Public- Use Microdata Sample A; Technical Documentation*. Washington, DC: U.S. Government Printing Office.

_____. 1984. *1980 Census of Population, Characteristics of the Population*. Washington, DC: U.S. Government Printing Office.

_____. 1990. *Statistical Abstract of the United States, 1990* (110th Edition). Washington, DC: U.S. Government Printing Office. Tables 639 and 640.

U.S. President. 1984. *The State of Small Business: A Report of the President Transmitted to Congress, March, 1984*. Washington, DC: U.S. Government Printing Office.

Usselman, Steve W. 1992. "From Novelty to Utility: George Westinghouse and the Business of Innovation during the Age of Edison." *Business History Review* 66:251–304.

Velez-Ibanez, Carlos G. 1983. *Bonds of Mutual Trust: The Cultural Systems of Rotating Credit Associations among Urban Mexicans and Chicanos*. New Brunswick, NJ: Rutgers University.

Waldinger, Roger. 1984. "Immigrant Enterprise in the New York Garment Industry." *Social Problems* 32:60–71.

_____. 1986a. "Immigrant Enterprise." *Theory and Society* 15: 249–285.

_____. 1986b. *Through the Eye of the Needle; Immigrants and Enterprise in New York's Garment Trade*. New York: New York University.

_____. 1988. "The Social Networks of Ethnic Entrepreneurs." Paper presented at the 1988 Annual Meeting of the National Economic Association, New York City.

_____. 1989. "Immigration and Urban Change." *Annual Review of Sociology* 15:211–232.

Waldinger, Roger, Howard Aldrich, and Robin Ward. 1990. "Opportunities, Group Characteristics, and Strategies." Ch. 1 in *Ethnic Entrepreneurs: Immigrant Business in Industrial Societies*, edited by Roger Waldinger, Howard Aldrich, and Robin Ward. Newbury Park, CA: Sage.

Waldinger, Roger, Mirjana Morokvasic, and Annie Phizacklea. 1990. "Business on the Ragged Edge: Immigrant and Minority Business in the Garment Industries in Paris, London, and New York." Ch. 7 in *Ethnic Entrepreneurs: Immigrant Business in Industrial Societies*, edited by Roger Waldinger, Howard Aldrich, and Robin Ward. Newbury Park CA: Sage.

Waldinger, Roger, Robin Ward, and Howard Aldrich. 1985. "Trend Report: Ethnic Business and Occupational Mobility in Advanced Societies." *Sociology* 19:586–597.

_____. 1990. "Conclusions and Policy Implications." Ch. 7 in *Ethnic Entrepreneurs: Immigrant Business in Industrial Societies*, edited by Roger Waldinger, Howard Aldrich, and Robin Ward. Newbury Park: Sage.

Wallman, Sandra. 1979. "The Scope for Ethnicity." Pp. 1–14 in *Ethnicity at Work*, edited by Sandra Wallman. London: Macmillan.

Wall Street Journal. 1977. "Pepsi Co., Pizza Hut Reach an Accord on Proposed Merger." June 17:24.

_____. 1991. "Waiter There's a Rat in My Soup." May 31:A1.

Ward, Robin. 1985. "Minority Settlement and the Local Economy." Ch. 10 in *New Approaches to Economic Life*, edited by Bryan Roberts, Ruth Finnegan, and Duncan Gallie. Manchester: University of Manchester.

_____. 1987. "Ethnic Entrepreneurs in Britain and Europe." Ch. 6 in *Entrepreneurship in Europe*, edited by Robert Goffee and Richard Scase. London: Croom Helm.

Watts, H.D. 1987. *Industrial Geography*. Harlow, Essex, England: Longman Scientific.

Weber, Max. 1958. *The Protestant Ethic and Spirit of Capitalism*. New York: Scribner's.

_____. 1968. "The Economic Relationships of Organized Groups." Ch. 2 in *Economy and Society*, Vol. 1. New York: Bedminster.

_____. 1978. "Anticritical Last Word on the *Spirit of Capitalism* by Max Weber." Translated by Wallace M. Davis. *American Journal of Sociology* 83:1105–1131.

_____. 1981 [1927]. *General Economic History*. New Brunswick, NJ: Transaction.

Weiss, Linda. 1988. *Creating Capitalism*. London: Basil Blackwell.

Wells, Mirriam. 1991. "Ethnic Groups and Knowledge System in Agriculture." *Economic Development and Cultural Change* 39:739–771.

Werbner, Pnina. 1984. "Business on Trust: Pakistani Entrepreneurship in the Manchester Garment Trade." Pp. 166–188 in *Ethnic Communities in Busi-*

ness, edited by Robin Ward and Richard Jenkins. New York: Cambridge University Press.

_____. 1987. "Enclave Economies and Family Firms: Pakistani Traders in a British City." Pp. 213–233 in *Migrants, Workers, and the Social Order*, edited by Jeremy Eades. London: Tavistock Publications.

_____. 1990. *The Migration Process: Capital, Gifts and Offerings Among British Pakistanis*. New York: Berg Publishers.

White, L. J. 1982. "The Determinants of the Relative Importance of Small Business." *The Review of Economics and Statistics* 64:42–49.

Whitley, Richard. 1991. "The Revival of Small Business in Europe." Ch. 9 in *The Culture of Entrepreneurship*, edited by Brigette Berger. San Francisco: ICS.

Wicker, Allan, and Jeanne King. 1989. "Employment, Ownership, and Survival in Microbusiness: A Study of New Retail and Service Establishments." *Small Business Economics* 1:137–152.

Wilensky, Harold L. 1963. "The Moonlighter: A Product of Relative Deprivation." *Industrial Relations* 3:105–124.

Wilken, James. 1979. *Entrepreneurship: A Comparative and Historical Study*. Norwood, NJ: Ablex.

Will, George F. 1987. *The New Season*. New York: Simon and Schuster.

Wilson, Kenneth L., and Alejandro Portes. 1980. "Immigrant Enclaves: An Analysis of the Labor Market Experiences of Cubans in Miami." *American Journal of Sociology* 86:295–319.

Witkin, Gordon. 1991. "The Men Who Created Crack." *U.S. News and World Report* 111:44ff.

Wong, Bernard. 1978. "A Comparative Study of the Assimilation of the Chinese in New York City and Lima, Peru." *Comparative Studies in Society and History* 20:335–358.

_____. 1987. "The Role of Ethnicity in Enclave Enterprises: A Study of Chinese Garment Factories in New York City." *Human Organization* 46:120–130.

Woodrum, Eric. 1985. "Religion and Economics among Japanese Americans: A Weberian Study." *Social Forces* 64:191–204.

Yoon, In-Jin. 1991. "The Changing Significance of Ethnic and Class Resources in Immigrant Business: the Case of Korean Immigrant Businesses in Chicago." *International Migration Review* 25:303–331.

Young, Frank W. 1971. "A Macrosociological Interpretation of Entrepreneurship." Pp. 139–149 in *Entrepreneurship and Economic Development*, edited by Peter Kilby. New York: Free Press.

Young, Philip K. Y., and Ann H. L. Sontz. 1988. "Is Hard Work the Key to Success? A Socioeconomic Analysis of Immigrant Enterprise." *The Review of Black Political Economy* 16:11–31.

Young, Ruth C. 1988. "Is Population Ecology a Useful Paradigm for the Study of Organizations?" *American Journal of Sociology* 94:1–24.

Yu, Eui-Young. 1982. "Occupation and Work Patterns of Korean Immigrants." In *Koreans in Los Angeles*, edited by Eui-Young Yu, Earl H. Phillips, and Eun

Sik Yang. Los Angeles: Koryo Research Institute: Center for Korean-American and Korean Studies, California State University, Los Angeles.

Zelinsky, Wilbur. 1985. "The Roving Palate: North America's Ethnic Restaurant Cuisines." *Geoforum* 16:51–71.

Zenner, Walter P. 1991. *Minorities in the Middle*. Albany: State University of New York.

Zucker, Lynne. 1983. "Organizations as Institutions." *Research in the Sociology of Organizations* 2:1–47.

_____. 1986. "Production of Trust: Institutional Sources of Economic Structure, 1840–1920." *Research in Organizational Behavior* 8:53–111.

Index

Acs, Zoltan J., 15
Affirmative action, 83
African Americans
  demand effects, 81, 83, 88
  demand; variables of, 134; and
    immigrant entrepreneurs,
    195–200, 223; and labor market
    disadvantages, 163, 165, 168,
    171–174, 175; and settlement
    patterns, 200–201, 202; and
    supply effects, 141–142, 143
  entrepreneurship of, 76, 78,
    141–142, 213, 219, 226
  ethnic resources of, 64, 65
  income-defined self-employment,
    63
  legal constraints, 83
  self-employed income of, 52
  self-exclusion of, 84
Aggregated characteristics, 41
Aiken, Leona S., 64, 72n. 40, 113n. 30,
    128, 144nn. 9, 11, and 19, 145nn.
    26, 29
Alberta, Canada, 212
Aldrich, Howard, 74, 75, 76, 78, 150
Alger, Horatio, 205, 206, 227nn. 1, 2
Altoona Pa., 91
Amsterdam, the Netherlands, 18
Archer, Melanie, 3
Asia, 226
Asians, 41, 42, 45
  entrepreneurship, 78, 213, 219
  ethnic resources, 61, 62, 63, 72n. 36,
    85; and demand effects, 81; and
    economic closure, 86; legal
    constraints and, 83
  intercategory rates of, 56–57, 60, 61,
    129, 132, 134, 138, 220
  self-employment, income of 52, 214;
    rates of, 183, 203n. 4

supply variables, 139, 141; in
    Britain, 150; in the labor market,
    157, 163, 165, 168, 173, 174, 178n.
    14
Asian Indians, 52
  and supply variables, 126
Atlanta Ga., 150, 157
Atlantic City N.J., 84
Audretsch, David, 15
Australia, 156

Bach, Robert, 22, 98
Bailey, Thomas R., 79
Balkin, Steven, 211, 212, 215
Barrett, Giles, 150
Bates, Timothy, 213
Bearse, Peter, 111 n.6
Bechofer, Frank, 11
Becker, Eugene H., 151
Bell, Daniel, 8, 11
Bendix, Reinhard, 20
Benson, John, 205
Berg, Ivar, 111n. 9
Berlin, Germany, 18, 150
Birch, David L., 14
Blacks (See African Americans)
Boissevain, Jeremy, 12
Bonacich, Edna, 17, 19, 20, 24, 77, 79,
    115, 157, 227n. 3
Borjas, George J., 83, 112n. 17
Boston, Mass., 211
Boulton, William R., 2
Bourdieu, Pierre, 28nn. 29, 30
Bozorgmehr, Mehdi, 17, 227n. 9
Boyd, Robert, 32, 96, 98, 197
Brearley, Sally, 2
Britain, 85, 150, 211
Brockhaus, Robert H., 2
Bronars, Stephen G., 83, 112n. 17
Brown, Charles, 14

249